THE IVP NEW TESTAMENT COMMENTARY SERIES

1-2 Timothy & Titus

Philip H. Towner

Grant R. Osborne
series editor

D. Stuart Briscoe
Haddon Robinson
consulting editors

INTERVARSITY PRESS
DOWNERS GROVE, ILLINOIS, USA
LEICESTER, ENGLAND

InterVarsity Press
P.O. Box 1400, Downers Grove, Illinois 60515, U.S.A.
38 De Montfort Street, Leicester LE1 7GP, England

InterVarsity Press®, U.S.A., is the book-publishing division of InterVarsity Christian Fellowship®, a student movement active on campus at hundreds of universities, colleges and schools of nursing in the United States of America, and a member movement of the International Fellowship of Evangelical Students. For information about local and regional activities, write Public Relations Dept., InterVarsity Christian Fellowship, 6400 Schroeder Rd., P.O. Box 7895, Madison, WI 53707-7895.

Inter-Varsity Press, England, is the book-publishing division of the Universities and Colleges Christian Fellowship (formerly the Inter-Varsity Fellowship), a student movement linking Christian Unions in universities and colleges throughout the United Kingdom and the Republic of Ireland, and a member movement of the International Fellowship of Evangelical Students. For information about local and national activities write to UCCF, 38 De Montfort Street, Leicester LE1 7GP.

USA ISBN 0-8308-1814-6
UK ISBN 0-85111-676-0

Printed in the United States of America ⊗

Library of Congress Cataloging-in-Publication Data

Towner, Philip, 1953-
 1-2 Timothy & Titus/Philip H. Towner.
    p.   cm.—(The IVP New Testament commentary series)
 Includes bibliographical references.
 ISBN 0-8308-1814-6
 1. Bible. N.T. Timothy—Commentaries. 2. Bible. N.T. Titus—
Commentaries. I. Title. II.Title: 1-2 Timothy and Titus.
III. Series.
 BS2735.3.T68 1994
 227'.8307—dc20   94-413
                                                      CIP

British Library Cataloguing in Publication Data

A catalogue record for this book is available from the British Library.

17	16	15	14	13	12	11	10	9	8	7	6	5	4	3	2	1
08	07	06	05	04	03	02	01	00	99	98	97	96	95	94		

For Anne

General Preface

In an age of proliferating commentary series, one might easily ask why add yet another to the seeming glut. The simplest answer is that no other series has yet achieved what we had in mind—a series to and from the church, that seeks to move from the text to its contemporary relevance and application.

No other series offers the unique combination of solid, biblical exposition and helpful explanatory notes in the same user-friendly format. No other series has tapped the unique blend of scholars and pastors who share both a passion for faithful exegesis and a deep concern for the church. Based on the New International Version of the Bible, one of the most widely used modern translations, the IVP New Testament Commentary Series builds on the NIV's reputation for clarity and accuracy. Individual commentators indicate clearly whenever they depart from the standard translation as required by their understanding of the original Greek text.

The series contributors represent a wide range of theological traditions, united by a common commitment to the authority of Scripture for

Christian faith and practice. Their efforts here are directed toward applying the unchanging message of the New Testament to the ever-changing world in which we live.

Readers will find in each volume not only traditional discussions of authorship and backgrounds, but useful summaries of principal themes and approaches to contemporary application. To bridge the gap between commentaries that stress the flow of an author's argument but skip over exegetical nettles and those that simply jump from one difficulty to another, we have developed our unique format that expounds the text in uninterrupted form on the upper portion of each page while dealing with other issues underneath in verse-keyed notes. To avoid clutter we have also adopted a social studies note system that keys references to the bibliography.

We offer the series in hope that pastors, students, Bible teachers and small group leaders of all sorts will find it a valuable aid—one that stretches the mind and moves the heart to ever-growing faithfulness and obedience to our Lord Jesus Christ.

Author's Preface

I suppose it was natural that after working on the Pastoral Epistles during my postgraduate research I should desire the chance to bring out their practical implications in a useful way. And I am grateful to the IVPNTC editors, Grant Osborne and James Hoover, for giving me that opportunity. But I have discovered that the task of bringing any insight gained at that level to bear on the actual situations in which churches and Christians find themselves today is about equivalent to the challenge one faces coming fresh out of theological training into the real world. Life on the inside of the university or theological seminary may have little to do with life on the outside. And ministry that is relevant, whether it is preaching or writing a book, requires engagement in the world and its struggles.

However much it reflects it, this book had its start and development during my introduction to life after theological training. I had just taken up my first full-time teaching post and had done so in a foreign culture. There is no better way to flush from the system naive notions about the spiritual life or easy formulas for Christian living. What I may have begun to wonder about as a student became absolutely clear to me as a teacher: this life is resistant to the easy answers of the classroom. Anyway, I think my own attempt to come to terms with the mysteries of life has influenced the shape of this book, hopefully for the good.

I am indebted to many commentators who have gone before me, and not simply to those with whom I might agree. It would be difficult to draw up a fair list, but certainly Donald Guthrie, Gordon Fee, J. N. D. Kelly, Martin Dibelius and Hans Conzelmann, and Jerome Quinn, among others, would have to be included. In the case of some, at either end of the theological spectrum, it has been the sheer tenacity with which they hold to their views that has moved me. Others who stand in the middle and hold opposing views in tension have influenced me with their courage. If we cannot agree on all interpretive matters, I hope we can at least agree that these three letters at the back end of the Pauline corpus have something important to say to Christians today, and that we must make every effort to put this message into accurate and understandable terms.

Of the many others who have played a part in this work, I am especially grateful to Rüdiger Fuchs, who has shared much with me from a great distance; to Warren Heard for his friendship, insights and support; and to my students at China Evangelical Seminary in Taipei and Covenant Theological Seminary in St. Louis, on whom much of the material was tried out. Above all I owe a debt of thanks to my wife, Anne, and to my daughters, Rebekah and Erin, for their love and patience.

Introduction

None of the Pauline letters have found it as difficult to gain a hearing in our times as 1 and 2 Timothy and Titus—the Pastoral Epistles. Why? For one thing, they occur near the end of Paul's writings. For another, the majority of modern scholars doubt that Paul wrote them. Even the evangelical church, which is generally less concerned with the question of authorship, has been somewhat ambivalent about their contents. I have heard many messages and whole series of messages on the first nine letters of Paul, but only a handful of sermons on texts from the Pastoral Epistles. This may be due to the perception that these letters were meant solely for ministers, like Timothy and Titus. Or the problems of false teachers, apostasy from the faith and bizarre doctrines they address may seem quite unlike those we face. But actually 1 and 2 Timothy and Titus need to be heard today as much as any of the letters of Paul.

What do these three letters have to do with our present situation? Consider the agendas for Christian action and evangelical response being set in many quarters of the church today. At the forefront are a number of very pressing items: the church's role in a changing society, the church's responsibility to the poor and the disfranchised, the Christian message among competing messages, the secularization of Christianity, church and state. Consider some of the perennial issues: a Christian attitude to wealth and materialism, the church's response to the cults, spiritual lifestyle, leadership and authority, the role of women, discipline in the church. Finally, consider some of the items on our personal agendas: the true meaning of godliness, faithfulness to the gospel, suffering and life in the Spirit, responsibility to those in authority, the importance of Christian witness. For the church that seeks to understand its role in a complex world and for the individual Christian "who wants to live a godly life in Christ Jesus" (2 Tim 3:12) today, the Pastoral Epistles make very relevant reading.

□ The Situation of the Pastoral Epistles

One of the first tasks in determining the message of a New Testament writing is to place the writing within its original historical, cultural and literary setting. We must understand its original relevance before we try to bring the biblical message across the centuries to apply in our own time. To understand the author's original thrust, we must understand, if we can, the conditions of the church he addressed and the terms in which he addressed it. Of course, this applies to all of the New Testament writings, but the Pastoral Epistles present some particular challenges in this respect:

1. Where do 1 and 2 Timothy and Titus belong in the historical framework of Paul's ministry?

2. How should the content, topics and distinctive interests of the letters be explained?

These two large questions actually involve several smaller ones, which will be treated below under the categories of the situation and teaching of the Pastoral Epistles. Once we have considered these questions, we will examine the problems related to authorship.

Post-Pauline Origin and Fictitious Setting? With the works of such nineteenth-century scholars as Schleiermacher and Baur, the authenticity of the Pastoral Epistles came under heavy suspicion. Differences in style, vocabulary and theology and descriptions of a heresy that, they held, must be second-century Gnosticism tipped the scales away from the traditional view. The majority of modern scholars maintain that the Pastoral Epistles are pseudepigraphical—that is, written pseudonymously (in Paul's name) sometime after Paul's death (so Dibelius and Conzelmann, Brox, Barrett, Hanson, Houlden, Karris, Hultgren). Most today locate these three letters around the turn of the century, suggesting that the author aimed to revive Pauline teaching for his day or to compose a definitive and authoritative Pauline manual for denouncing heresy in the postapostolic church. Therefore, according to this view, the situations that emerge in the letters are fictional. Dibelius and Conzelmann (1972:66) maintain that the author does not describe a particular heresy or heretical group but "heresy" in general.

As Michael Prior points out, the nature of the pseudepigraphical theory makes it virtually impervious to disproof: "All that needs to be done is to propose that some unknown person, on some unknown occasion, and for some supposed reason produced his own theological viewpoint under the guise of Pauline letters" (1989:23). But is the theory necessary for the Pastoral Epistles to make sense? And are the assumptions it rests upon sound? The first of these questions will be addressed below. The second perhaps reveals a weakness. What most proponents of the theory assume is that pseudepigraphy was an accepted practice among Christians (see Donelson 1986). But in fact the number of undisputed Christian pseudepigraphical works does not provide overwhelming evidence of an accepted literary practice within the early church. Furthermore, the early church seems to have been quite consistent in denouncing as inauthentic and inferior the pseudepigraphical writings that came to its attention (see Guthrie 1962:43-59). Consensus or no, then, there would still seem to be room for considering other explanations that link the Pastoral Epistles to Paul.

The Letters Within Paul's Ministry In the first place, since the Pastoral Epistles are three in number, one would assume that there are actually three (more or less) separate situations that need to be ascertained. Still, the interests and language of these letters, and perhaps also the time period in which they were written, make them a "corpus" within the whole of the Pauline writings. But where do we place these letters within Paul's ministry? The majority of scholars who believe the letters to be authentic prefer to locate them after the end of Acts, because the details within them do not seem to correspond with Luke's account.

Gordon Fee (1988:3-5) provides one reconstruction. First Timothy and Titus depict Paul traveling east of Rome after his release from an initial Roman imprisonment (Acts 28). These travels included a visit to Crete, with Titus, during which churches were planted; since opposition was encountered, Titus was left behind to see the work further along (Tit 1:5). Then, during a stopover in Ephesus on their way to Macedonia, Paul and Timothy discovered that false teaching had arisen due to the influence of some defected leaders (Hymenaeus and Alexander are named in 1 Tim 1:19-20). Timothy was subsequently left to sort these matters out, as Paul continued on to Macedonia (1 Tim 1:3). Paul wrote back to his coworkers (1 Timothy and Titus) from Macedonia (c. A.D. 62-65). Timothy's instructions at this point were to stay put; Titus, on the other hand, once relieved, was to travel to Nicopolis, where Paul planned to spend the winter months (Tit 3:12). At some point in the course of additional travels, Paul was rearrested, and he apparently returned to Rome to await his final trial. At this point (c. A.D. 65), with the end in sight, a more somber Paul wrote to Timothy to exhort him in his work and to encourage him to get to Rome with all speed (2 Tim 4:21).

Some questions remain. First, that Paul was indeed released from the imprisonment in Rome recorded in Acts 28 is somewhat conjectural. But Luke's silence on this point in the ending of Acts does not rule out the possibility (see Ellis 1989:107-11). Second, Paul's original plans for further travel seem to have envisioned movement in a westward direction (Rom 15:23-29). But an eastward change in Paul's itinerary already seems to be indicated in Philippians, Colossians and Philemon, letters that Paul may have written during that Roman imprisonment and in which he intimates his expectation of release (Fee 1988:4; on the possibility of a Caesarean origination of the prison letters, see Gunther 1972:91-121).

E. Earle Ellis (1989:107-11; see also Prior 1989:61-90) enters another detail that may be of importance in reconstructing the final stage of the Pauline mission. His conclusion concerning the end of Acts is that Luke closes Acts on the note of Paul's "rather mild detention" because he knows of Paul's subsequent release but chooses not to publicize it. More to the point, there is fairly firm tradition that Paul did in fact complete his plans to travel to the west. The Muratorian Canon and the Acts of Peter (1-3; 6), both written in the second century, indicate that Paul left Rome for Spain. First Clement, written by Clement of Rome in the last decade of the first century, describes Paul as having traveled to the "extreme limits of the west" (5:6-7), which from the perspective of a Roman can only be Spain. Then, according to Ellis, after preaching in Spain, perhaps while returning eastward, he received news of problems in Ephesus and Crete. To aid Timothy and Titus, he wrote the letters 1 Timothy and Titus. On this reconstruction the Cretan churches would presumably have been planted sometime prior to the initial Roman imprisonment, despite Luke's failure to mention it. But since Luke's account is not exhaustive, this is not necessarily an insoluble problem. Perhaps Paul never personally ministered there; Titus 1:5 possibly means "I left you in that position." In any case, the above association of 2 Timothy with a second, final Roman imprisonment also fits Ellis's explanation.

As I pointed out, it is widely acknowledged that Luke's account of Paul's travels is not exhaustive. In recent times several significant attempts have been made to locate the Pastorals within Acts. Knight (1992:15-17) draws attention to the difficulties that most of these approaches face in matching events or movements noted in the Pastorals with Luke's recounting of the details. However, the argument of J. van Bruggen (1981) deserves more attention than it has received, for it does not depend on cross-matching in the same way.

The basic argument is that Paul wrote 1 Timothy and Titus during his third missionary journey (Acts 18:23—21:15) and 2 Timothy from prison in Rome (Acts 28). Most crucial is the locating of 1 Timothy and Titus in Acts, since Luke does not mention Timothy's ministry in Ephesus or Titus's in Crete. Van Bruggen posits a gap in Luke's account between 19:20 and 21, during which Paul made a round trip from Ephesus to Corinth and back. The trip in essence breaks the Ephesian ministry into two stages. What merits notice in this approach is not the gap itself but the substantiation from the Corinthian letters of a two-stage Ephesian ministry and a trip to Corinth.

Both Acts and the Corinthian letters suggest two stages in the Ephesian ministry. Stage one was about two years (and three months?) in length (Acts 19:8-20). Stage two, described in 19:21-40 and including additional work in Ephesus as well as a wider ministry in Asia Minor, is implied by the summary reference to three years in 20:31. The same division is noticeable by a comparison of 2 Corinthians 1:8 (where Paul writes from the perspective of ministry in Asia = stage two; Acts 19:23-40) and 1 Corinthians 15:32 and 16:8 (where Ephesus is specifically in view; stage one, probably near the conclusion). At this point, references to a "third" visit to Corinth in 2 Corinthians 12:14 and 13:1 raise the question, When did Paul visit the second time (see 2 Cor 13:2)? First Corinthians and Acts 18 assume that only one visit had thus far been made. But 1 Corinthians 4:18-19 mentions an upcoming visit. This upcoming "second" visit is probably also in view in 1 Corinthians 16:5-11. And the description there seems to be of a proposed stopover visit in Corinth as part of a broader itinerary; the movement would correspond to a round trip, beginning (just after Pentecost—May) and ending at Ephesus (sometime in the following spring, when sea travel became possible), that lasted about a year. Since Luke restricts stage one (19:8-20) to two years (and three months?), it is not likely that a trip lasting about one year can be inserted into this period. There is also probably not time for this round trip in the second stage (19:21-40).

Does Luke reveal any knowledge of this proposed round trip and break in the Ephesian ministry? Acts 19:29 mentions Paul's "traveling companions from Macedonia" who were seized by the Ephesian mob and dragged into the theater. This is possible confirmation of a trip to Macedonia, which brings into line 1 Corinthians 16:5 and 1 Timothy 1:3 as references to the same trip.

It remains to reconstruct Timothy's and Titus's movements in connection with Paul's. First, 1 Corinthians 16:10 (written from Ephesus prior to the round trip) reveals that at that time Timothy, having been dispatched to Corinth (1 Cor 4:17), had not yet returned to Paul. However, once he had returned, Paul gave him his orders and departed for Macedonia and Corinth (1 Tim 1:3). At this point (perhaps toward the end of the first stage) troubles with false teachers had already begun; Paul alludes to such troubles in 1 Corinthians 15:32 ("I fought wild beasts in Ephesus"). When Paul writes back to Timothy, probably from Macedonia or Achaia, he addresses this situation and expects to return to Ephesus soon (1 Tim 3:14).

Titus may have been sent to Crete from Ephesus by Paul prior to the round trip. Titus 1:5, which some view as an obstacle to such a reconstruction since it seems to imply that Paul and Titus visited Crete together, need mean no more than that Paul "left" him there in the sense of "dispatching" or "assigning" him to duty there. Paul wrote to Titus somewhat after he wrote 1 Timothy (Tit 3:12 suggests that his plans were more settled than when he wrote 1 Tim 3:14). By this time, earlier plans possibly to spend the winter in Corinth (1 Cor 16:6) were changed so that Paul would go to Nicopolis in the same province, probably because his second visit to Corinth proved to be a painful confrontation (2 Cor 2:1).

Acts 19:21-22 picks up the story again after Paul's return with a general summary, reference to Paul's future plans and a general description of the second stage as "a little longer in Asia." But shortly after Paul's return the riot occurred (vv. 20-41).

According to van Bruggen, Paul wrote 2 Timothy from Rome during his first (and possibly only) imprisonment there (Acts 28). But a problem emerges. When Paul writes (presumably from Rome) to the Philippians, the Colossians and Philemon, Timothy is with him; but 2 Timothy is written to Timothy from Rome. However, the three former letters, which reflect a more optimistic tone, could well have come from the early stage of the imprisonment, which lasted two years (Acts 28:30), during which Timothy was with Paul (Paul may mention certain Roman Christians by name because Timothy had met them; 2 Tim 4:21). There would be ample time for Timothy to have been dispatched back to Ephesus/Asia Minor before Paul's execution.

Whether this third explanation is an improvement on the first two remains to be seen. One of its most attractive features is the way it allows the situation of false teaching and spiritual enthusiasm in Ephesus to be seen in the direct light of similar developments in Corinth (see below). The close relationship of these two churches in Paul's ministry (Acts 18—20), the correspondence of persons (Aquila, Priscilla, Apollos, Paul) and the striking similarity of the churches' theological misunderstanding all make van Bruggen's explanation one worth considering.

Consequently, in combination or separately, Fee and Ellis provide conceivable reconstructions of Paul's travel plans. Van Bruggen's is no less conceivable, although it runs the risks connected with identifying and filling in the gaps left by Luke's account (whereas Fee and Ellis take up where Luke left off).

The Recipients and the Churches The Pastoral Epistles are probably best understood as letters written to individual coworkers of Paul, Timothy and Titus, which were meant to be read to the congregations in which they were working (so each letter closes with a benediction addressed to "all"—1 Tim 6:21; 2 Tim 4:22; Tit 3:15).

During Paul's first missionary journey (Acts 13—14), he and Barnabas stopped and preached the gospel in the region known as Lycaonia (in what is now Turkey) in the cities of Lystra and Derbe (Acts 14:1-20). It is possible, though we cannot be certain, that Timothy, son of a Jewish mother and a Greek father, believed in response to Paul's message. In any case, when Paul returned to these parts on his second journey, Timothy's good reputation among the believers impressed him so that he invited the young man to join his team (16:1-3). To appease the sensibilities of local Jews who knew of Timothy's mixed blood, Paul first circumcised him.

The accounts of Acts establish a pattern for Timothy's ministry with Paul that Paul's own letters elaborate on and confirm. Timothy could be trusted to be sent ahead or left behind to carry on the apostle's work (19:22; 20:4). We learn from Paul of at least three other instances in which Timothy was called on to return to churches planted by Paul— in Thessalonica, Corinth and Philippi—to carry (in the first two cases) and implement Paul's instructions to them (1 Thess 3; 1 Cor 4:16-17; 16:10-11; Phil 2:19-24). The fact that Paul trusted him with the difficult situation in Corinth shows how highly he regarded his young assistant. Paul's recommendation of him to the Philippian church ("I have no one else like him," Phil 2:20) leaves us in no doubt of Timothy's worth.

It is hard to know how far to take certain references to Timothy's disposition and age in assessing his character. Apparently he was of an age that might have led some in Ephesus to question his authority (1 Tim 4:12). Depending on the placement of 1 Timothy into Paul's ministry (see above), as few as five to seven or as many as ten to fourteen years had passed since the time Paul enlisted him in Lystra. Fee is confident that Timothy was older than thirty by the time he was left in Ephesus to oppose the false teachers (1988:2). Some maintain that he was timid in nature (2 Tim 1:6-7), easily discouraged or frightened (1 Cor 16:10-11; 2 Tim 1:8) and prone to sickness (1 Tim 5:23). But if so, Paul nevertheless continued to use him and trust him, and his affectionate epithets ("my son whom I love"—1 Cor 4:17; "my true son in the faith"—1 Tim 1:2; "my dear son"—2 Tim 1:2) indicate an intimate relationship of mutual love.

In comparison, we know very little about Titus. We meet him first in Galatians, where we learn that he was a Gentile (2:3) who had been with Paul as early as (perhaps even prior to) the time when Barnabas went to Tarsus to bring Paul back to Antioch (Gal 2:1; compare Acts 11:25-30). Whether he was a convert of Paul's ("my true son"—Tit 1:4) remains unclear (see commentary). As the situation in Corinth continued to develop, it was Titus whom Paul called on to deliver his corrective teaching and represent him in the matter of the collection for the Christians in Jerusalem (2 Cor 2:3-4, 13; 7:6-16; 8:16-24). In light of this, it comes as no surprise that Paul left (or dispatched) him to strengthen and correct the churches in Crete.

Ephesus was a city located on the western coast of Asia Minor (modern Turkey). Its location along a major trade route made it (like Corinth) a natural point for the church to be planted and from there influence other parts of the Roman Empire. Paul's initial preaching and later three-year period of teaching in the city were undoubtedly major factors in the church's establishment and growth (Acts 18:19-21; 18:24—20:1; 20:13-38). Ephesus was famed for its cult and temple dedicated to the worship of Artemis, around which a good deal of the city's commercial interests revolved. It also had a large Jewish colony. Ephesus presented the gospel with a formidable challenge in that it was a center of pagan worship. From its inception here (see Acts 19) the church was very much in the public eye. When we speak of "the church" in Ephesus, we should understand a system (more or less) of house churches (compare 1 Cor 16:19).

Crete is an island in the Mediterranean, situated south of Greece and

Asia Minor on a north-south line bisecting the Aegean Sea. Although Luke reports that Paul, as a prisoner being escorted by ship to Rome, visited Crete (Acts 27:7-17), it does not appear that he had enough time for evangelistic activity, even if he had had freedom to engage in it. The people of Crete had inherited a nasty reputation, as the quote of Epimenides shows (Tit 1:12). Paul applies the quote specifically to a group of agitators in the church, but if there was any truth to the ancient assessment of Cretan character, then we can easily imagine that church planting and the nurturing of young Christians in Crete must have been an especially arduous undertaking. What we know of the church there comes from the letter to Titus. The task left to Titus—to complete and put in order what was unfinished (1:5; see commentary)—suggests a church (probably house churches in most of the districts) considerably younger and less organized than the church in Ephesus.

The Occasion for Writing A quick scan of these letters makes it clear that Paul's central concern in writing was to give instruction for confronting false teachers and restoring the stability of the churches. Although the descriptions in 1 Timothy and Titus are very similar, the opponents are not precisely the same. They may be "separate manifestations of a general contemporary tendency" (Guthrie 1957:35). If the two letters were written at roughly the same time, this might help to explain the similarity. These emerging parties have been labeled "opponents," "false teachers," "errorists," "spiritual enthusiasts," "pneumatics" and "heretics," and each label reflects one or more of the various facets of their doctrine, methods and behavior. In any case, the presence of the opposing movements in Ephesus and Crete was determinative for the shape of Paul's message in the Pastorals.

Several passages indicate that the opponents originated within the churches rather than invading from the outside (as in the case of the Galatian and Corinthian situations—Gal 2:4; 2 Cor 11:4). First, directions to Timothy and Titus to "command," "urge," "rebuke" and "warn" (1 Tim 1:3; 6:2; 2 Tim 2:14; 4:2; Tit 1:13; 3:10) imply that the false teachers were members of the community and, at least in principle, therefore subject to the church's authority. Then the reference to Hymenaeus and Philetus (2 Tim 2:17-18), who seem to have been leaders in the opposition movement, and Hymenaeus's excommunication (1 Tim 1:20; see commentary) point in the same direction. Similarly, the reference to a prophecy in 1 Timothy 4:1 (see Paul's warning to the Ephesian elders—Acts 20:28-31), which predicted the defection of some from the faith, and the repeated description of the heretics as deviating from or denying the faith (1 Tim 1:6; 6:21; 2 Tim 2:18) imply that the false teachers had once been "of the faith." Finally, 2 Timothy 2:19-21 depicts the church as a mixture of true and false Christians and lends support to the idea that the false teachers (particularly in Ephesus) emerged from within the church.

In light of some additional clues it seems likely that some of the false teachers in Ephesus were elders in the church (Fee 1988). First, Paul emphasizes the need for extreme care in selecting elders (1 Tim 3:1-7; 5:17-25) and deacons (3:8-13). Second, they seem to have been able to influence the communities in the role of teachers, a function that corresponds to the office of elder/overseer (3:2; 5:17). If the reference in Titus 1:11 to "whole households" is to house churches, then there again Paul may be expressing his concern for the influence of defected leaders on the church. In any case, the situations that arose in Crete and especially in Ephesus correspond closely to Paul's prophetic warning: "Even from your own number men will arise and distort the truth in order to draw away disciples after them" (Acts 20:30).

Very little can actually be discerned of the false doctrine. But probably a central feature, in the case of Ephesus, was a misunderstanding of the resurrection. The key passage is 2 Timothy 2:18, which attributes to Hymenaeus and Philetus the teaching of the doctrine that the resurrection (of believers) has already occurred. Furthermore, to judge from similarities between this passage and 1 Timothy 6:20-21, which mentions the "falsely called knowledge" of the heretics, this resurrection doctrine was at least one (probably major) element in their "knowledge." This belief, as paradoxical as it might strike us, has a parallel in 1 Corinthians 15:12-58. The effect of the similar teaching in either case seems to have been to convince adherents that spiritual "fullness" is completely available now (1 Cor 4:8).

We can only speculate on how this doctrine might have developed. One possibility is that Paul's teaching about baptism and present participation in Christ's resurrection (Rom 6:3-8; 1 Cor 4:8; Eph 2:5; Col 2:12; 2 Tim 2:11-13), which draws a fine line between our present and future experience of salvation, was misunderstood. By asserting that all was available now, the heretics' understanding of salvation became too realized (see Towner 1989:29-42).

The false teaching affected the communities in several ways, and there are a number of parallels between the Corinthian situation and that reflected in 1 and 2 Timothy. In each case, Paul's instructions seem to address or anticipate some sort of unrest or unsanctioned behavior among women (1 Cor 11:2-16; 14:33-35; 1 Tim 2:9-15; 5:15; 2 Tim 3:6; Tit 2:3-5) and perhaps slaves too (1 Tim 6:1-2; Tit 2:9-10; compare 1 Cor 7:21-24). The relevance of the institution of marriage was being either denied outright (1 Tim 4:3) or questioned (1 Cor 7:1-16). And in the Pastorals Paul's teaching may indicate a general disregard on the part of the errorists for the institution of the family, which may also have been linked to its too-realized view of salvation.

How the false doctrine, or the view of salvation that it seems to indicate, would influence behavior in this manner is not entirely clear. But presumably in the case of women and slaves the belief that the fullness of salvation was at hand "now" could have led them to implement promises of equality associated with the Pauline gospel (see Gal 3:28), which a rigid social structure resisted. Marriage and rigidly defined social institutions such as the household could easily be regarded as belonging to the "old" era of incompleteness. Such developments can indeed be found in later Gnostic writings, but admittedly these connections are nowhere near as certain in the situations described by the Pastoral Epistles or 1 Corinthians and so must be pursued with caution.

Another distinctive element in the false teaching was the opponents' use of the Old Testament. "Myths and endless genealogies" (1 Tim 1:4), "myths" (1 Tim 4:7; 2 Tim 4:4), "Jewish myths" (Tit 1:14) and "genealogies" (Tit 3:9) are probably all descriptions of a speculative use of the Old Testament creation material and stories about famous personages, from which proof texts and spiritual lessons (or bizarre doctrines) were drawn (Quinn 1990:100-101, 245-48; see 1 Tim 1:4 commentary and notes). Further allusions to their interest in (and misuse of) the Old Testament law point in the same direction. This practice, which the rabbis of that time also engaged in, is possible evidence that the heretics were Jewish Christians. Perhaps the movement in Crete was Jewish in flavor as well. But the presence of the resurrection heresy suggests that in Ephesus there was something more than a return to Judaizing legalism (as in the Galatian church) at work. Somehow the Ephesians' use of the Old Testament supplied or substantiated their special "knowledge." And it is possible that support for their bold behavior and ascetic tendencies was derived from their arcane use of the Bible.

The opponents in Ephesus prohibited marriage, and there is evidence of food restrictions in both churches (1 Tim 4:3; Tit 1:15). In the case of marriage, similar thinking is evident among later Gnostics (Irenaeus *Against Heresies* 1.24.2), earlier (or perhaps contemporary) Essenes (according to Philo *Apology* 380) and in the more closely related Corinthian situation (1 Cor 7:1-7). Although some see in this aspect of the heresy an underlying Gnostic disregard for women, it is not necessarily a good idea to jump to much later documents to explain this phenomenon. The whole strain of developments seen in the Corinthian letters, Colossians (for common elements here, see Knight 1992:11-12, 28) and the Pastorals may be the reflection of the influence of Hellenistic-Jewish speculation on Christian thought (see Fee 1988:8-9). The Corinthian church provides a closer point of comparison. There, as pointed out above, the church was also under the influence of an unbalanced view of the times, and some of its members were questioning the continuing relevance of marriage (1 Cor 7:1-7). There, and in 1 Timothy 4, the problem Paul addresses is more likely the growing suspicion that marriage belonged to the "old" order which had passed away, or that the model for living in the resurrection age was to be found in descriptions of life before the fall into sin (Gen 1—2; see 1 Tim 2:11-15).

Abstinence from certain foods reflects some type of dualism, whether Jewish (Col 2:16-23; Tit 1:15; see Knight 1992:28), Greek or eschatological. Some foods were regarded as unclean.

Finally, a word should be said about Paul's method of denouncing the false teachers. He criticizes the opponents and their teaching with numerous harsh adjectives. Their teaching is "godless" (1 Tim 4:7), "chatter" (1 Tim 6:20), "meaningless talk" (1 Tim 1:6), "foolish and stupid" (2 Tim 2:23), "foolish controversies" (Tit 3:9), "old wives' tales" (1 Tim

4:7) and so on. The false teachers themselves are "hypocritical liars" with "seared" consciences (1 Tim 4:2) who "understand nothing" (1 Tim 6:4; see 1:7) and "have been robbed of the truth" (1 Tim 6:5; see 2 Tim 3:13). The effect of this sort of characterization (see the lists of vices: 1 Tim 1:9-10; 6:4-5; 2 Tim 3:2-5) was to create a stereotype in the minds of the faithful that would keep them from associating with the false teachers and their doctrines.

□ **The Teaching of the Pastoral Epistles**
Most of Paul's statements in the Pastorals and the manner in which he makes them are governed by the presence of heresy in the churches. The three focal points in Paul's message are Timothy/Titus, the churches and the false teachers. Although the opposition movements determine the shape of the message, there are still limitations on how far each piece of teaching can be pressed to yield specific information about the opponents and their beliefs (as we saw above in considering the false teaching and its effects). Still, to miss the fact that the rise of false teaching in the Ephesian and Cretan churches precipitated these letters is to miss their point and severely restrict their application to our modern situations.

Forms and Sources Generally speaking, 1 and 2 Timothy and Titus are letters. But the nature of their content has led some German scholars to conclude that especially 1 Timothy represents a stage in literary development on the way to the church order. Of course, the extant church orders are much later than the New Testament, and this conclusion about the Pastorals relies heavily on the assumption that their date of composition is at least as late as A.D. 100. According to Ellis (1989:107-11), the Pastorals contain a number of teaching materials originally written by others to deal with such issues as church organization and false teaching. Paul incorporated these materials into letters addressed to his coworkers for their use in Ephesus and Crete. The much different focus of these letters compared with Paul's earlier letters (church organization instead of theological interpretation) was related to the increase in the number of churches whose loose organization opened them up to the common problem of false teachers. It remains to be seen whether Ellis's explanation is an improvement on the traditional view (that the Pastorals are simply three letters written by Paul to specific situations), but it certainly provides a reasonable alternative to the church order hypothesis.

All agree, however, that the materials in the Pastorals come from a variety of sources. In two places, 1 Timothy 3:1-13 and Titus 1:5-9, Paul employs (and adapts) codes that regulate selection of overseers/elders and deacons. It is not certain where they originated (possibly in the church at Rome—Ellis 1989:111), but secular office codes may have provided a model (see Dibelius and Conzelmann 1972:50-51, as well as my commentary on these passages).

The early church's common ethical teaching was the source of Paul's "household code" instruction: 1 Timothy 2:8-15; 5:1-2; 6:1-2; Titus 2:1—3:8. Initially, such material gave instruction concerning appropriate conduct within the various relationships found in the household and in society: husband-wife, parent-child, master-slave, citizen-state.

While 1 Timothy's specific teaching concerning widows (5:3-16), elders (5:17-25) and the wealthy (6:17-19) exceeds the bounds of the traditional New Testament household codes (compare Ephesians, Colossians, 1 Peter), the tendency to address the Ephesian believers according to socioeconomic or official categories may be patterned after the household code, and it is possible (though not necessary) that the instructions in these passages represent teaching that was current beyond the Pauline churches.

The early church had also accumulated a collection of theological material: hymns, creeds, baptism and (perhaps) ordination pieces and other preaching formulas. Paul clearly adapts such material for use in 1 Timothy 1:15-16; 2:3-6; 3:16; 2 Timothy 1:9-10; 2:8-13; and Titus 2:11-14; 3:5-7. The so-called faithful saying formula sometimes introduces theological material (1 Tim 1:15; 2 Tim 2:11; Tit 3:8) and sometimes ethical material (1 Tim 3:1; 4:9).

Other sources are also apparent. On a couple of occasions the source of material seems to be Jesus' own teaching (1 Tim 5:18; 6:19). Paul also draws from secular popular wisdom (1 Tim 6:10; Tit 1:12) and from the Old Testament and the intertestamental Wisdom and apocryphal traditions (1 Tim 6:7-8; 2 Tim 2:19; 3:8). In several places Paul may have made use of his own earlier teaching or compositions (1 Tim 5:17; 2 Tim 2:11, 20).

A final source that should be mentioned is Hellenistic ethics. Many ethical terms in the Pastorals probably derive from the pagan ethicists. To cite but one of many instances, Titus 2:12, in describing the new Christian life, makes use of three of the Greek cardinal virtues: "self-controlled, upright and godly." But Paul does not endorse a secular ethic; he rather makes use of widely known terminology to communicate the Christian message.

Despite Paul's obvious use of prepared material, the Pastorals are original in their message. In fact, the materials he used were chosen for their suitability to the issues and audience he was addressing or the themes he was creating. In many cases the fact that the materials were well known by the churches would have given them added credibility within messages designed to call them back to the genuine Christian faith.

Theology Paul is especially concerned to drive home the fact that salvation is a present reality (compare Dibelius and Conzelmann 1972:8-10 and Towner 1989:75-119). To do this he incorporates at various points pieces of the early church's traditional teaching: 1 Timothy 1:15-16; 2:3-6; 3:16; 2 Timothy 1:9-10; 2:8-13; Titus 2:11-14; 3:4-7. Each piece announces in its own way that salvation is a matter of historical record because Christ entered history and accomplished it. However, in response to the false teaching that apparently misunderstood the partial nature of the salvation experience "now" (2 Tim 2:18), Paul presents salvation as unfinished.

He does this in several ways. First, he describes the present age itself as terminal and evil ("the last days"—2 Tim 3:1; 1 Tim 4:1), and so we look forward to the return of Christ (1 Tim 6:14; 2 Tim 1:12, 18; 4:1, 8; Tit 2:13), which will mark the completion of salvation, the passage of the present imperfect age, and the full arrival of the age to come (1 Tim 4:8; 6:19). Second, the striking use of "epiphany" (meaning "appearance") language in reference to both the first advent (2 Tim 1:10; Tit 2:11; 3:4) and the awaited second advent (1 Tim 6:14; 2 Tim 4:1, 8; Tit 2:13) of Christ characterizes salvation and the present age in a unique way. Salvation is depicted as intrinsically related to both of these epiphanies: it began with Christ's first appearance but will be brought to a full conclusion only with his second appearance. The present age stands between these two poles, and life therein—Christian life—alternately experiences the life of the dawning new age and the death of "the last days."

If salvation is incomplete, so is the church's mission. An often-overlooked concern of these three epistles is mission. The church exists for many reasons, but one of the most primary is to spread the gospel. The false teaching threatened the church and the message entrusted to it, and Paul reminds his colleagues and the churches of their responsibility to this task. The whole of 1 Timothy 2 and 3 is devoted to mission: prayer, the appropriate behavior of men and women, and the organization of the church's leadership all figure in the effectiveness of the church's participation in God's salvation program. In the same way the evangelistic mission sets the tone for Titus (1:1-3). Paul also defines his and his coworkers' task largely in terms of mission (1 Tim 1:11-12; 2:7; 2 Tim 1:8, 11-14; 2:8-13; 4:1-5; Tit 1:1-3). And in giving commands to safeguard the message (1 Tim 6:20; 2 Tim 1:14), Paul clearly has in mind the danger to the mission posed by distortions of the gospel. Furthermore, the underlying motive of much of the ethical teaching is the good witness that leads others to Christ (1 Tim 3:7; 5:14; 6:1; Tit 2:5, 9; 3:2, 8). God's will, the readers are reminded, is the salvation of "all" (1 Tim 2:4; see 4:10).

Ethics Much of the body of each of these letters is taken up with teaching related to various aspects of the Christian life. Again, disturbances in the churches caused either directly or indirectly by the false teaching almost certainly prompt this part of Paul's message. Paul's goal when speaking to certain social groups (men, women, slaves, the affluent), to church leaders (overseers/elders, deacons), to believers in general or to his coworkers is to restore stability to the churches and encourage the Christian life of witness. In Crete, whole households (or house churches) had been upset by the false teaching (Tit 1:11), and Titus 2—3 is a call to return to responsible Christian behavior. In Ephesus, the emancipationist behavior of some women and slaves, possibly related in some way to mistaken notions about the "times" circulated by the enthusiasts, called for correction (1 Tim 2:11-15; 6:1-2).

In general, Paul sought to splice back together the belief and practice dimensions of Christian living that the heretics had separated with their emphasis on special knowledge and their careless disregard for conduct. Consequently, when Paul described genuine Christian living, his focus was very much on the observable life. He drew from a popular vocabulary terms such as "self-control" (1 Tim 3:2; 2 Tim 1:7; Tit 2:12), "modestly," "decency," "propriety" (1 Tim 2:9), "respectable," "hospitable" (1 Tim 3:2), "gentleness" (1 Tim 6:11; Tit 3:1), "uprightness" (or "righteousness"—1 Tim 6:11; 2 Tim 2:22; Tit 2:12), all of which focus on behavior that is observably superior. But far from simply adopting pagan notions of respectability, Paul grounded this observably superior life in the salvation brought by Christ (Tit 2:11-12). For Paul, genuine faith in God must have observable results. In fact, Paul's favorite term in the Pastorals for genuine Christian life, "godliness" (eusebeia, 1 Tim 2:2; 3:16; 4:8; 5:4; 6:3, 5, 6, 11; 2 Tim 3:12; Tit 1:1; 2:12), which he may have borrowed from the heretics' own teaching (1 Tim 6:5; 2 Tim 3:5), envisions Christianity as the combination of faith in God and the observable conduct that faith produces.

We might ask why Paul chose to use such a heavy concentration of Hellenistic ethical terms in the Pastoral Epistles. Paul was very sensitive to his culture, and very disturbed that the behavior of Christians in Ephesus and Crete was bringing criticism on the church from outsiders (1 Tim 3:7; 6:1; Tit 2:10; 3:2). For him to encourage the churches to live a life that would measure up even to pagans' critical estimate was sound evangelistic technique. The mission motive behind the life he called for is obvious.

A concern for outside opinion and for restoring order to the churches also underlies the teaching concerning the offices of overseer/elder (1 Tim 3:1-7; 5:17-25; Tit 1:5-9) and deacon (1 Tim 3:8-13). The office codes and the instructions concerning the selection of elders aim at establishing "blamelessness" of reputation and, as far as possible, a proven track record. In Paul's mind, the believability of the gospel and the credibility of Christian conduct are inseparably linked. This goes doubly for the Christian leader.

□ Authorship

According to the letters themselves, Paul is the author. But according to the consensus of modern scholarship, someone other than Paul, perhaps a disciple or a later church leader, wrote in his name. Among the commentators who maintain that the Pastorals are inauthentic (or pseudonymous) are Dibelius and Conzelmann (1972), Quinn (1992), Brox (1989), Karris (1979), Barrett (1963), Hanson (1982), Houlden (1976), Easton (1948) and Hultgren (1984). Among those in favor of authenticity are Fee (1988), Kelly (1963), Guthrie (1957), Spicq (1969), Jeremias (1975), Hendriksen (1957) and Johnson (1987). Lock (1924) seems to have been uncertain. For the view of the Pastorals as letters incorporating Pauline fragments, see Barclay (1975) and Harrison (1921; Barclay's use of the argument is far more positive). The questions involved are not necessarily easily answered, and a definitive solution is not likely to be forthcoming.

The arguments advanced by Dibelius and Conzelmann (1972:1-5) in support of pseudonymity are representative:

1. The external evidence indicative of authenticity is not very strong. The Pastorals are not included in Marcion's canon or the Chester Beatty Papyri (P^{46}). And there is not much evidence that the early fathers (specifically Ignatius and Polycarp) knew them.

2. The style of the polemic against heresy is unlike that of the earlier (authentic) Pauline writings.

3. The situations reflected in the Pastorals do not seem to fit the life of Paul as told by Acts and Paul's undisputed writings.

4. The church organization in the Pastorals reflects developments that are best located at the turn of the century or later.

5. In general, the Pastorals depict a "bourgeois," middle-class Christianity, concerned mainly with peaceful coexistence with the world, that cannot possibly be reconciled with authentic Pauline thought (39-41).

6. The Pastorals contain a good deal of vocabulary foreign to the other Pauline epistles.

No defense of Pauline authorship of the Pastoral Epistles can hope to resolve all doubts raised by the points above. Nevertheless, a plausible response is possible.

1. In fact, the external evidence pointing toward authenticity is nearly as strong as the evidence for any other of the Pauline epistles. Polycarp may well have referred to them (*Philippians* 4. 1) sometime prior to

c. A.D 135. Irenaeus (c. A.D. 180) accepted them as Pauline *(Against Heresies* 2. 14. 7; 3. 3. 3). While it is true that Marcion did not include them in his canon (c. A.D. 150), he may have rejected them because they contained teaching in opposition to his own (especially 1 Tim 4:1-5; see Tertullian *Against Marcion* 5. 21), not because he regarded them as inauthentic. By the close of the second century the Pastorals were clearly a fixture within the canon (see further Guthrie 1957:12-15; 1970:585-88).

2. While it is arguable that the polemic against opponents in the Pastorals differs from that of other Pauline epistles, the difference may be more a matter of intensity and concentration than of actual style or content. Most, if not all, of the elements of the polemic can be found elsewhere in Paul. For example, the derogatory labels in 1 Timothy 4:2 are no harsher than those occurring in Philippians 3:2 and 2 Corinthians 11:13. The vice lists of 1 Corinthians 5:10-11 and Romans 1:29-31 serve similar purposes to those of 1 Timothy 1:9-10 and 6:4-5. The use of the Pauline "model" to introduce a contrast with the opponent in 1 Timothy 1:5-16 is comparable to the ploy of 2 Corinthians 11—12. True, the Pastorals deal less directly with the opponents than do the other Pauline epistles. But on the one hand, the development of theological and ethical themes does indeed present a corrective to the false teaching and its effects. On the other hand, the letters purport to have been written directly to Timothy and Titus, so a less direct engagement with the opponents is to be expected. In fact, if the marked difference in situations addressed by the Pastorals in comparison with the other Pauline epistles is taken into account (not to mention the possible influence of a secretary), this part of the argument against authenticity becomes groundless.

3-5. In discussing the placement of the Pastorals within Paul's ministry, I have already noted the possibility that the situations that gave rise to 1 Timothy and Titus belong to a period after the conclusion of Acts. I have also outlined a possible solution that places the Pastorals within the Acts framework. For the latter possibility and for the argument from Acts against authenticity, it simply depends how one reads between Luke's lines. Actually, if we keep in mind the post-Acts solution, however helpful corroborative evidence in Acts might be, it cannot be considered a prerequisite for the authenticity of the Pastorals.

The charge that the church order reflected in the Pastorals surpasses anything possible in the lifetime of Paul is also open to question. On the one hand, we must keep in mind the reference to the offices of overseer and deacon in Philippians 1:1 (see also Acts 20:28-31). The Pastorals are indeed unique in the depth of treatment they give to the selection of overseers/elders and deacons, but the particular circumstances that the letters purport to address could easily account for this. That 1 Timothy 3:1 gives evidence of a monarchical episcopate (rule by a single bishop), a post-Pauline development, is not a necessary conclusion. The singular "overseer" of 3:1 is possibly a generic reference to overseers in general, which belongs to the code of qualifications (3:1-7; compare Tit 1:5-9) that Paul adapted for use. The further observation that an office of widows had developed, impossible for Paul's time, is significant only if in fact an office and not simply a system for maintaining needy widows is in view (see commentary; 1 Tim 5:3-16).

Equally uncertain is the argument that the author of the Pastorals portrays Christianity as "middle-class" or "bourgeois." The claim is that, with the delay of Christ's return and the prospect of a lengthy stay in this world, the church had to find a way to ensure its survival. A tendency toward conformity and peaceful coexistence is said to be reflected in the author's ethical teaching, which admittedly emphasizes conduct that is socially responsible and observably superior, and which employs Greek ethical terminology. But on the one hand, the author's hope in the return of Christ is vivid (1 Tim 6:14; Tit 2:13). On the other, the lifestyle he endorses is meant to recommend Christianity to the pagan, as well as to restore the balance disrupted by the false teaching. Once again, it seems that it is the distinctive nature of the situation that shapes the message.

6. The linguistic argument for pseudonymity is the most difficult one, and it can only be introduced here (see Prior 1989:25-35; Harrison 1921; Guthrie 1957:46-48; Kelly 1963:21-27; Barrett 1963:5-7; Lock 1924:xxvi-xxxi). As often noted, the vocabulary of the Pastorals includes words of importance that Paul did not use elsewhere: "godliness" *(eusebeia)*, "self-controlled" *(sōphrōn)*, "appearance" *(epiphaneia* instead of Paul's more normal "coming" *[parousia];* but see 2 Thess 2:8). It omits others that seem characteristic of Paul (for details see Hanson 1982:2-3). Other

terms or ideas of importance in Paul's other letters are used in different ways in the Pastorals: for example, "righteousness" *(dikaiosynē)* for "uprightness" of living (1 Tim 6:11; but see Tit 3:5-7). More telling in terms of style are the differences, in comparison with the major letters, in usage of prepositions and connecting particles (see Turner 1976).

Do these differences force us to the conclusion that Paul is not the author of the Pastoral Epistles? Not necessarily. The different situations in the churches and different thrusts of these letters are factors that complicate any conclusions to be drawn from comparisons of the Pastorals with the remaining Paulines. And considerations of methods of composition raise even more questions. What effect would Paul's use of a secretary have on style and language? In a study originally published in 1965, C. F. D. Moule (1982:113-32) pointed out that many of the non-Pauline terms seem to be Lukan terms. Stephen G. Wilson (1979) developed this line of thought still further, concluding that Luke (though one different from the companion of Paul), the author of Luke and Acts, wrote the Pastoral Epistles toward the end of the first century (see also Quinn 1978 for the argument that the Pastoral Epistles represent Luke's third volume). On the strength of such evidence, Luke has emerged as a strong candidate for the position of secretary in the writing of these three letters (2 Tim 4:11; see also Ellis 1989:104-11; Knight 1992:50-52; Fee 1988:26). Nevertheless, the reviews of the studies mentioned above (for which see Knight 1992:48) advise caution in attempting to solve the problem in this way. But the fact remains that Paul did make use of secretaries (Rom 16:22) and often employed traditional materials that someone else had written (hymns, creeds, Old Testament quotations and other teaching materials), and this makes questionable the need for an immediate retreat to a theory of pseudonymity.

Prior's 1989 study (37-59) puts an even sharper edge on this question. He concludes that the Pastorals are distinctive in style and expression among the Paulines not because they are pseudonymous but because they "are private letters in a double sense" (50). He means that unlike most (perhaps all) of the rest of the Paulines, which appear to have been coauthored (Timothy himself is so named in six, and possibly influenced the contents and expression of even more) and are addressed to groups, Paul was the sole author of the Pastorals and they were written to individuals. If the Pastorals are in fact uniquely Pauline in this way, some (at least) of the differences between them and the rest of the Paulines not only are to be expected but are actually entirely logical.

The studies of both Ellis and Prior demonstrate how far from "assured" is the case for pseudonymity (see Guthrie 1962:43-59). If an amanuensis enters the equation, "vocabulary, idiom, and theological expression can no longer be used in any precise way to determine the Pauline authorship of the letters ascribed to him" (Ellis 1989:104). If sole Pauline authorship is considered, differences between the Pastoral Epistles and the other (coauthored) Pauline epistles may well signify authenticity. Either way, we can be confident that the Pastoral Epistles express Paul's messages to Timothy and Titus and the churches in which they were at work.

Outline of 1 Timothy

5:17-25 ——**Instructions Concerning Elders**

5:17-18 ——Proper Regard for Faithful Elders
5:19-21 ——Discipline of Elders
5:22-25 ——Careful Selection of Elders

6:1-2 ——**Instructions Concerning Slaves**

6:2-16 ——**Final Orders to Timothy**

6:2-5 ——Opposing False Teachers
6:6-8 ——The Christian View of Money
6:9-10 ——Greed: A Love That Consumes
6:11-16 ——Timothy: Man of God

6:17-19 ——**Instructions Concerning the Wealthy**

6:20-21 ——**Final Charge to Timothy**

COMMENTARY

1 Timothy

☐ Greeting (1:1-2)

"Cynthia's a lemming" is a phrase I heard for the first time at a faculty prayer meeting in a Taiwan seminary. Throughout the year that followed, I detected the same phrase over and over again in the prayers of the seminary's president. That I could possibly hear such a thing can only be explained as the combination of his accent and my unaccustomed ear as I was struggling to learn Chinese. I was told that good language learners were to take note of peculiar phrases, and this one seemed to qualify. It was voiced so frequently and with so much feeling that I was convinced of its deep significance. In this at least I was correct. I eventually learned that what sounded like "Cynthia's a lemming" had nothing to do with anyone named Cynthia or that puzzling suicidal rodent. The phrase was an appeal to God, meaning "Give us grace and mercy." Its frequency in the president's prayers revealed his conviction that the foundation of Christian life and service is God's grace and mercy.

Paul's opening lines to Timothy reflect that same deep conviction. As in his other epistles, the greeting takes the form typical of that day: he identifies himself as the sender (v. 1) and Timothy as the recipient (v. 2), and then includes a word of greeting and blessing (v. 2). But this is no form letter.

What I didn't mention above is that when I asked my Chinese colleagues what the phrase meant, they hadn't even noticed it! It was too familiar to attract their attention. This often happens with Paul's greetings in our study of his letters. The language seems familiar or perfunctory, so we tend to pass quickly over it. But actually the greeting is an integral part of the whole message. In his opening words Paul (1) establishes his (and his letter's) authority, (2) introduces the letter's dominant theme and (3) identifies himself closely with Timothy.

The Sender (1:1) Paul calls himself *an apostle of Christ Jesus,* one sent by God. The term designates an office that he held by the command of God and the choice of the risen Christ (1:11; 2:7; Rom 1:1; 1 Cor 1:1; 2 Cor 1:1; Gal 1:1). This was not simply biographical data that might interest the readers. Rather, Paul's reference to his office signifies the authority from God by which he preaches, teaches and writes. Although he did not need to convince Timothy of this, the letter was meant to be aired before the whole church (see on 6:21). Paul wanted his hearers/readers to know that his teaching is authoritative, and the delegate who administered it to the community, Timothy, was to be regarded as an extension of the apostle himself. In view of the difficult task that faced him, this may have been an encouraging reminder for Timothy as well.

But this reminder is also a timely one for us today. Questions have arisen within the church concerning the authority of Scripture. Cults and sects continue to multiply, and their ability to confuse the unwary with their doctrinal subtleties is as threatening to the church today as it was when Paul wrote. It falls to ministers of the gospel and church leaders to guide the church through this murky water, while at the same time attempting to address issues like those Paul addressed through Timothy centuries ago. Where does our authority for this task come from? Like Timothy, we depend on the apostle whose writings are invested with the authority of God.

Paul's reference is to *God our Savior.* It is a designation that Paul

Notes: 1:1 The designation of God as *Savior,* unusual in Paul, is in keeping with the Old Testament presentation of God (Deut 32:15; Ps 24:5; 27:1; Is 12:2; 17:10). It described the God who delivered his people from their bondage in Egypt and many times thereafter as the initiator and originator of salvation. In the New Testament, of course, God as the Savior is the initiator of the program of deliverance through Christ.

1:2 That Timothy may have been Paul's convert is arguable from Luke's description of this coworker as coming from a region in which Paul had preached (compare Acts 14:1-20 and 16:1-3; see introduction, under "The Recipients and the Churches"). Similar terminology

confined to the Pastoral Epistles, and with this phrase the apostle introduces his main theme, salvation. He chose with equal care the additional reference to *Christ Jesus our hope*. At the core of the false teaching Timothy faced was an out-of-balance view of salvation: the heretics proclaimed that the End had come and the resurrection had occurred (2 Tim 2:18; see introduction), and the return of Christ was all but forgotten. Here at the outset Paul begins to assert his balanced theology: this is the age of salvation, but salvation's completion awaits the Second Coming of Christ, *our hope*.

The Recipient (1:2) Timothy was the immediate recipient of the letter. He is linked to Paul in Acts 16:3, and though it is not clear that he was the apostle's convert, it is apparent that he became Paul's trusted assistant (1 Thess 3:2), so that Paul could say that Timothy served with him "as a son with his father" (Phil 2:22). Paul here injects a note of intimacy and fatherly love in calling him *my true son in the faith*. But this is also a pronouncement of Timothy's genuine faith in Christ. For Timothy this undoubtedly came as a vote of confidence for the difficult task ahead. The church was to recognize this as the apostle's stamp of approval on Timothy's doctrine, particularly in the light of the current doctrinal controversy.

The Blessing (1:2) The blessing that follows occurs regularly (minus *mercy*) in Paul's introductions. He calls down the benefits of God's covenant, which no one merits but God freely gives. *Grace* refers generally to all God's gifts and his loving disposition toward his people. *Peace* describes the one who is at rest in God. *Mercy* in this instance denotes God's special care of an individual in need. At the outset, Paul thus reminds Timothy that God's unearnable love and peace will overshadow his servant even in the most difficult of circumstances. Today, this is our promise—as sure as the authority of Scripture.

---

in 1 Corinthians 4:15, 17 may lend support to this view (Knight 1992:63-64).

In adding *mercy* to his usual greeting, "grace and peace" (Rom 1:7; 1 Cor 1:3; 2 Cor 1:2; Phil 1:2; Tit 1:4), Paul combines a Jewish greeting, "mercy and peace" (see Tobit 7:12; Gal 6:16), with a Greek greeting, "rejoice" *(chaire)*, which he has Christianized as *grace* (Gk *charis)*. That this added nuance *(mercy)* occurs only in 1 and 2 Timothy and Galatians may indicate an added measure of concern for churches troubled with doctrinal misunderstanding and schism.

□ **Timothy's Standing Order: Stay and Fight (1:3-20)**

When it comes to heresy or even misguided enthusiasm in the church, it is fairly obvious that history repeats itself. Early misconceptions about Christ and his relationship with the Father and the Holy Spirit (was he really human or did he just seem to be? was he simply adopted by God because of his moral purity? was he really divine?), from which heretical movements developed, are still with us today in popular quasi-Christian movements well known for their vigorous proselytizing. The denial of the deity and resurrection of Christ currently fashionable in parts of Christendom also presents parallels. Spiritual elitism/enthusiasm, confusion about the times and subtle systems of interpretation—things that characterized certain Gnostic-Christian communities and troubled earlier New Testament churches—can also be found in certain quarters of the modern church. Justification by works (legalism) is yet another modern delusion (even in some "evangelical" churches) with roots going back well before the time of Pelagius in the fourth century. A close look at our situation will uncover many points of contact with the situation Timothy was to face in Ephesus.

Heresy is to the church what treason or sedition is to the state—a divisive force made treacherous by the fact that it begins within the organization and exploits lines of trust and positions of authority. In the church's experience, false teachers often rose to prominence within the Christian community. Once censured by church leaders, they and their followers could choose either to repent or to depart. Much of what the early church fathers wrote was in response to false teachers who had departed and continued to challenge the faith with their own "enlightened" versions. Strangely, given all the emphasis on interpretation and knowledge, the appeal and staying power of any such cult often owed more to the personality or charisma of the leader(s) than to its distinctive doctrine.

Yet *heresy* is a term that needs to be carefully defined. As Harold O. J. Brown points out, the term, originally meaning "party" (Acts 5:17), gradually took to itself negative connotations as it was applied to factions that had deviated or split from the apostolic faith (1 Cor 11:9; Brown 1984:2). But the term is used so loosely today (as it has been down through history) that still further definition is necessary. *Heresy* in reference to a doctrine denotes one "that was sufficiently intolerable to destroy the unity of the Christian church. In the early church, heresy did not refer to simply any doctrinal disagreement, but to something that seemed to undercut the very basis for Christian existence" (Brown 1984:2). Some today (as, again, down through history) would place things like infant baptism or tongues-speaking into this category. Yet to judge from the New Testament and the early fathers of the church, the early church's greatest concern was for deviations in doctrines pertaining to God and Christ and the nature of salvation and justification, because the very substance of the gospel message and the salvation that rests on it lies in these things. Teachings that tend to characterize and distinguish the various Christian denominations (views about baptism, Communion, church government, gifts of the Holy Spirit and the role of women in ministry, among others) may certainly be held to with passion, but the differences here derive mainly from biblical passages capable of more than one reasonable explanation. The term *heresy* is not appropriate in this latter context.

As Paul saw it, heresy posed a dual threat. It endangered the church and individuals who would be drawn into error, perhaps beyond the reach of salvation. It threatened the church's evangelistic mission in the world, by contaminating the gospel. Thus Paul's charge to Timothy is equally a charge to us.

The logical structure of 1:3-20 recommends that we consider it as a unit.

A The Charge to Timothy to Oppose the False Teachers (vv. 3-5)

  B The False Teachers (vv. 6-7)

    C The Law: Mishandled by the False Teachers (vv. 8-10)

    C' The Authorized Doctrine (vv. 10-11)

  B' The Testimony of a Faithful Teacher (vv. 12-17)

A' The Charge to Timothy Repeated (vv. 18-20)

Paul denounces the heresy forcefully at the outset by introducing a contrast between true and false. False teachers are contrasted with Paul. False doctrine and misuse of the law are contrasted with the genuine gospel. And opening and closing charges to Timothy bracket this contrast. This juxtaposing of true and false and instructions to Timothy will carry on through the whole of the letter.

Opposing False Teachers (1:3-5) The responsibility of opposing error in the church falls mainly to Christian leaders. So in Ephesus it fell to Timothy. At the time Paul wrote, he planned to visit again (or return) soon (3:14; see introduction). He had already invested a great deal of time and effort in building this church, and he was quite concerned about recent developments there (Acts 18:19-21; 18:24—20:1). Ephesus was a city located on the western coast of Asia Minor (modern Turkey). It was famed for its cult and temple dedicated to the worship of Artemis, around which a good deal of the city's commercial interests revolved. It also had a large Jewish colony. Ephesus presented the gospel with a formidable challenge in that it was a center of pagan worship. From its inception here (see Acts 19) the church was very much in the public eye.

False Doctrine (1:3) Paul learned that certain men within the church were teaching *false doctrines.* Their probable position as leaders or elders in the church (see introduction and note) called for immediate action. Timothy was to command these individuals not only to stop teaching false doctrine but also to put an end to their speculative system of interpretation.

False doctrines literally means "different doctrines" (compare 6:3), those that diverged from the accepted teaching of the Old Testament, Christ and the apostles. The little we know of the specific content of these teachers' doctrine suggests that its central feature was a misunderstanding about the resurrection of believers (2 Tim 2:18). Perhaps due to some confusion over the Pauline teaching that believers even now participate in the death and resurrection of Christ (Rom 6:4-5, 8; 2 Tim 2:11), they believed and taught that the resurrection of believers had already occurred in a spiritual sense (see further 2 Tim 1:5 and introduction).

Notes: 1:3 On the nature of the false beliefs, see further the introduction and 2 Timothy 1:5; 2:18.

It is implicit that those Timothy was to correct were at least members in the church; otherwise Timothy's authority would have been of little use. Some may have been elders: we should not ignore the prediction of the defection of certain leaders in the Ephesian church, as recorded in Acts 20:17-35 (see Fee 1988:7-9).

1:4 In terms of content, the descriptive phrase *myths and endless genealogies* has been taken by some scholars as an indication that the heresy was Gnosticism, which in some of its manifestations held to the belief that God related to the created world via a system of

That such a mistake could be made may seem strange to us. But the fervency of the first-generation church's hope of Christ's return and certain carryovers from the pagan religions out of which believers came (see comment on 2 Tim 1:5) could have led some to the conclusion that all of salvation's blessings were to be experienced now. A modern parallel is what we might describe as Christian triumphalism (or the "health and wealth" gospel), which tends to present the Christian message as the quick solution to all of life's problems. The same basic mistake seems to be involved. In any case, the heretics' special insight into spiritual matters, which they termed "knowledge" (6:20), also had ethical implications, as allusions to their asceticism would suggest (4:3).

Speculative Interpretation (1:4) In verse 4 Paul criticizes the errorists' *myths and endless genealogies.* As the term is used in the New Testament (always in the plural—1 Tim 4:7; 2 Tim 4:4; Tit 1:14; 2 Pet 1:16), *myths* is consistently a pejorative and polemical classification. It classifies material not simply as untrue or legendary but as pernicious in its (or its author's) purpose to justify immoral or improper behavior on the basis of a divine or traditional pattern. Thus grounds for certain immoral practices could be found in the behavior attributed to the gods. Paul uses the term similarly in the Pastorals to categorize the false teaching in Ephesus as dangerous and immoral. But the actual content of this false teaching is more clearly in view in the term that follows. *Genealogies,* as a description of a literary type, is broader in meaning than lists of families and descendants (such as 1 Chron 1—9; Mt 1:1-17; Lk 3:23-38); it referred to the part of history concerned with persons and so meant "personal histories or biographies" (so Quinn 1990:245). The false teachers probably used such stories to support their doctrine (see comment on 2:11-15), and their "knowledge" and its ethical demands

---

angels (called *archons),* here supposedly alluded to in *endless genealogies.* The preoccupation with stories about creation (here indicated by *myths?)* evident in some Gnostic literature allegedly further supports this view (Dibelius and Conzelmann 1972:16-17; Hanson 1982:57; Brox 1989:35). Jeremias and Strobel (1975:14-15) understand *myths* and *genealogies* to refer respectively to creation stories and the traditions about the patriarchs. Others (Sandmel 1972:158-65; Quinn 1990:246-47) argue that *genealogies* (see also Tit 3:9) refers to biographical stories about the historical Jesus.

While it may not be possible to be that precise, it is important to note that the Jewish (and Hellenistic Jewish) interest in *genealogies* or "generations" (Hebrew *toledoth),* as seen

were somehow linked to this source. The rabbis were well known for intricate and fanciful interpretations of such Old Testament texts. Several decades later an interest in the Old Testament "genealogies" is evident among a Gnostic sect called the Ophites.

While Paul does not elaborate, his reason for rejecting the false teachers' system is clear: instead of serving God's salvation plan, as proper interpretation of Scripture should, their esoteric approach causes only "controversy" (compare 6:4). Evidently their conclusions were not all readily accepted, and the debates and arguments that followed did more to divide than to edify the congregation. In fact, Paul goes on to say that God's "plan" of redemption (NIV has *work;* see Eph 3:9) is apprehended by faith, that of genuine believers, not by novel schemes of interpretation. And with this word (and what follows) Paul sets the beliefs and activities of the false teachers totally outside the bounds of true faith in Christ and service to God. For this reason Timothy must oppose the new interpretation.

The Goal of Admonition (1:5) But there is more than an impersonal interest in preserving correct doctrine in all of this. For the *goal* of this admonition is *love,* flowing out of a cleansed heart, a good conscience and a genuine faith. *Faith* and *love* in the Pastorals and throughout Paul's letters signify a correct and personal knowledge of and belief in God, and its proper, active outworking in the life of the believer (see notes on 2:15). *Pure heart* and *good conscience* are technical terms in the Pastorals. The heart was regarded as the inward part of the person and the center of one's spiritual and thought life. The total inner life of the believer, cleansed from sin, could be depicted with the term *pure*

---

in Philo (*Moses* 2. 46-47; compare *On Rewards and Punishments* 1-2) and in the writings of Qumran (1QS 3:13-15) make it clear that the term itself was a reference not just to lists of family names and descendants but also to edifying stories about significant Old Testament figures (see also Josephus *Against Apion* 1. 16). The Jewish/Judaizing features connected with the occurrences of the words and phrase in these letters (1:8; Tit 1:14; 3:9) suggest that Paul is criticizing some sort of speculative interpretation based on the Old Testament stories. For the view (adopted here) that the term *myths* is mainly a negative qualitative assessment (for which see the discussion in Quinn 1990:100-101, 111) and *genealogies* identifies content, see also Quinn (1990:100-101, 245-48). Paul's readers would not miss the derogatory tone in *myths and endless genealogies* (see also Guthrie 1957:58; Fee 1988:41-42).

The term *controversies* (*ekzētēseis;* see 1 Tim 6:4; 2 Tim 2:23; Tit 3:9 for the related *zētēseis*)

heart. For Paul and for us, the *conscience* is that part or faculty of the mind that gives awareness of the standing of one's conduct as measured against an accepted standard.

But we who are modern Westerners should not read into Paul's term all of our understanding. The concept of individuality bred into us in the West was foreign to Paul's culture. *Conscience* tends to function individualistically in us to produce feelings of guilt. For Paul and the ancient Mediterranean culture in general, *conscience* was the internal judgment of one's actions by that one's group—"pain one feels because others consider one's actions inappropriate and dishonorable" (Malina 1981:70). Honor and shame, rather than guilt, were the operative feelings. Therefore, Paul's readers would perceive the conscience as sending internal signals evaluating the rightness or wrongness of behavior (past, present or future) as a member of a group. We, on the other hand, view the conscience as concerned with right and wrong on an individual basis, not necessarily taking into account what others think and expect about us.

Now just as the qualifier *pure* defines the condition of the true believer's *heart*, so *good* (1:19) and "clear" (3:9; 2 Tim 1:3) refer specifically to the *conscience* of the one rightly aligned with God. As the opposing references to the "seared" (4:2) and "corrupted" consciences (Tit 1:15) of the false teachers reveal, it is the acceptance or rejection of correct doctrine (the Word of God) that determines the condition and effectiveness of the *conscience*. That is, the standard of behavior accepted by the group (the community of faith or church) is the Word of God properly interpreted. It is necessary to operate with this standard for the *con-*

---

refers almost technically to argumentative questions about interpretation of the Bible.

The phrase *God's work (oikonomia)* has parallels elsewhere in Paul (Eph 1:10; 3:2, 9; Col 1:25), where the reference is to the revelation of God's grace in Christ that Paul has been commissioned to preach.

1:5 The concept of the *pure heart* (literally "cleansed heart," *kathara kardia*) which Paul uses to define genuine Christianity (2 Tim 2:22) represents the new life in Christ in its totality, the redeemed and renewed inner person. For the biblical concept of the heart as the seat of thought and intentions, the inward part of the person and the center of spiritual life, see Deuteronomy 4:29; 10:12; 11:13; Romans 1:21, 24; 5:5; 6:17.

Conscience (syneidēsis) means literally "with-knowledge," "a knowledge with others, individualized common knowledge, commonly shared meaning" (Malina 1981:51). For differences between ancient and modern perceptions, see Malina 1981:51-70.

science to perform its function of encouraging correct behavior (the behavior deemed appropriate by the Christian community).

Thus the *goal* Paul sets for Timothy in opposing the errorists through teaching is to encourage the development of "whole" Christians: cleansed by God, directed by his effective Word, producing visible fruit. While the main concern is to reach believers who have been threatened by false doctrine, the goal embraces the heretics themselves, if they repent and return to orthodox beliefs (see 2 Tim 2:25-26).

The False Teachers (1:6-7) As Paul's analysis of the situation continues, he uses language that expresses regret and irony to describe these disguised "wolves." There is more to false teachers than false doctrine.

First, they have lost their spiritual bearings. They have *wandered* (v. 6)—an image of slow but steady movement away from some point. Perhaps in the beginning these teachers only drifted aimlessly. But as they hardened in their disbelief and became argumentative in their attempts to convince others of their views, their lives came to be characterized not by love but by controversy, impure hearts and ineffective consciences. They have *wandered* from the faith.

Second, they speak and teach foolishness (v. 6). Having left the faith and diverged from the standard of approved teaching, their doctrines and discussions are *meaningless talk,* devoid of truth (6:4-5). In choosing the word he does, Paul places their doctrine into the category of idolatry and paganism (compare Acts 14:15; 1 Pet 1:18).

Third, verse 7 reveals that they claim authority for their teaching. *Teachers of the law,* a title given to the rabbis (Lk 5:17; Acts 5:34), were regarded as the authoritative interpreters of Scripture. These enthusiasts were not interested in simply offering their ideas for consideration. Rather, they "taught" them as God's message and expected them to be received.

Finally, Paul's description of their "confidence" implies in this context stubbornness, a refusal to be denied. We might say they are dogmatic, which (along with the claim to authority) Paul regards with irony, since

Notes: 1:6 *Meaningless* ("foolish" or "empty"; *mataios),* here used in the compound *meaningless talk (mataiologia),* is a word used to describe false religious claims (Jas 1:26; 2 Pet 1:18).

they have no real understanding of the matters they teach. Error, the claim to authority and dogmatic insecurity make a deadly combination to be sure, especially if these heretics began from positions of leadership in the church, as may well have been the case.

These characteristics make a timeless portrait of the false teacher. Doctrinal subtleties, special interpretation, spurious claims to authority, controversy and dogmatism ought to make God's people suspicious. At the same time, evidence of these same tendencies in our own lives ought to cause alarms to go off. From the human perspective, it is often a deeply rooted, though sometimes well-concealed, insecurity that drives one to take the lead in a heretical movement. We would do well to ask ourselves whether stubborn dogmatism that takes us beyond discussion to argument and anger is not motivated by such a fear. No rigid doctrinal structure can dispel this fear. An awareness of God's permanent love for us is integral to the solution, though there may be other elements that only skilled counseling can help us address. Then, while a desire to learn the deep truths of God's Word is commendable, if this leads us to embrace arcane views that run counter to the main lines of biblical teaching, we are headed for trouble. The remedy is not to stop thinking, for there is much yet to be discovered. However, theological investigation must be done in dialogue with the church. The individual needs the balance and testing that discussion with other mature believers will provide.

The Law (1:8-10) Placed in the position of this church, we might well have wondered about the purpose of the Old Testament law. The false teachers, who were just becoming visible as such within the church, were putting the Old Testament in a new light. It had a new kind of usefulness, if approached in the right way. Perhaps some who were not caught up in the trend noticed the increase in arguments over interpretation or how attention had shifted away from God and his demands toward human "knowledge."

In any case, Paul noticed it. He reminds the readers that *the law is good*

1:7 *Teachers of the law* is a term used by Luke to describe Jewish teachers (Lk 5:17; Acts 5:34). The term is not meant to identify the false teachers as "Judaizers" (that is, Christians who wanted to return to legalistic observance of the law; though compare Tit 1:10).

if one uses it properly (v. 8). Some commentators understand this assessment of the law to contradict Paul's earlier views. In Romans 7:16 Paul said that the law, which intends life but provokes sin, is good. The demands of the law exceed our ability, and the knowledge of our sin that comes from these demands leads us to repentance. But, it is argued, this is not the meaning of 1 Timothy 1:8. Yet what Paul refers to here is the legitimate or appropriate use of the law, and there is in this a none-too-veiled glance at the heretics' misuse of it.

Verse 9 *(law is made not for the righteous but for lawbreakers)* amplifies "proper use": the purpose of the law was not to approve the conduct of righteous people, but to expose and condemn that of sinners. Against God's ethical standard revealed in the law, human sin stands out in bold relief. The heretics' interpretation of the Old Testament (used to support a gospel that promised too much too soon) obscured this revelation, so that sinners were no longer directed toward the genuine gospel. Their use of the Old Testament was illegitimate because it did not accord with God's purpose.

The list of sins in verses 10-11 is all-encompassing. The first three pairs *(lawbreakers and rebels, the ungodly and sinful, the unholy and irreligious)* introduce the range of sinful behavior, outward, inward and defiantly rebellious. What follows is a more specific catalog of the worst sort of sins which bears unmistakable resemblance to the Ten Commandments: *those who kill their fathers or mothers* (Ex 20:12: honor your father and your mother), *murderers* (Ex 20:13: you shall not murder), *adulterers and perverts* (Ex 20:14: you shall not commit adultery), *slave traders* (Ex 20:15: you shall not steal), *liars and perjurers* (Ex 20:16: you shall not give false testimony against your neighbor). The list concludes with the catchall *whatever else is contrary to the sound doctrine*—that is, the doctrine that bears the apostolic seal of approval.

In that final phrase Paul completes the statement of the purpose of the

Notes: 1:9-10 Though Paul often used such lists of vices to categorize unregenerate life (Rom 1:29-31; 1 Cor 5:11; 6:9-10; Gal 5:19-21; 2 Tim 3:2-4), no two are exactly alike.

1:10 The reference to *adulterers (pornoi,* literally "fornicators") is better translated more generally as "the immoral," referring to illicit sexual activity.

Perverts (NIV), a rather vague translation of *arsenokoitai,* is an explicit reference to male homosexuals. This may be an allusion with local flavor, for according to an ancient report,

law: it reveals sins and sinners for what they are and points in the direction of the gospel. The false "teachers of the law" saw in the Old Testament law, especially in its "genealogies" (see above on v. 4) and creation stories, the basis for their extreme manner of behavior and the justification for their superspiritual claims. Their teaching missed the law's emphasis on God's demands and human need. False teachers are lawbreakers, who, without necessarily personally committing the sins listed here, become responsible for such sins by causing others to misunderstand or ignore God's moral demands.

The Authorized Doctrine (1:10-11) In contrast to the erroneous doctrine taught by the false teachers stands the approved doctrine of the church. Paul intended the contrast to be obvious, and his description of Christian doctrine reveals three critical points of departure.

What is the difference between Christian doctrine and false doctrine? First, as Paul describes it, apostolic teaching is *the sound doctrine* (v. 10). This is not an allusion to consistent and compelling logic, for all competing doctrines make this claim. *Sound* means "health-producing," and Paul means that in the widest sense. On the one hand, the Christian faith produces new life in those who accept it. Christianity is much more than assurance of a place in heaven; it involves a thorough renovation of the person, which begins with the way one thinks about God and oneself and continues from there to affect every part of a person's life. Thus *the sound doctrine* produces new people who are morally and conceptually healthy, those marked by love, pure hearts and good consciences (1:5). Christian health builds relationships through service and sacrifice. Here is where today's (like yesterday's) false religions often diverge from the intent of Christian doctrine. Impressive outward expressions of piety and self-denial may have nothing to do with relationships.

Second, Christian doctrine differs from false doctrine in that it *con-*

during the latter half of the first century Ephesus was filled with homosexuality (Hanson 1982:59).

Apparently the main crime involved in the business of the *slave trader* (some versions read "kidnapper") was regarded as being robbery, not particularly an abuse of human rights.

1:10 The designation *sound doctrine* (1:10; 2 Tim 4:3; Tit 1:9; like "sound instruction," 6:3, and "good teaching," 4:6) is polemic in thrust, as the passages in which the term occurs reveal. By implication the heresy is "unsound," incapable of producing health.

forms to God's message of salvation, *the glorious gospel* (v. 11). Paul means that the message that Christ proclaimed and passed on to his apostles (1 Cor 15:1-3) is the source and "standard" of Christian doctrine. But there is also an implication of results. Correct doctrine produces genuine Christian life, beginning with repentance and forgiveness of sins, then supplying power for godly conduct. Also, this new life is a gift from God, for Paul rightly says that it is "God's" gospel. So it has been said that Christianity is not our search for God, but God's rescue of us. Correct doctrine is God's revelation, which directs us in our proper response to him. Genuine Christianity must come out of the gospel that saves. Anything else may be similar in some respects, but will lack the staying power that is available to the Christian by faith in Christ.

Third, the Christian message bears apostolic authority. This is Paul's meaning when he says of the gospel in verse 11 that it was *entrusted* to him. He rejects the false teachers' claim to authority. He has seen the risen Christ and has received God's special commission to carry the gospel to the Gentiles. The implication of this is that if some competing doctrine conflicts with the apostle's, its source is something other than God (Gal 1:6-9).

"Conformity to approved Scripture" and "apostolic endorsement" were the "canons" applied by the church fathers to various Christian writings as they sought to set the limits of Scripture. These tests, which Paul applies here himself, are very appropriate for us today. We can approach competing claims to authority, those made by the cults, by beginning with Scripture. Missionaries of one particular cult say that their scriptures are authoritative because they stem from God. Its elders usually insist that the Holy Spirit will "move in the heart" to confirm the veracity of their teaching. But when their doctrines do not pass the more objective test applied by the church fathers, what does it matter how one "feels" about their teaching? Such counterclaims to authority are clearly wrong.

Coming to final conclusions concerning this doctrine or that is a difficult task and one that requires the attention of the church's leaders. We have a measuring stick—Scripture—and doctrines, interpretations and whole systems must conform to this standard. The doctrine that Paul approved for Christian use must produce whole Christians, must be founded on or flow out of the gospel and must bear the apostle's seal. But a cautionary note is again in order: let us not think that every doctrinal disagreement is capable of an easy solution, or that complete agreement on every teaching in Scripture is necessary within the church. There are essential issues which need to be addressed and nonessentials in which freedom to hold diverse views must be allowed. Above all, there should be a commitment to open dialogue, particularly in those areas in which the teaching of Scripture may be interpreted in more than one way (see the discussion of heresy above).

The Testimony of a Faithful Teacher (1:12-17) After mentioning his reception of the gospel, Paul continues in verses 12-17 to reminisce about his calling out of sin into Christ's service. He presents himself as a model for Timothy, other church leaders and all believers to follow (see v. 16). He also presents himself as the antithesis of the false teacher, as the stress on "faithfulness" and repetition of "faith" words in verses 12-16 indicate. As this testimony unfolds, Paul reveals several essential qualities to be found in the Christian, which the leader/teacher must exemplify.

Dependence on Christ (1:12) This is not the first time in his writing that Paul saw fit to "give his testimony" (2 Cor 10—12; Phil 3:4-11). When he chose to do so, however, he seems to have had a good reason. What is most interesting in this is how he starts with the importance of Christ in his life. Even if there is a hint of personal defense in his presentation, it is a defense built on the work of Christ.

First, *strength* for Christian life and ministry comes from Christ. Paul's ministry was marked by the manifestation of spiritual "power"—his work brought results, but he does not explain them on the basis of his seminary education, up-to-date methods or personal charisma. Instead, he credits and thanks Christ for empowering him.

Second, the right to participate in ministry is established solely by Christ. Paul's thanksgiving extends to the consciousness of having been considered faithful to be appointed *to his service.* Such faithfulness is borne out only by actual ministry, and Paul clearly felt that his own record bore witness to Christ's selection of him. But there is a sense in which this particular trait, faithfulness or trustworthiness, ought to be evident initially in those who would serve the Lord (see below on 3:1-13; 5:17-25). The false teachers mentioned above, regardless of the promise they might have shown at first, had proved themselves unfaithful.

Paul's ministry was sustained by and originated in Christ. We who would share Paul's goals and vision for life and ministry must also share his complete dependence on Christ.

Experience of God's Grace and Mercy (1:13-14) Paul was fully aware of the change in direction that the *grace* of God brought to his life. Before encountering the risen Christ on the road to Damascus (Acts 9), his life was lived for the sole purpose of persecuting the church right out of existence. He did this out of commitment to God! He was truly a religious, anti-Christian fanatic. In fact, we first meet him as he stood by in approval of the stones being thrown at Stephen, the first Christian martyr (Acts 7—8). Here is Luke's portrait of him: "But Saul began to destroy the church. Going from house to house, he dragged off men and women and put them in prison" (Acts 8:3; see 9:1-2). To be honest, this brings to mind the terror of Nazi Germany or Idi Amin's regime. From his Christian perspective, Paul described himself in the past as *a blasphemer and a persecutor and a violent man* (1 Cor 15:9; Gal 1:13-14), yet he experienced God's *mercy* (v. 13). He was saved. The outpouring of grace from the Lord produced in him *faith and love* (v. 14)—that is, genuine spiritual life (see notes on 2:15).

Paul's references to *faith* and *love* and to his prior condition of ignorance and unbelief are again directed at the false teachers. On the one hand, he seriously questions any "Christian" spirituality that is not marked by *faith and love,* belief and godly response. On the other hand, the false teachers' Christian background—they know the gospel and have been members and probably even leaders in the church—makes the game they play an extremely dangerous one (compare Heb 6:4). Their history is marked by movement away from the faith, while Paul's

Notes: 1:13 *Blasphemer* takes us back to Acts 26:11, where Paul admits to having forced others to blaspheme—that is, to deny the Christ. Here Paul refers to his own former blasphemy/denial of Christ, the forgiveness of which illustrates profoundly the depth of God's mercy: according to the law, blasphemy was punishable by stoning (Lev 24:10-16). See notes on 1 Timothy 1:20; 6:4.
1:14 *Grace* here refers to that undeserved favor which God shows to sinners in bringing them to salvation.

life reflects growth in the faith. The false teacher and the Christian teacher are opposites.

Committed to the Gospel and God's Plan of Salvation (1:15-16) With the turn in thought that occurs at this point, Paul continues his contrast of the faithful teacher and the false teacher. In teaching false doctrine, the false teachers are diverging from the authorized gospel and God's plan of redemption (1:4). In contrast, the faithful teacher will follow Paul in fully affirming God's plan.

First, at the center of this plan is the gospel message. Paul was fully convinced of its reliability. He signals his commitment and calls others to do likewise with a formula, *Here is a trustworthy saying that deserves full acceptance,* and a succinct statement of the gospel, *Christ Jesus came into the world to save sinners.* As he clearly states here, the basis of salvation is the historical ministry of Christ. As he has stated elsewhere (1 Cor 1:18-31; 2 Tim 1:10), this "ministry," executed in the past (Christ *came),* continues in the present day to be effective in the preaching of the gospel. This is God's plan: salvation is linked solely to Christ and the message about him. Commitment to anything but the apostolic gospel is heresy.

Second, God's redemptive plan is imperturbable, as Paul's own experience taught him. It reaches to the depths of depravity. Paul's self-confessed pre-Christian history (as *the worst of sinners* [v. 15], a reference to his persecution of Christians [v. 13; compare Gal 1:13]) made him, ironically, the perfect illustration of the effectiveness of the gospel, the boundless grace of God and the inexhaustible *patience* of Christ (v. 16).

Third, the readers are reminded that salvation requires "belief" in Christ (v. 16). Furthermore, Paul's language *(believe on him)* indicates that he means personal faith in Christ, not simply adherence to a dogma. In order for this kind of belief to occur, the gospel must be kept pure.

1:15 *Here is a trustworthy saying that deserves full acceptance* is a formula that also occurs (with slight variations) at 3:1, 4:9, 2 Timothy 2:11 and Titus 3:8. In this case the saying follows the formula (so also 3:1; 2 Tim 2:11-12; but compare 4:8-9 and Tit 3:3-8). Its function seems to be to emphasize that the related teaching is widely accepted as authoritative (see Knight 1979:1-30).

1:16 *His unlimited patience* (NIV) is better translated "the full extent of his patience."

Finally, the ultimate goal of the plan of salvation is *eternal life* (v. 16; compare 4:8; 6:12, 19; 2 Tim 1:10; Tit 1:2; 3:7). Paul's connection of ideas makes it clear that the believer's personal faith in Christ is the necessary stepping-stone to the ultimate goal of eternal life. It is this plan of salvation that Paul's life verified.

Most of us would be reluctant to do what Paul has done here. We are certainly no match for the apostle. But humility aside, each Christian's spiritual history is filled with poignant reminders of God's grace and mercy. While it will not do to live in that past, from time to time we must take our bearings from it as we move forward on a path that may not be clear. Paul's testimony of his personal encounter with Christ demonstrated the power of the approved gospel. Paul knew in his heart and was fully convinced that this message was true. And it is essential that every Christian share this conviction borne out of experience. We must remember, however, that this proof cannot be based solely on a mystical encounter with God; it must be backed up by a changed life (v. 14). Could the false teachers with their version of the gospel make the same claims as Paul? No! God's salvation plan is linked solely to the Christian gospel. It requires faith and produces a new manner of life.

Testimony Leads to Worship (1:17) Paul could not reflect on God's grace in his life and the promise of *eternal life* without being moved to worship. Verse 17 takes the form of a doxology (see 6:15-16). It imparts a powerful vision of the majesty and mystery of God. *King eternal* ascribes to God absolute sovereignty over all the ages. *Immortal* recalls Romans 1:23, where God is contrasted with images of mortal humans and animals. By nature God lives eternally; death is foreign to him. He is also *invisible* (6:16). For a sinful human to see God is to bring death (Ex 33:20). Finally, God is "one" (2:5), *the only God,* a thought that returns to the first commandment, the starting point of the Christian faith.

1:17 Doxologies such as this one and the one at 6:15-16 belong to the early church's liturgy and may have stemmed originally from Jewish synagogue worship. They provided the congregation a form in which to express corporately adoration of God. *King eternal,* literally "king of the ages," is a Jewish designation (Tobit 13:7, 11), reflecting the belief that God rules over all the ages of his creation. For *immortal* and *invisible* see Romans 1:20, 23 and Colossians 1:15, respectively.

Only God (see 2:5; 1 Cor 8:4-6) is a title that emerged from the Jewish encounter with

The source of Paul's life and ministry was the eternal God. As we see here, he went back to that source regularly. The one who would serve God must do so as well (see further below, on 6:15-16).

Timothy, Fight the Good Fight (1:18-20) Before moving on to instructions to the whole church, Paul returns to underline Timothy's standing orders concerning the heretics. It is this purpose of instructing Timothy that controls the entire first chapter. The *instruction* of verse 18 is the *command* of verse 3 and all that has followed. Now, however, in repeating the charge to Timothy, Paul speaks to him as to the minister whose special calling by God carries with it special obligations.

The Obligation (1:18) Persons who accept positions of power and importance in this world must also accept the obligations and responsibilities that go with them. The same is true in the church. Here Paul calls to mind Timothy's God-given responsibility to serve. The instructions, Paul reminds, were part of the "package" that Timothy agreed to when he responded to God's call. The event of appointment to ministry (the modern parallel would be ordination), referred to here obliquely as *the prophecies once made about you,* involved the recognition of gifts appropriate to ministry, God's selection and the prophetic announcement of God's choice to the congregation, as depicted by the (public) laying on of hands (4:14; compare Acts 13:1-3). Ultimately, the minister's enlistment is in God's service, not simply in a church which, should it happen to falter or split, the minister could choose to leave behind. Appointment to ministry involves commitment to service even when it is under less than ideal circumstances. Thus Timothy's "package" includes the instruction to oppose false teachers.

But Paul calls Timothy's appointment to mind for another reason as well. The event involves more than vows to serve God. As Paul reminds Timothy, the prophecies or proclamations surrounding his assistant's

---

pagan polytheistic idolatry and was taken over readily by the church.

1:18 Apparently what Paul refers to is the pronouncement of the Holy Spirit, via prophets in the church, associated with the commissioning of someone to God's work. From Acts 13:2 (compare 1 Tim 4:14) it seems clear that the prophetic pronouncement was accompanied by the laying on of hands, a public indication of God's selection (see further Aune 1983:265-66). First Timothy 1:18 and 4:14 refer to the same event of Timothy's setting apart for the work of ministry (see also Fee 1988:57-58).

commissioning also announced God's promise of support to him (see below on 6:13-14).

Paul's instructions to Timothy are *in keeping with* Timothy's call to ministry in that the task of opposing heresy belongs to the ministry. By keeping in mind his earlier commitment to God and God's commitment to him, Timothy will be able to *fight* well.

The Fight (1:18) The gravity of the situation is apparent from the military imagery Paul employs to describe Timothy's task: *fight the good fight.* Here the believer is cast in the role of a soldier who is ordered out into battle. The weapons of this soldier, however, are not clever argumentation or inescapable logic, things that we might think best suited to debates with false teachers. On the contrary, Timothy is to avoid debates (2 Tim 2:23-25). Nor is the soldier's objective the destruction of his opponent. Appropriate strategy includes instructing, correcting erroneous views and urging repentance (see 2 Thess 3:14-15). The minister's weapons for this *fight* are the gospel and godly concern for the spiritual condition of the opponent. The goal is to protect the faith of those whom the false teachers seek to influence and, if possible, to win back those who have strayed (1:5). Only the gospel is sufficient for such work, as Paul has just taken great care to illustrate (1:11-16).

The Danger (1:19-20) Luke tells the story of the seven sons of Sceva, Jewish priests who had gone into the business of casting out demons (Acts 19:13-16). Having no power of their own, they would invoke the names of Jesus and Paul to command the demons to come out of the possessed victims. One day their scheme backfired on them. In response to their formula, a demon, having admitted to knowledge of Jesus and Paul, denied the priests' right to draw on their names and used the possessed man to give them all a sound beating. One thing is clear: these Jewish priests did not realize the danger of the one with whom they thought to do battle.

Paul clearly does recognize the dangers involved. For this reason he qualifies the command of verse 18 by referring, without a break in the sentence, to the believer's personal spiritual condition in verse 19.

1:20 The propagation of false doctrine is a sin specially singled out for severe disciplinary action (Rom 16:17-18; 2 Jn 10-11). Paul puts this sin into the category of blasphemy, public

The qualifying phrase, *holding on to faith and a good conscience*, considers the spiritual life from two perspectives. *Faith* here means a correct knowledge of God and Christ (or the gospel). *Good conscience* is that inner faculty that causes faith to issue in godly conduct (1:5). According to Paul, the purity of one's faith is directly related to the effectiveness of one's conscience (4:1-2). The concern here is that while opposing the false teachers and their subtle doctrines Timothy could, if inattentive or unprepared, suffer a severe blow to his faith. It is like the doctor who risks infection while attempting to treat a sick person. But in the Christian's case, one has to remember that the enemy is Satan (compare 4:1; 2 Cor 11:1-15), and his powers of deception and persuasion are not to be taken lightly or ignored.

Some Christians in Ephesus—Paul singles out two leaders, Hymenaeus and Alexander (v. 20)—made this mistake (and Paul's language, *rejected* and *blaspheme,* suggests that it was a conscious one), with devastating results to their relationship with God. *Shipwrecked* raises images in the mind of "destruction," not "setback." Furthermore, the disciplinary measures taken are severe. *Handed over to Satan* refers to excommunication from the church back into Satan's realm.

We should not misunderstand the nature of this process. It was not simply intended to "cut out a cancer" in order to preserve the rest of the body, as some churches view it today. Neither is it a practice that the church today can afford to ignore, as if it were an aberration belonging to the Inquisition. Taken together, Matthew 18:15-17, 1 Corinthians 5:5, 2 Corinthians 2:5-11 and 2 Thessalonians 3:14-15 reflect the development of a carefully measured process. Each step was designed to bring the erring individual to the point of admission and true change of mind and behavior. Even if the individual persisted in a stubborn refusal to change (like the two mentioned here), the final step of expulsion from the fellowship back into the hostile world was ultimately intended as a means (desperate and last-ditch though it be) of reclamation. To be *handed over to Satan* (compare 1 Cor 5:5) is to be exposed, without the protection God promises to his people, to the dangers of sin. For some

---

defamation of God, which in the Old Testament carried the death penalty (Lev 24:16).

it takes being cast off into the sea to realize the advantages on board ship.

No faithful Christian can avoid engaging the enemy (2 Tim 3:12), and the danger involved is real. This goes doubly for ministers and Christian leaders. They must stand in the gap and fend off attacks on the gospel message, because of the threat to the church and to its mission in the world. God's people must take their place in the battle lines.

□ Behavior in God's Household (2:1—3:16)

For as long as there have been households to belong to, there have been rules to direct household life. Most who are able to recall their teenage years will remember the words "As long as you live in *this* house, you'll abide by the rules!" As one of six boys under the same roof, I certainly heard them spoken on one or two occasions.

Naturally, the head of the household has the privilege of establishing those rules. Though they may seem arbitrary to other, less-privileged members, in principle the rules are meant to provide the household with some semblance of order.

In Paul's day the concepts of household and order in society were inseparable. One could not think of household without immediately thinking of such things as authority structure, rules of propriety and responsibilities. Orderliness and efficiency began with the authority of the master. But the degree to which success in these things could be achieved depended on the household members' response to the master.

It was particularly with the ideas of responsibility and order in mind that Paul drew on the household analogy to describe life in the church (3:15; 2 Tim 2:20-21). Christians have a common Lord and are related to him as to a father. Moreover, they are brothers and sisters in Christ. But there is more to the analogy. Just as the earthly household has a human authority structure and different classes of people, so God's household has officers, men and women, parents and children, different generations, masters and slaves, who must all relate to one another in proper ways and carry out certain responsibilities. Paul reminds his readers that the Master establishes the rules, and that believers' responsibility

Notes: 2:1—3:16 Verner (1983:91-125) argues that the image of the church as God's household, which surfaces in 3:15, is the letter's center, out of which the author's ethical concerns naturally flow to explain how to live in such a household. However, rather than

in obeying them is directly related to the accomplishment of the Master's goals.

The main theme of 2:1—3:16 is summed up in 3:15: proper conduct within God's household. Paul treats three issues, each of which can be seen to relate more or less directly to the disturbance caused by the false teaching in Ephesus. His first concern was to encourage the church to pray. Second, he gives instructions that pertain to men and women, in which he particularly addresses the matter of women teaching men in the church. Finally, the apostle lays down some guidelines for selecting church officers.

Ethical instruction in the New Testament exhibits certain recurring patterns which suggest that the early church held a common view of what constituted "Christian" social conduct. This agreement is perhaps best seen in teaching on marriage (Eph 5; 1 Pet 3), the relationship of men and women (1 Cor 14; 1 Tim 2; Tit 2), the relationship between slaves and masters (Eph 6; Col 3; 1 Tim 6; Tit 2; 1 Pet 2) and the posture of the church toward the state (Rom 13; 1 Tim 2; Tit 3; 1 Pet 2). The characteristic verbs are *submit* and *obey*. Although there is certainly variation from one passage to the next, both the content and the form of the teaching suggest a set teaching device. Because of the interest in rules of behavior for members of a Greco-Roman household (husband-wife, parent-child, master-slave, citizen-state), scholars have come to call this device a *household code*.

Many have argued that the New Testament household codes were borrowed or adapted from Greek or Hellenistic Jewish ethical thought. But there are no exact parallels to substantiate this. What we do find as the nonbiblical and biblical writers are compared is a shared interest in the behavior of members of a household and adherence to a patriarchal structure. But the biblical teaching differs from the secular by grounding the given relationships and appropriate behavior within them upon a Christian foundation. Furthermore, the New Testament household codes reveal development toward a Christian understanding of the traditional household relationships (as manifested in the church) which might best

being the dominant theme or cornerstone of the message (since other important images are used to depict the church), it may have served instead as the best rubric under which to organize a wide-ranging collection of ethical teaching.

be described as "reformation" (Witherington 1988:42-61). Still, the biblical teaching reflects a sensitivity to ideas about respectability current outside of the church. This teaching tool enabled the church to start with the social structure as it existed, affirm much of it and at the same time introduce changes demanded by the new status "in Christ." In this way, the church might keep open the lines of communication with the world it was meant to be reaching. The likelihood that the household codes were drawn upon to stabilize situations in which traditional rules of relationships were being discarded (for theological reasons) suggests that sensitivity to the surrounding culture was an important feature of early Christian ethical teaching. To threaten institutions that the secular ethicists held to be essential to protecting the status quo would have been to equate Christianity with revolution. The message of the resurrection was revolutionary enough.

When Paul heard that women were forging ahead toward emancipation, he drew on what had become accepted teaching about men and women to call them back to appropriate conduct. When he addresses the church concerning its prayer, he includes teaching about the church's respect for the state. And the rules he issues governing the selection of leaders emphasize dignified behavior of a standard that would also meet with outsiders' approval.

Prayer for the Church's Mission (2:1-7) Whoever coined the phrase "can't see the forest for the trees" could easily have had in mind the local congregation's view of its task in the worldwide church's mission enterprise. "Local" work is certainly important and in need of prayer. Yet sometimes we lose sight of the fact that this work is a part of a larger task that has been set before the worldwide church to accomplish in unison. Today's church is perhaps already fragmented beyond the point of achieving such unity. But wherever cooperation is possible, the original plan to reach all nations calls for the parts to recognize the whole.

When Paul turns to the matter of instructing the church, the subject he first broaches is that of prayer. The instruction, which runs through

---

2:1 *Thanksgiving* was an essential part of the prayer process (Eph 1:15-16; Phil 4:6; Col 1:12), signaling the believer's trust in God. *Requests (deēseis)* emphasizes the thought of need (5:5), while *intercession (enteuxeis)* carries the thought of addressing a petition to

verse 7, has two parts. First is the command to pray, which is itself twofold. The church is to pray for all people and for kings and those who are in authority. Each aspect of this prayer is directly related to the church's evangelistic mission. Then comes the rationale behind the command: the salvation of all people everywhere is God's will. The subsequent creedlike material demonstrates the universal scope of God's will to save, reflecting on God's nature and Christ's sacrifice. A final personal reference submits the apostle's call to the Gentiles as proof of God's expansive redemptive plan and the church's need to be involved in it.

Prayer for All People (2:1) Isn't it true that people tend to be most concerned for those on the outside when they happen to be outsiders themselves—that once on the inside they tend to forget whence they came? It seems to me that we who have experienced God's grace ought to be all the more concerned for those who have yet to do so. Although we cannot be certain of the reason, the church in which Timothy was ministering apparently had been neglecting to pray widely for the salvation of people in the world. In response, Paul does not lay down a detailed, four-stage program of prayer in asking that *requests, prayers, intercession and thanksgiving be made for everyone.* Rather, he calls for prayer in a comprehensive sense that attends to all details. In fact, seeing this removes the apparent vagueness from the command to pray *for everyone.* He does envision a prayer ministry, one that will be attentive to every aspect of the gospel enterprise, from the initial planning and opening of doors for preaching (Col 4:3), to seed-sowing and boldness to preach (Eph 6:19), to thanksgiving for changed lives (1 Thess 1:2). The prayer he has in mind is specifically related to the evangelistic mission. Notice the rationale given in verses 3-4: the will of *God our Savior* is that *all men . . . be saved.* This prayer is expansive in scope, reaching to all people, and the repeated occurrence of *all* throughout the passage reminds the readers to "think big" when they pray this prayer (vv. 1, 2, 4, 6).

Two obvious conclusions may be drawn from this instruction. First, all believers have a necessary part to play in the church's worldwide mission. Second, each local gathering of believers is to participate directly

---

a superior (see Guthrie 1957:69). *Prayers (proseuchas)* is the generic term, encompassing all elements.

and corporately in this work when coming together for worship. Since Paul mentions this as being a matter of *first* importance, we ought to give careful thought to the place we give this task within our worship service and other church activities.

Prayer for the State (2:2) A vital aspect of this prayer for the church's mission is prayer for the state. This practice began with the worship of the Diaspora Jews, who were thus to ensure the people's prosperity in a pagan environment (Jer 29:7). Back in the Jews' own land, this prayer was coupled with offering sacrifices for the king, the whole of which came to be an expression of loyalty (Ezra 6:9-10; 1 Macc 7:33).

These two ideas, with a slight twist, seem to have come together in the New Testament church's thinking. On the one hand, the church was to respect state rulers and to submit to the institution of the state. The theological rationale for this obedience was the fact that the state and human government are a part of God's creative will (Rom 13:1; 1 Pet 2:13). But from a more practical standpoint, a submissive posture toward the state would lend the church credibility in the eyes of the world (1 Pet 2:15). The church was to express its submission by paying taxes (Rom 13:7), honoring the ruling authorities (Rom 13:7; 1 Pet 2:17) and praying *for kings and all those in authority.*

The twist comes in that while the immediate goal of prayer for the state is that it fulfill its God-given function of maintaining an orderly, peaceful environment (v. 2: *that we may live peaceful and quiet lives),* this goal is meant to serve a higher end. What is sought is the best of conditions for expanding God's kingdom, not simply a peaceful life. The context determines the overriding interest in salvation, from which the meaning of verse 2 must be derived. Furthermore, the description of the manner of Christian living *(in all godliness and holiness)* contains hints

---

2:2 *Godliness (eusebeia)* is an important ethical term in the Pastorals. Paul possibly borrowed it from the false teachers' special vocabulary (1 Tim 6:5; 2 Tim 3:5) in order to correct their erroneous views about the spiritual life. From Paul's discussions of their misunderstandings about it, it appears that for them "godliness" was largely something to be attained at the cognitive level through "knowledge" (1 Tim 6:20; 2 Tim 3:5; Tit 1:16) but that had little or no bearing upon outward behavior. Thus Paul's use of the term stresses correct knowledge of God (1 Tim 6:3; Tit 1:1) that produces an observable Christian manner of conduct (1 Tim 2:2; 4:8; 5:4; 6:11; 2 Tim 3:12; Tit 2:12). This genuine *godliness* is a product of Christ's redemptive work (Tit 2:12) and the life-changing gospel (1 Tim 6:3; Tit 1:1).

of witness. *Godliness* is Paul's term in the Pastorals for "genuine Christianity"; it brings together knowledge of and faith in God and the observable response of lifestyle. *Holiness* (NIV), better translated as "seriousness," suggests a deportment of respectability that is evident to observers. The manner of life here described has the evaluating eye of the observer in mind (1 Tim 3:7; 6:1; Tit 2) and is meant to recommend the gospel to those who look on.

Prayer That Accords with God's Will (2:3-7) Having issued these instructions, Paul goes on to ground them in the will of God: *This is good, and pleases God our Savior, who wants [wills] all men to be saved and to come to a knowledge of the truth* (vv. 3-4). The reason does indeed suggest that Paul's primary concern here is the church's prayer for the salvation of *all* people. *Come to a knowledge of the truth* (v. 4) was a formula that described conversion as a rational decision about the gospel. This statement qualifies how the universality of God's will to save is to be understood. We do not have here grounds for saying that all people will be saved regardless of their disposition toward the gospel. Rather, the emphasis is on access: the gospel is to be preached to all nations. Certain references such as this one reveal that God's will is as broad as his entire plan of redemption and yet can be expressed in terms of specific standards of behavior (compare 1 Thess 4:3, 18; 1 Tim 5:4; Tit 3:8). Of course, unlike the human will, God's is unchanging and accompanied by his imperturbable power which makes its ultimate accomplishment certain.

Because of this belief, ordinarily an appeal to God's will was sufficient grounds in itself for apostolic instructions. But the importance of prayer support for world mission apparently called for further substantiation of God's far-reaching redemptive plan. For this Paul draws on well-known

---

"Seriousness" (NIV *holiness;* Greek *semnotēs),* a favorite term with Greek ethicists, also contributes to Paul's description of the observable new life of faith (2:2; 3:4, 8, 11; Tit 2:2, 7). The respectability it denotes is connected with the believer's witness to unbelievers.

2:4 Appeal to God's will to enjoin proper conduct was normal for Paul (1 Thess 4:3, 18; 1 Tim 5:4; Tit 3:8).

The condition of the faith-response is close to hand in other New Testament affirmations of the universality of salvation (see Jn 1:12; 3:16-17; 1 Tim 4:10; 2 Pet 3:9).

With the formula *to come to a knowledge of the truth* (2 Tim 2:25; 3:7; Tit 1:1; compare 1 Tim 4:3), Paul emphasizes the rational aspect of belief, thereby creating a visible link between belief and correct doctrine *(truth).*

formulations; they may be parts of the early church's hymns or creeds, and the readers would have recognized them immediately.

God's expansive unity (2:5). Verse 5 makes two main points. First, God's desire to reach all with the gospel is a logical corollary of his unity: *for there is one God and one mediator between God and men, the man Christ Jesus* (v. 5). In pre-Christian times the Jews employed this "there is one God" formula, which echoes the thought of the Shema (Deut 6:4), to counteract the polytheistic claims of the pagan religions. Paul went a step further and drew on the oneness of God to demonstrate that all have access to God's salvation: the fact that there is one God of both Jews and Gentiles means salvation for the Gentiles too (Rom 3:29-30; Eph 4:4-6).

Second, the reference to the oneness of *the mediator* pins this universal access to the ministry of Christ. He as *mediator* stepped between God and sinful humankind to make possible a new relationship between the two parties. What he "mediated" was the new covenant (Jer 31:31-34; Heb 8:6; 9:15; 12:24). The final phrase, *the man Christ Jesus,* locates his mediating activity in his earthly ministry, which takes Paul on to the next stage of his logic.

But before we go on, what are the implications of Paul's logic? His main point is simply that the existence of only one God implies that the gift of salvation is extended to all. Therefore, the church's participation in the mission enterprise must involve earnest prayer for all people. Yet at the same time there is an exclusiveness implied by Paul's logic. Salvation is linked solely to the one mediator, Christ, and therefore to the gospel about him. The church as the sole guardian of this message (3:15) is the sole means by which God's salvation can be extended to

---

2:5 Hanson's suggestion (1968:56-64; 1982:68-69) that *mediator* (and *man*) comes from the Greek version of Job 9:33 and therefore contains no "covenant" ideas is doubtful. Given the immediate reference to Jesus' redemptive death in verse 6 and the relation of Jesus' humanity with his death in the New Testament generally, it is the use of "mediator" in Hebrews that offers the better background.

Some commentators suggest that *the man Christ Jesus* may have found its way into this tradition by way of Paul's Adam-Christ teaching (compare Rom 5:15; Kelly 1963:63; Fee 1988:65). Others maintain that it is an abbreviation of "the Son of Man" as it occurs in Mark 10:45 in keeping with the reference to that Jesus-tradition in verse 6 (Jeremias 1975:17). The strong tradition that explains that the purpose of Christ's humanity was his redemptive death (Rom 8:3; Gal 4:4-5; Phil 2:7-8; compare Guthrie 1981:344-52) is a more informative background.

2:6 The change of prepositions that occurred in the tradition (from "in place of" [*anti;*

all. Consequently, the church's prayer for the salvation of all people is
not optional or subsidiary in the least. It is intrinsic to the church's reason
for existing and to the accomplishment of the larger evangelistic goal.

Christ's inclusive sacrifice (2:6). The tradition Paul cites includes next
a piece of material that goes back to Jesus' own preaching about himself
(Mk 10:45). Its purpose is to clarify the meaning of the ministry of
mediation fulfilled by *the man Christ Jesus* (v. 5). Although it is brief,
it nevertheless reflects a deep understanding of the meaning of Christ's
death.

First, the change from the original "many" (Mk 10:45) to *all* stresses
that Jesus' sacrifice was inclusive. Paul may have selected this piece of
tradition because of this particular emphasis. According to the earliest
tradition, the church believed and emphasized that Jesus' death was
meant to reach to "all" people (2 Cor 5:14-15).

Second, Jesus' gospel-sacrifice was voluntary; he *gave himself.* His
death, far from being an unexpected, senseless accident, came about
because God was in full control of the situation (Jn 10:18; Acts 2:23;
2 Cor 5:19). Christ's death is integral to God's redemptive plan.

Then, this sacrifice amounted to a payment that obtains the release of
slaves, or a *ransom.* Life without God is bondage to sin. Christ paid the
price of our release (see also Tit 2:14 commentary).

Fourth, Paul's citation reminds that Jesus died as a representative. The
fact that *the man* stood between God and sinful humans as our *mediator*
reveals the intimate degree of his representation. But the meaning of his
mediation is amplified in verse 6. The preposition *for* ("in behalf of")
which precedes *all men* defines "mediation" as his death for humankind.

Mk 10:45] to *for [hyper])* is characteristic of Paul's use of this part of Jesus' teaching
(compare Gal 1:4). The compounding of the preposition *anti* with the noun meaning
"ransom payment" *(lytron)* probably indicates some development in the early church's
understanding of the substitutionary meaning of Jesus' death (on which see Morris 1955:48;
Guthrie 1981:441).

By virtue of the contexts in which the term occurs, the *proper time (kairoi idioi,* in which
the possessive *idioi,* meaning "one's own," gives the sense of "appointed" or "appropriate")
refers in the Pastoral Epistles to times, whether past (1 Tim 2:6; Tit 1:3) or future (1 Tim
6:15; compare 1 Thess 2:6), when God acts. The events so indicated refer respectively to
the incarnation and return of Christ.

The awareness of a special calling to the Gentiles was one of the most dominant aspects
of Paul's self-understanding (Acts 9:15; Rom 9—11; Gal 2:7; Eph 3:7).

Finally, the description also emphasizes the substitutionary nature of his sacrifice. It accomplishes this by adding to the original word for *ransom (lytron;* Mk 10:45) the preposition *anti,* which means "in place of." Jesus gave himself not only as our representative but also in our place.

Consequently, the universal scope of God's will to save is also demonstrated by the teaching of Jesus. The church knew this teaching by heart and through continued reflection delved ever deeper into its meaning: a voluntary sacrifice made in behalf of helpless sinners, so effective that it reaches to all.

Paul's extensive mission (2:6-7). The final point to demonstrate the breadth of God's saving will comes not so much from accepted theology as from the early church's common understanding that in giving Christ to the world God began actively to preach the gospel. That is, God actively implemented his will for all to see. The advent of Christ was God's *testimony given in its proper time* (v. 6). God himself, at the moment of his choice (compare Gal 4:4), initiated the proclamation of the gospel. But as verse 7 proceeds to show, this God-initiated work of proclamation passed into Paul's hands and, just as important, into the church's. Paul's was the universal mission to the Gentiles, which he carried out as God's "herald" and Christ's "sent one" (1:1). The fact that the Gentiles were being reached for Christ was further demonstration of God's will to save all people.

At the last, lest the readers forget the setting out of which the teaching grew, the apostle underlines the veracity of his message *(I am telling the truth . . . [I am] a teacher of the true faith to the Gentiles).* He knows his claim may well be challenged, just as *the true faith* had been in that church.

The church's prayer for all people is an essential aspect of its participation in the Great Commission. It is prayer that seeks the gospel's penetration into all parts of the world and every aspect of life. The closely related prayer for those whom God has placed in charge of government finds its ultimate purpose too in the accomplishment of God's plan of salvation. Perhaps it is worth noting that we find Paul praying not for the liberation of the land from Roman rule, but for the responsible administration of that rule. The importance that Paul attached to this facet of our conduct in God's house suggests the need to rethink the place we give to it in all of our gatherings.

Men and Women in Worship (2:8-15) How are men and women to behave and relate to one another in the church? This question and this particular passage have been on the minds of many in recent times. For many, the passage before us has been regarded as a major hill to be taken in an interpretive battle. But the teaching of 2:11-15 is just one piece in a larger puzzle, and by itself it is incapable of providing a complete answer. Specific circumstances required Paul to answer the question asked above in specific ways. The concern here will not be to generalize those specifics but rather to set out the issues that Paul addressed and those that we must consider in the church today.

When Paul instructed men and women (some think husbands and wives were specifically in view) in his churches (see also 1 Cor 11:2-16; 14:33-35), the immediate problem was disturbances in the worship service. On the one hand, changing attitudes about the man-woman relationship led women to assert themselves in the worship service in ways that threatened unity and perhaps also reflected a disregard for biblical and cultural distinctions between men and women. Disruptions by women included inquiring about the meaning of prophecies (1 Cor 14:33-35) and teaching men (1 Tim 2:11-12). But the present passage also reveals that the anger and arguments of some men were contributing to the disruption of the church's worship service. As pointed out above (see on 2:1), Paul drew upon certain material in such cases in order to restore peace to the community by encouraging appropriate behavior. In this his concern both for biblical patterns and for the perceptions of those outside of the church is evident.

His instructions are given in two parts. First, they encourage cooperative behavior among men in the worship service in relation to the specific task of prayer outlined above. Second, women are instructed concerning appropriate dress and then concerning appropriate behavior in the worship setting in relation to teaching.

The Appropriate Demeanor of Men (2:8) The NIV omits the word "therefore," which in the original Greek sentence connects the instructions to men with the preceding instructions about prayer. A connection is intended, as in fact Paul now lays down two principles to ensure the effectiveness of the church's prayer.

First, prayer that is acceptable must come from *holy,* purified hearts. The physical lifting of hands was important in the Jewish act of prayer. But the purity of the hands, originally a physical prerequisite to be fulfilled before one approached God (Ex 30:19-21), came to be symbolic of the condition of the heart. The early church understood such purity to be a condition of acceptable prayer (Jas 4:8). When we pray, our communication is with a holy God. He requires of us that we deal with our sins before making our approach.

Second, prayer that is acceptable must come from people in right relationship with one another. For this reason Paul adds the stipulation that our prayer be *without anger or disputing.* This principle too was widely known in the early church and goes back to Jesus' own teaching (Mt 5:23; 6:12, 14-15; Jas 4:3; 1 Pet 3:7). Simply put, difficulties in our relationship with God or in our relationship with fellow believers can hinder our prayer. The reference to arguments has the dissension caused by the false teachers in mind (1 Tim 1:6-7; 6:4-5; Tit 3:9-10). A divisive spirit had invaded the worship service, where unity was to be most evident. Interpersonal harmony is a resource of incalculable value for the prayer life of the church.

The Appropriate Demeanor of Women (2:9-15) As is customary in this type of "household code" teaching, instructions to one member of the pair are followed by corresponding instructions to the other (Eph 5:22—6:9; Col 3:18—4:1; 1 Pet 3:1-7).

Notes: 2:9-10 The connection with the teaching in 1 Peter 3:3-5 is obvious: each passage discourages showy outer adornment (forms of *kosmos, kosmios, kosmeō* occur; *braided hair or gold or pearls or expensive clothes* here as compared to "braided hair and the wearing of gold jewelry and fine clothes," 1 Pet 3:3), and each encourages inner adornment (that is, *good deeds* here, like "the unfading beauty of a gentle and quiet spirit," 1 Pet 3:4).

However, the phrase *with decency and propriety* adds a note concerning appropriate outer adornment in 1 Timothy 2:9 that is not in 1 Peter 3 (which focuses entirely on inner adornment). See Kelly (1963:66) and Fee (1988:71) for the view that the instruction is sexual in tone. For the cultural caricature of women who lavishly adorn themselves see Juvenal *Satires* 6. 492 and Petronius *Satire* 67.

2:9 A verb needs to be supplied to complete the thought. Most understand the initial *I want* of verse 8 to be implied here too, which is then completed with *to dress modestly* (NIV). But it is possible that Paul meant the whole thought—*I want [women] to pray*—to be repeated, so that as a condition for effective prayer, a woman's modest adornment

Appropriate adornment (2:9-10). One source of the disruption being caused by women was their dress. Paul addresses this by drawing from the church's accepted teaching about the adornment of women (compare 1 Pet 3:3-5). He prescribes a manner of dress with three very similar terms stressing modesty and discretion (NIV *modestly, with decency and propriety*). Some commentators suggest that the tone of this instruction is "sexual," Paul's intention being to discourage women from dressing in a way that would distract men in the worship service. But perhaps the more acute problem was that of insensitive women flaunting their dress, jewelry and hairstyles in a way that hurt the feelings of the poor and disturbed the church. The kinds of adornment mentioned *(braided hair . . . gold . . . pearls . . . expensive clothes)* all belonged to that culture's critical caricature of wealthy women.

While today this manner of dress is not nearly as exclusive as it was in Paul's day, nor indeed restricted to women, its effects can be the same. I am reminded of a visit to a large, upper-middle-class church in Dallas (it could have been any large city or suburb). When I entered the sanctuary, the first thing that struck me was the glitter of jewelry, the expensive clothing and the fashionable hairstyles. The craning necks as people sized one another up gave the impression that for many the purpose of gathering together that Sunday morning was to display economic status. A newcomer of modest economic means could not help but feel a sense of exclusion.

According to Paul's instruction, what is to be noticeable about Christian women (and men) is not showy apparel, which sends an unsettling message (even to outsiders), but the power of God in spiritual deeds.

corresponds to a man's holy hands and cooperative spirit (compare Witherington 1988:119 and note 203). Even if the former explanation is preferable, Paul did not exclude women from praying in the worship service (1 Cor 11:5).

2:10 *Good deeds* belongs to Paul's special ethical vocabulary and is thematic in the Pastorals, occurring (in one configuration or another) fourteen times (1 Tim 3:1; 5:10 [2x], 25; 6:18; 2 Tim 2:21; 3:17; Tit 1:16; 2:7, 14; 3:1, 8, 14; compare the verb "to do good" *[agathoergein]* alongside the noun in 1 Tim 6:18). As the references in Titus 2:14 and 3:8 (compare Eph 2:10) demonstrate, good deeds in the Christian sense are the result of salvation. *Good deeds* thus describes the visible dimension of the genuine Christian life from the perspective of "doing": works done in the power of the Spirit.

The term *worship God (theosebeia)* within the phrase *profess to worship God* is equivalent to "godliness" *(eusebeia;* see above on 2:2). Paul implies that their claim to be genuine believers was contradicted by their behavior.

Good deeds (v. 10) speaks of genuine Christianity, the observable life-style that flows out of faith in Christ. This is the *appropriate* "adornment" for those who profess to be genuine Christians. Among other things, Paul sought to prevent Christian women from being typed by those outside. In some parts of the world today, the "prosperity gospel" has put showy apparel at a premium and minimized good deeds, but the discerning unbeliever can tell the difference between genuine and nominal Christianity. At the same time, it is the invisible force behind *good deeds,* love for others, that creates and sustains unity.

The woman-man relationship in the worship service (2:11-15). Today, among those who take the Bible seriously, two main positions have emerged in the discussion of this passage and its implications. As the following brief outline of each position will show, the passage needs to be considered as a whole, for the instructions of verses 11-12 (and also vv. 9-10) are grounded in some way by verses 13-15.

One position (here called position 1) generally maintains that verses 11-12 prohibit women from teaching and holding authority over men. Within the worship setting their appropriate role is that of the learner. Women will be quiet during the teaching portion of the service—that is, they will not teach or question. And they will be fully submissive to men's authority. Furthermore, on the basis of the Genesis material in verses 13-14, the arrangement sanctioned by Paul is held to be permanent. Verse 13 grounds the subordinate position of the woman in the order of creation, the man having been created first. The allusion to Eve's deception in verse 14 presents an illustration of the negative consequences that result when the divinely willed structure is disturbed. In one way or another verse 15 then refers positively to the acceptable role of women.

The second position (which I shall call position 2) insists that the passage contains a temporary restraining order issued to curb the activities of a group of women who (most argue) were teaching the heresy in Ephesus. Thus the relegation of women to the role of learners, who

---

2:11-15 Representatives of position 1 are Hurley (1981:195-223), Moo (1980:62-83), Clark (1980:191-208) and Knight (1992:138-49). For position 2 see Scholer 1986:193-224, Fee 1988:72-77 and Evans 1983:100-107. For additional bibliography see Scholer 1986:194.

Some scholars argue that Paul's teaching was particularly directed against women who were teaching the heresy (Fee 1988:73; Scholer 1986:194-200; Payne 1981:169-97). However, this remains uncertain, for the nature of their involvement is not clear (compare 5:15;

must be quiet and submissive to the imposed (male) authority structure, represents a local rather than a universal rule. Similarly, the prohibition from teaching in verse 12 was a stopgap measure, and the reference to holding authority over a man is better understood as "wrongfully usurping" his authority. As far as Paul's use of Genesis goes, verse 14 provides an example or explanation, showing how just as the deception of Eve had drastic results, so also did the deception of some women in Ephesus. Verse 13 is somewhat problematic for this position.

The contemporary debate seems to turn on the question of the rule's limits of applicability, local and temporary versus universal and timeless. And the determining factor usually ends up being the interpretation of Paul's use of the Genesis allusions. But there is more to be considered.

First, the passage must be assessed within the whole of Paul's teaching, and particularly in light of other statements he made about the relationship of men and women (and husbands and wives). Those of position 2, in attempting to understand the relevance of 1 Timothy 2:11-15 for today, have rightly pointed to a Pauline theme of equality within the social structure, as registered by the triad of texts Galatians 3:28, 1 Corinthians 12:13 and Colossians 3:11. Further, it is certainly arguable that Paul's acknowledgment of the role of women in his ministry (Rom 16:1; Phil 4:3) and in the church's worship (1 Cor 11:10) is the outworking of that principle of equality. The apparent discordant note struck in the present passage (and in 1 Cor 14:33-35) should alert us to the fact that Paul's program of social equality was not unconditional, but it does not necessarily nullify the basic principle. As F. F. Bruce explained, in Galatians 3:28 "Paul states the basic principle . . . if restrictions on it are found elsewhere . . . they are to be understood in relation to Gal. 3:28, and not *vice versa*" (1982:190).

But Galatians 3:28 was almost certainly not meant as a proclamation of liberty to be experienced immediately and fully in all dimensions of life. If it were this simple, Paul would have been far more forthright in

2 Tim 3:6). It may be that the heresy, with its misunderstanding about the times (compare 2 Tim 2:18), indirectly influenced some women and slaves to agitate for emancipation in the church. Parallels in Corinth (1 Cor 11; 14) suggest that Paul's "equality principle" (1 Cor 12:13; Gal 3:28; Col 3:11) may have figured in this emancipationist thinking. See further Towner 1989:38-41, 210-12).

urging the abolition of slavery. Also, Galatians 3:28 addresses three kinds of fundamental relationships or distinctions (racial, economic [perhaps], gender), but they do not have the same origin. Slavery was already common to Hebrew culture when God claimed his people. What he did was provide guidelines for its regulation. It may be argued that racial distinctions between Jews and Greeks (Gentiles) were encouraged for a time, but clearly bigotry and exclusive claims to spiritual superiority have human origins. Of the three pairs, only distinctions related to gender trace directly back to God's creative activity. This by no means automatically substantiates position 1. It merely suggests that Galatians 3:28 is not a simple declaration of the immediate eradication of all social distinctions. Paul's own approach to the three relationships ought to be evidence of that.

There are at least two other factors that need to be considered in discussing Paul's approach to these institutions and to movement in the direction of freedom. The first is his understanding of and sensitivity to culture. On the one hand, Paul and other New Testament writers seem to have viewed their world and its structures as a part of God's design. They could encourage the church to "submit to" the institutions of the world (1 Pet 2:13) and (as far as possible) through generally acceptable behavior to make a redemptive impression in it (1 Thess 4:11-12; 1 Tim 3:7; 6:1). But this was a view held in tension with a firm belief that the world is an evil force at war with God. Consequently, the church was by no means to allow culture or society to dictate its policies; however, where possible, peaceful coexistence would be a help to the church's evangelistic mission. The New Testament household codes give some evidence of social awareness and cultural sensitivity, but they never advocate conformity for conformity's sake, and when we are reading them, we need to distinguish between categories of relationships as we do in Galatians 3:28. Ultimately, it is reasonable to think that Paul or any other New Testament writer would have stopped short of advocating the immediate abolition of slavery because the culture might perceive it as a threat. But it does not automatically follow that his concern was precisely the same when he addressed the woman-man relationship.

The second factor is Paul's (and the New Testament's) understanding of salvation. It leaves us in a state that has been described as "already and not yet." Salvation is a combination of things to be realized progressively in this life (victory over sin, growth in godliness) and promises to be fulfilled only with the return of Christ (resurrection, the final victory over sin). Salvation in relation to the social structure within the church and in relation to personal sanctification is progressive, under way but not finished, "already" but "not yet." But that the distinctions inherent in the female-male relationship belong to the category of things that may or should pass away in this age (as it is argued in the case of slavery or racial distinctions) is a proposition in need of theological demonstration. Jesus' statement in Matthew 22:30 may have been misinterpreted to mean that all significant male-female distinctions will eventually disappear; but whatever it means, it applies to the resurrection and remains a promise. To judge simply from Paul's teaching elsewhere, it is doubtful that Galatians 3:28 implies that all male-female distinctions ought to be done away with as soon as the church is able to carry this program out. But even if Paul means more, it does mean that, with respect to value and position as heirs, no cultural distinctions that might support male superiority have a bearing on salvation or usefulness in the church. With respect to function and authority in the church, it is probably ill-advised to draw conclusions directly from either Galatians 3:28 or 1 Timothy 2:11-15. A broader theological program is needed.

A final question bearing on the interpretation of the passage is the degree to which Paul is countering effects of the false teaching. Two views should be introduced briefly.

1. At a bare minimum, it is reasonable to understand the rise of women to teaching positions as the indirect result of the false teaching. The doctrine of a realized resurrection (2 Tim 2:18; see introduction) was current and may have led women (and perhaps slaves) to enact promises (even if they misunderstood them) such as those connected with the well-known teaching of Galatians 3:28. Even Jesus' teaching (Mt 22:30) could have figured in their thinking. Some scholars have suggested that the women in mind had actually been enlisted by the false teachers to teach the heresy. The latter is difficult to prove, but it remains a possibility.

2. It is also within the realm of possibility that the passage speaks with even more precision to false doctrines that affected the thinking and

behavior of women. In this case too the resurrection misunderstanding and the connected overrealized view of salvation would be central. Perhaps the false teachers drew on Jesus' teaching on marriage in the resurrection (Mt 22:30) to support their doctrine of celibacy (1 Tim 4:3). They may have construed their present "resurrection existence" in terms of pre-Fall existence. From the first three chapters of Genesis they might have concluded that since sexual distinctions, sexuality and childbearing came after the Fall, they no longer pertain to the new age. In the same way, they might have argued that "subordination" was enforced only as a result of the Fall (Gen 3:16) and that the eating of meat was a sign of depravity (Gen 9; 1 Tim 4:3). In this case, the *myths and endless genealogies* Paul mentions (1:4) might have included proof texts of such doctrines drawn from the creation materials. And in this case, 2:13-15 may take up and correctly apply the Old Testament material.

We cannot be certain of either view. But it is extremely likely that the false resurrection doctrine had an effect on views of sexuality and perhaps blurred distinctions between the sexes, affecting marriage and certain functions in the church. It seems all the more likely in view of the close parallels between the resurrection misunderstanding and questions about marriage, men and women, and foods in Corinth and Ephesus (see introduction).

These considerations provide a framework within which to explore the meaning and intent of the instructions to women. However, the complexity of the whole issue and the range of texts involved suggest that we should think in terms of possibilities rather than certainty at several points.

Paul actually encourages women to learn, which sets him apart from his contemporaries in Judaism. But it is the manner in which they learn that will settle the disturbances they have been causing in the church:

2:11 On *full submission* as complete submission to the authority of men, see Hurley 1981:200-201. For submission as "participation" in social institutions see Goppelt 1982:168. The precise meaning of *submission (hypotassō)* must be determined by its context. Indications of a hierarchical arrangement can be found in the term's use in Romans 8:20, 1 Corinthians 15:27-28, Ephesians 1:22 and Philippians 3:21. But the note of willingness indicated by the middle voice must not be overlooked (Rom 13:1; 1 Cor 14:34; Eph 5:21-22; Col 3:18; Tit 2:5, 9; 3:1; 1 Pet 2:13, 18; 3:1).

2:12 Knight's attempt (1992:141-42) to limit the meaning of *to have authority (authen-*

in quietness and full submission (v. 11). Paul does not mean that women are to be absolutely silent during the service (compare 1 Cor 11:5). Rather, he instructs them to exhibit *quietness* (in spirit) instead of taking the lead, or to "be silent" in the sense of not teaching. Even as learners, perhaps, they are to refrain from entering into public discussions about interpretation of the Old Testament and prophecies (1 Cor 14:33-35).

Full submission is the more general description of the appropriate demeanor of the woman learner. It seems clear from this passage that to be in *full submission* meant for those women to refrain from teaching (men) and probably also to dress in appropriate ways. Certain questions, however, continue to be asked: Is this a universal or temporary rule? Does the teaching here need to be understood as an exception to the principle of Galatians 3:28, necessitated by the imprudent actions of some women? Positions 1 and 2 answer these questions in different ways (see above). Below we will consider the matter further.

Teach and *have authority over a man* (v. 12) may be references to separate activities that Paul restricted to men. Or the first term might represent a specific example of activity that falls under the general rule that follows: women's teaching in the public assembly would violate the given authority structure. In either case, we should notice that Paul did not employ his usual term for "the normal exercise of authority" *(exousia)*. He chose an unusual word *(authenteō)* that could carry negative connotations such as "to usurp or misappropriate authority" or "to domineer." The unusual term probably signifies an unusual situation. In the Ephesian context at least, women had misappropriated authority by taking upon themselves the role of teacher.

Thus verses 11-12 aim to restore peace in the worship service by placing certain limits on the role of women. Probably as a result of the influence of the false teaching, some women had assumed the role of

---

teō) to a positive description of "authority" (such as would go with positions of teaching and leadership) is inconclusive. The work of Kroeger (1986:225-44) and Osburn (1982:1-12) suggests that a meaning such as "usurp or misappropriate authority" or "domineer" is also possible.

For Paul's preferred term *(exousia)* in discussions about "authority," see Romans 13:1-5; 1 Corinthians 6:12; 7:4; 8:9; 9:4-6; 11:10; 15:24; 2 Corinthians 10:8; 13:10. See the discussion in Scholer 1986:205.

teacher. This step led Paul to invoke a subordination rule; it seems to have precluded women from teaching men, since to do so constituted *authenteō*—that is, the wrongful appropriation of authority over men.

In handling the supporting material that follows, verses 13-15, our first concern should be whether any special significance is to be attached to Paul's citation of material from the creation narrative of Genesis to support some argument or other. It is difficult to establish a hard and fast rule. On the one hand, Paul in 1 Corinthians 11:7-9 alludes to the same Genesis passage (2:21-23) that 1 Timothy 2:13 does in order to ground the covering of the woman's head in worship. But this practice, most would argue, was bound to a particular culture. On the other hand, the reference to Genesis 2:24-25 in Ephesians 5:31 is indeed meant to remind Christians that marriage is an institution to be continually honored (compare Mt 19:5). Therefore, the allusion to Genesis 2 in the words *for Adam was formed first, then Eve* (v. 13) is best considered on its own.

What are the possibilities? First, it can hardly be denied that Paul appeals to the order of creation. While it is usually thought that this statement substantiates the prohibition of verse 12 (Knight 1992:142-43), it may ground all of verses 9-12, with *full submission* understood as encompassing aspects of dress and function (Fee 1988:74). But the question of precise intention remains. Did Paul intend the Genesis allusion to mean that the created order still pertained and that distinctions between the sexes and an authority structure existed even prior to the Fall (compare 1 Cor 11:7-9)? Did he mean that the conditions of the curse,

---

Notes: 2:13-14 Many have argued that the reasoning of the author (who in their estimation is not Paul) reflects rabbinic attitudes about women. The oft-quoted references are *y.Sota* 3. 4 and 19a. 7: "Better to burn the Torah than to teach it to a woman." See also *m.Sota* 3. 4; *Qidd.* 29b, 34a; *b.Sanhedrin* 94b; Hanson 1968:65-77; Dibelius and Conzelmann 1972:47-48. Verse 14 tends to be the linchpin of this interpretation, for allegedly here we find a reference to the rabbinic teaching that Eve as the original sinner was more culpable than Adam. Moreover, some assert that the verb *deceived (exapataō)* implies the belief that Eve's sin was sexual in nature. Although it seems that Jewish writers had begun to speculate on the fall into sin by the first century (but the dates of some of these writings are questionable: 4 Macc 18:6-8; Philo *Quest. Gen.* 1. 47; *Leg. All.* 3. 59-61; *Life of Adam and Eve* 9-11; *Apoc. Mos.* 22), it is only in the later (second-century and beyond) literature (mostly rabbinic) that we find explicit references to the serpent's sexual seduction of Eve *(Prot. Jas.* 53. 1; *Gen. Rab.* 18; *b.Sota* 9b; *Ber. Rab.* 18; see further Ellis 1957:61-62). Furthermore, the verb *exapataō* does not necessarily imply sexual transgression.

A final argument designed to demonstrate that Paul knew and employed rabbinic tradition

which promised painful childbearing and placed the wife under the husband's rule (Gen 3:16), were still in effect? Was he addressing the false teachers' twisted interpretations of the creation accounts which had influenced the thinking of women (see above)?

Verse 14 is almost certainly a local reference to the deception of some women in the Ephesian church (see the notes for other explanations). The deception of Eve had become a model to illustrate the dangers posed to the church by false teaching (compare 2 Cor 11:3). Paul's use of the model here probably sent the signal that by taking the role of teachers (and possibly in what they taught) these women had been deceived by heretics. It also implies that this activity was sinful.

Verse 15 sounds strange to the ears in any version: *But women will be saved through childbearing.* Not surprisingly, its meaning is debated. The NIV has rightly interpreted the singular verb (literally, "she will be saved") as a general reference to women. But as the promise continues, a condition limits its applicability to those women who *continue in faith, love and holiness with propriety.* That is, the promise applies to women whose conduct (here *propriety* refers back to the appropriate conduct prescribed in vv. 9-12) bears the marks of genuine Christian existence. But what does *saved through childbearing* mean? With original sin and the pronouncement of the curse as the background, some have understood the definite article ("the") which precedes *childbearing* in the Greek sentence to denote "the birth"—that is, the birth of the Christ. Following the guilty verdict of verse 14, *saved* would then mean primar-

---

is based on 2 Corinthians 11:3, the relevant portion of which reads "but I am afraid that just as Eve was deceived by the serpent's cunning." As the argument goes, the imagery of the "pure virgin" (v. 2) is an allusion to Eve prior to her sexual seduction, which is hinted at in *exapataō,* and points to the rabbinic reflection on the fall into sin (Hanson 1968:71). But this is surely to draw more out of the marriage imagery than Paul originally intended. He applies the allusion to Eve to the whole Corinthian church, which, being deceived by false teachers (vv. 14-15), was being led into sin (vv. 3-4). More likely the main theme in that passage is that the serpent (Satan) was the prototype of false teachers (compare the extension of this motif in 1 Tim 4:1 and 5:15); for Paul envisages doctrinal perversion ("minds . . . led astray," v. 3; see also vv. 4, 14-15), as the context confirms, and thus draws upon the model of Eve's deception (and "deception" is the focal point) to make the Corinthians acutely aware of the danger of false doctrine. On the motif in 2 Corinthians 11:3 see further Furnish 1984:500-502 and Harris 1976:385.

Another view that somehow clings to life argues that verse 14 actually affirms the belief that women are inherently more susceptible to deception than men and therefore less suited

ily salvation from sin, and the allusion would be to the "protoevangel-ion"—the promised seed of the woman who will crush the serpent's head (Gen 3:15). While this reading is possible, one wonders why such an ambiguous reference to Christ would be made (unless Paul here is simply making use of the false teachers' language and text to adjust their teaching). The same background perhaps leads more naturally to a promise that God will provide physical protection for godly women under the curse, an emblem of the final complete removal of the curse to come. Finally, some point to 5:14, where the term *childbearing* de-scribes a part of the life appropriate for young widows, to argue that Paul endorses here the domestic life of the housewife as the normative, ac-ceptable role that women are to pursue. Serving God in this capacity, they will "work out their salvation."

Clearly, none of these interpretations is free of problems, and the best we can do is to narrow down the possibilities. It may be that what seems to us as allusiveness in Paul's references to the creation material actually represents his counterarguments using the kinds of texts the heretics themselves employed. But while we have no way of knowing the precise lines of the false theology, we can be reasonably sure that it was trium-phalistic in thrust (2 Tim 2:18). Consequently, we can at least see that 2:15 does pull the readers back to reality, either (from the theological perspective) by asserting that this life is still marked by the curse/sin and God's promise to save or (from the ethical perspective) by teaching that life must yet be lived in the confines of a mundane social structure that still awaits the eschaton.

---

to leadership in the church (Clark 1980:203-4, 382-33). The social-scientific evidence mar-shaled (rather selectively) by Clark seems to suggest that "women tend to perceive things more as an entire person—with mind, body, and emotions integrated. Their response is more immediate in time; they invest less time in a distanced analysis of a situation." On the other hand, men tend to respond with more detachment (Clark 1980:382-83). Allegedly this explains why historically women have found cults (such as Gnosticism and Montanism) so attractive. However, the statistics in Asia and Latin America (if applied superficially) might also suggest that these same characteristics make women better suited to embracing the gospel, for the female population in the church far outnumbers that of the male. In any case, a commonsense look at both church history and our present situation, each testifying amply to the deceitfulness and susceptibility to error of key male church/cult leaders, ought to be sufficient to recommend a balanced reevaluation of the social-scientific defense of this view.

2:15 For the view that a typical, socially acceptable role is endorsed in the reference to *childbearing (teknogonia;* compare 5:15), see also Fee 1988:75-76, Scholer 1986:195-200,

We run the risk of misusing 2:8-15 if we make it a proof text in our modern debate. The passage as a whole calls for men and women to relate to one another in the church according to the standards of acceptability, in awareness of the theological realities of the age in which we live. Although Paul's reference to the creation story cautions against viewing his teaching as simply suited to his culture, his sensitivity to culture should also be considered in addressing questions related to the role of women in the church today. There is a need to explore the degree to which there existed in the apostle's thinking about the female-male relationship a difference between nonnegotiables (aspects of this relationship that seem to stem from God's creative will) and negotiables (aspects of behavior within the relationship that may be expressed differently from one culture to the next). If 2:15 envisions an acceptable role for women, then, depending on the culture within which we find ourselves, verse 15 may well need to allow room for astronauts, surgeons and business executives in addition to missionaries, church workers of various sorts and, indeed, housewives. But in any role godliness will need to be found in this incomplete age through our reliance on God's promise in the continuing struggle with sin. As for the role of women in ministry, the church must continue to wrestle with this issue, and this passage will have its place. But easy answers that *either* simply impose culture on God's will *or* neglect culture altogether must be resisted.

Leadership Qualifications (3:1-13) If a church were to place an ad

---

Moo 1980:71-73 and Kelly 1963:69. For the possible explanation that Christ's birth is in view, or that actual physical safety in childbearing is meant (a reference to protection in spite of the curse) see Lock 1924:32-33 and Payne 1981:177-79.

Paul's use of a list of virtues to describe the Christian life is typical in the Pastorals (see below on 1 Tim 4:12; 5:10; 6:11). *Faith* and *love,* prominent in these lists, are combined nine times in the Pastorals (1 Tim 1:5, 14; 2:15; 4:12; 6:11; 2 Tim 1:13; 2:22; 3:10; Tit 2:2) and eight times elsewhere in Paul. This "summary" of the Christian life was prominent in early Christian teaching. Together they describe the vertical, personal relationship with God and acceptance of correct doctrine and the horizontal response dimension of Christian living. *Propriety (sōphrosynē* and related words) also occupies a dominant place in Paul's portrayal of visible Christianity (1 Tim 2:9; 3:2; 2 Tim 1:7; Tit 2:2, 4, 5, 6). It depicts ideas such as prudence, moderation, discretion and self-control, all ideas highly praised in Hellenistic ethical thought. Titus 2:12 specifically connects this virtue with the advent of Christ and salvation, a connection already made by Paul (Rom 12:3).

in a newspaper inviting applications for church leadership positions, what might it include? From visiting the board meetings of almost any modern church one might get the impression that successful business-men make the best elders—after all, management is management. On the other hand, books that deal with leadership training often highlight the sense of calling, dependence on God and perseverance that we see in the great biblical characters—Moses, Jeremiah, Paul—to provide a model. Of course, these figures were powerful leaders, and there is much to be learned about leadership from them. But if the question is "Who is fit to lead in the church?" and this decision falls to other church leaders, then the place to begin is with the kind of concerns raised in 1 Timothy 3:1-13.

At this point in the letter, the tone changes. What had been a discus-sion of what the church and certain groups in the church ought to *do* becomes a discussion of what leaders in the church ought to *be*. The moral lapse and defection of some of this church's leaders undoubtedly had left the fellowship in a state of instability. And the internal disruption was likely to be met by severe criticism from unbelievers. For these reasons the two lists included at this point describe the necessary qual-ifications for the offices of the overseer and deacon. In each case the focal point is the candidate's reputation among believers *and* unbeliev-ers, which is to be computed on the basis of proven moral character and maturity. Duties are hardly mentioned. The standard, *above reproach* (3:2) or blameless (3:10), is extremely high, but not out of proportion to the importance of the church's mission in the world (3:15-16), which always hangs in the balance.

Who were the overseers and deacons? The term translated *overseer* in the NIV was first used outside the church to refer to supervisors of

---

Notes: 3:1 Some take the formula *here is a trustworthy saying* as closing the paragraph about women in 2:11-15 (see Dibelius and Conzelmann 1972:44, 51). But 2:15 does not appear to be a "saying." The formula almost certainly affirms the office of overseer prior to the formal beginning of the overseer code (Fee 1988:79; Hanson 1982:75; see further Knight 1979:50-61).

The lists of qualifications for the office of the overseer in 1 Timothy 3:1-7 and Titus 1:6-9 exhibit the marks of a traditional code. (1) Each begins with a closely similar introduction (1 Tim 3:2; Tit 1:7; *above reproach [anepilēmptos]* and *blameless [anenklētos;* compare 1 Tim 3:10] are synonymous); (2) each joins "blamelessness" and "one-woman man" at

various sorts. As a description of one level of church leadership, it appears in Acts 20:28 and, again alongside "deacons," in Philippians 1:1. To judge from the account of Paul's farewell meeting with the elders (presbyters; compare 1 Tim 5:17) of Ephesus (Acts 20:17-38) and the instructions in Titus 1:6-7, the terms "overseer" and "elder" referred to the same office. Moreover, church leaders alluded to in Romans 12:8 ("leadership," "govern") and 1 Corinthians 12:28 ("those with gifts of administration") as well as in Ephesians 4:11, "pastors and teachers," would probably hold this office. Among the duties assigned to this office (though perhaps not exclusively) were preaching and teaching and generally leading or managing the church.

The office of deacons (which may have included women; see below on 3:11) probably emerged as the church grew in size and the demands on the leadership required that certain functions be delegated. The table-waiting deacons of Acts 6:1-6 may have been prototypical of the office referred to here and in Philippians 1:1. Teaching and ruling are not specifically mentioned in connection with deacons; they were apparently subordinate to the overseers and generally charged with seeing to the fellowship's practical needs. Nevertheless, some deacons would have been active in preaching the gospel (Stephen and Philip show how widely the preaching ministry extended).

Overseers: A Reputation Above Reproach (3:1-7) The second of Paul's "trustworthy sayings" (see 1:15) promotes the office of the overseer as a *noble task.* Perhaps the problems in Ephesus had led some to regard the offices with suspicion and disrespect. If so, a reminder of the honor and importance traditionally attached to the position might restore some of that respect and instill confidence in carefully chosen leaders. But as the following guidelines imply, the viability of the office

---

the head of the list (although rearrangement has occurred in Tit 1 in order to connect these requirements to the "elder"); and (3) the elements in the lists are generally comparable (see Dibelius and Conzelmann 1972:133). It is also quite likely that Paul adapted a code of duties then currently in use in the secular world (Dibelius and Conzelmann 1972:160 provide an example of this type of code). This would explain the focus on traits not specific to a church leader. However, he has clearly "Christianized" these tools (1 Tim 3:5-7; Tit 1:7, 9), and his reason for using them was probably to emphasize observable credibility with a view to missionary witness (1 Tim 3:7). As attributes of the genuine life of faith, such marks of respectability were the result of conversion (Tit 2:12; 3:2-7).

is closely linked to the one seeking to hold it. For us today, whose too-full schedules lead us rather to disregard offices in the church, the same reminder could well be taken as an exhortation to availability.

The code that follows in verses 2-7 gives guidelines for measuring a candidate's reputation, which *must be above reproach*. This requirement, one word in the original Greek, is the only one in the code that requires further definition. The items that follow give an idea of the directions that "irreproachability" should move in. Generally, the focus is on observable conduct. Most of the items of behavior that follow require little explanation. The reference to the overseer's marriage, however, is an exception.

Although we might cringe at the thought, most of us would probably admit that one's marriage sheds a good deal of light on one's character. Paul apparently held similar feelings. But the meaning of the condition that the overseer be *the husband of but one wife* (literally, a "one-woman man") continues to provoke discussion, and some of the interpretations bear a closer look.

1. The qualification prohibits polygamists from holding this office. However, this is not likely to have been Paul's intention. Monogamy was by far the norm of that day. Polygamy was generally regarded as abhorrent and did not need to be mentioned in such a list.

2. The qualification excludes those who have remarried after the death of a spouse. This is an equally unlikely suggestion. Remaining single, particularly in the case of widows, was often commended, but Paul seems to have allowed and even to have encouraged the remarriage of the surviving partner (1 Cor 7:39-40; 1 Tim 5:14).

3. The qualification specifically rules out those who have remarried after divorce. But even granting a fairly strong stand in the New Testament on the issue of divorce, exceptions to the rule prohibiting remarriage were made in the case of adultery (Mt 5:32; 19:9) and perhaps in the case of desertion by the unbelieving mate (1 Cor 7:15). Furthermore, there is nothing to exclude from consideration those who fall into this "excep-

---

3:2 For position 1 see Dibelius and Conzelmann 1972:52, Lock 1924:36-38 and Justin Martyr *Dialogue with Trypho* 100. 134. For position 2 see Kelly 1963:75-76, Verner 1983:130-31 and Brox 1989:142-44. For position 3 see Hanson 1982:75 and Jeremias 1975:24. For view 4 see Fee 1988:80-81, Barrett 1963:58-59 and Barclay 1975:87-91. The NIV interpretation *the*

tional" category (apart from this uncertain phrase, for which in any case there is no first-century evidence of its use in connection with divorce).

4. The qualification is a requirement of faithfulness in marriage. Given the context, this interpretation seems more plausible. Actually, the tone of the phrase is positive rather than prohibitive, which suggests a nuance of meaning different from the first three positions. The flow of thought in the list moves from personal to church life, from domestic to official functions. Implicit in this movement is an important axiom: what one does or is in one's private life has consequences for the church. It follows that within Paul's holistic outlook, which brings together personal and domestic qualities, it is far more likely that he would stress fidelity in marriage. So the point of the phrase is probably not how often one can be married, nor precisely what constitutes a legitimate marriage (that the marriage of the candidate is legitimate is assumed), but rather how one conducts oneself in one's marriage.

Without a break in the sentence, Paul inserts several personal qualities to amplify the meaning of *above reproach.* The candidate must be *temperate,* or better "sober," which taken figuratively, as probably intended here (in view of the prohibition of drunkenness in v. 3), means to be clear-headed or vigilant. Vigilance is the opposite of drunkenness or fuzzy thinking, which in this context has the life of faith in view. Christians are to guard against spiritual laziness and avoid habits that lull one to sleep (things and activities that draw us away from God).

Self-controlled, next on the list, is a quality Paul refers to frequently in the Pastorals as a basic element of the observable Christian life (2:9, 15; 2 Tim 1:7; Tit 2:2, 4, 5, 6). As a fundamental aspect of the new existence in Christ (Tit 2:12), it is the ability to take charge of the mind, and Christians have this possibility opened to them. This allows control over impulses (to overindulge the physical appetites, to think wrong thoughts about others and ourselves) which without control would drive us to excessive behavior.

Respectable refers to observable behavior that corresponds to inner

---

husband of but one wife seems to suit any of the first three positions (but see 5:9 where the counterpart "one-man woman" is translated more accurately as *faithful to her husband.* On *self-controlled* see note on 2:9.

self-control. It is behavior of all kinds (2:9) marked by self-discipline, order and balance. Paul's use of this traditional quality, especially in connection with self-control, sets before us the possibility and challenge of developing a life in which inner motivation and outer action achieve a harmonious balance. The ancients viewed inner control as the strength of life and outer balance as the beauty of life.

But Paul was not simply lauding traditional values that, some two thousand years later, are of no use to us. On the one hand, vigilance, self-control, respectability, and the balance of inner and outer life that Paul envisions are realities available to us in the Spirit. They are also necessities. Without vigilance (spiritual awareness and discernment) we will not exercise self-control. Without self-control we will indulge ourselves freely according to the advice of the world around us instead of setting the limits that produce godly balance.

Hospitality was a virtue also widely heralded in Greco-Roman culture. Within the church, however, the practice of hospitality was imperative. Some Christians had been forced out of their homelands by persecution or found it increasingly difficult to make a living. And this was always a prospect for Christians in the Roman Empire. The practical and sacrificial sharing of one's home and minimal resources might mean survival for someone. The New Testament enjoins all believers to practice hospitality (Rom 12:13; 1 Pet 4:9), but the Pastorals mention it only in connection with those who would serve (5:10; Tit 1:8), who are then to be examples.

Able to teach relates more directly to the ministry connected with the office of overseer. In the present context of heresy, this qualification would necessarily include teaching and preaching (5:17; 2 Tim 2:1) and refuting the heresy (2 Tim 2:24; Tit 1:9). In view of the apparent division of labor among the elders alluded to in 5:17, perhaps this qualification is typical and the ability to teach need not be equally in evidence in each candidate (compare Rom 12:6-8).

As the list continues to probe the background of the candidate for

---

3:3 *Gentle (epieikēs)* is the patient and winsome disposition toward all (but with special reference to the unbeliever) which encourages repentance; see Titus 3:2; 6:11.

Drunkenness was denounced by pagan and Christian ethicists alike. Paul places this vice into the general category of unregenerate behavior—1 Corinthians 5:11; 10:21; Galatians

leadership, it prohibits four characteristics of behavior. Tendencies toward *drunkenness* and violence (Tit 1:7) are clearly reasons for rejection. The church cannot afford to be led by those who allow themselves to be controlled by intoxicating substances (which enslave the user and inhibit decisive thinking) or emotions. But evidence of these traits in any believer calls for immediate action. They are signs of a loss of control. Maturity and strength are to exhibit themselves instead in gentleness, as they did in Christ (2 Cor 10:1).

At the same time, the overseer must not be *quarrelsome*. This tendency betrays an inability to get along with and accept the views of others, and perhaps deeper personality flaws as well. The false teachers in Ephesus were known for their quarrels (1:5; 6:4-5). A leader prone to this weakness will produce discord instead of harmony. But a leader, or any Christian for that matter, who promotes peace among people will create and preserve the relationships necessary for building a unified church.

Then, the overseer must not be a *lover of money*. This means the candidate's attitude toward material wealth ought to be one of healthy detachment, but certainly not irresponsibility. Such a leader can be a model of generosity and simplicity of lifestyle because of the knowledge that whatever one's economic status might be, all that one has belongs to God and so must be looked after faithfully before him (6:17-19). But this applies to every believer, and the issue raised by this characteristic is one we all ought to face. Many of us are capable of generating a comfortable income. How much is enough? How can we know if we have begun to put money and material things before God? What does responsibility mean in this area of our lives? These are hard questions, the kind we usually prefer not to ask. The very fact that these questions make us uncomfortable proves the relevance for us of Paul's word to overseers. All we can do here is suggest a beginning. Our attitudes and motivations where money and acquiring things are concerned must be brought before God for evaluation. God's Word and not the values of the society in which we live must be allowed to shape and correct our

5:21; Ephesians 5:18; compare Proverbs 23:30-35; Luke 21:34; *Epistles of Anacharsis* 3.
    For discussions about attitudes toward avarice and greed see on 6:3-10, 17-19 and notes. Recommended reading: White 1993, Sider 1977.

thinking and behavior in this area (Mt 6:19-24; 2 Cor 8—9; 1 Tim 6:5-10, 17-19).

The profile of the ideal candidate concludes with three conditions, each accompanied by a statement of rationale (vv. 4-6). First, Paul cites proficient management of the household (NIV *family)* as a prerequisite of church leadership (vv. 4-5). Indeed, if one's marriage hints at fitness for leading a church (3:2), then the effectiveness of one's attempts to lead and provide order in a home speaks volumes. Paul has in mind the typical householder of Greco-Roman society, who ordinarily would have been a citizen. Besides the male head of the house, household members included the wife, children and, depending on the economic status of the householder, slaves. In fact, some Christian householders in Ephesus owned slaves (6:2). The dwellings ranged from the spacious houses of the upper-class householder to the apartments (which varied in size) of middle- and lower-income households. Normally the authority structure of the household was strictly patriarchal, and at each level subordination to the householder was expected. Anything less than this kind of obedience to the householder was taken as a sign of disorder and even political subversion, for the stability of the household was regarded as fundamental to the well-being of society as a whole.

Given these values, it would have been unthinkable for Paul to sanction as church leaders those whose households belied their leadership skills. Society expected the householder to command the respect of his wife, children and slaves. To expect less from church leaders would have been to risk associating the church with charges of social disruption and political subversion. However, this particular condition was not meant to exclude the unmarried from holding positions of leadership in the church; in that day marriage was the almost universal rule.

Second, the overseer must not be a new believer (v. 6). The reason is not lack of leadership potential but lack of spiritual maturity. The new believer is more likely to see such a position of leadership as an opportunity for personal advancement and to fail to understand the gravity of

---

3:6 The qualification that the overseer/elder *not be a recent convert* must be limited in its application to churches that have been established for some time. It could not apply to churches of recent origin (compare Acts 14:23; Tit 1:6-9).

3:7 The appeal to the *good reputation* or the opinion of the outsider (which has "wit-

the task. The sense in this condition is well illustrated in the modern church, which has seen many recent converts who, because of influential position or fame in the world, are thrust into positions of church leadership that they are hardly ready to fill.

The danger, as Paul describes it simply, is becoming *conceited* (or "filled with pride") and falling under the devil's judgment (v. 6). The latter may mean *fall under the same judgment as the devil* (NIV) or, as seems more in keeping with the next verse, "be condemned by the devil." The point is that conceit, especially among church leaders, is just the kind of chink in the spiritual armor that the enemy often exploits. In Ephesus conceit was the bane of the false teachers (6:4; 2 Tim 3:4), who may well have been immature overseers. Their quick rise to this level of authority could easily have led them to think more highly of themselves (compare Rom 12:3) and their teaching than they ought, hardened them in stubbornness and caused no end of arguments in the church. Conceit and cooperation have nothing in common. Unfortunately, when the enemy discovers this breach in defense and a church leader falls into sin, the testimony of the church falls as well.

The final condition states clearly what has already been implied: the overseer must have a good testimony before *outsiders* (v. 7). Here the list of requirements concludes by returning to the general thought of "irreproachability" (3:2), but now with a particular audience, unbelievers, in mind. The good testimony is to be measured according to the preceding kinds of qualities. Deficiencies in the overseer's reputation or behavior that damage the testimony open the leader up to disgrace from outsiders—that is, *the devil's trap.* Perhaps in Paul's mind the greater danger lies in the fact that a fallen leader brings disgrace on the church and its message from those it is meant to reach (3:15).

To put the overseer code into proper perspective, the importance and urgency of the church's evangelistic mission require that its leaders be of the highest caliber (2:1-2; 3:14-15). They must be leaders whose management skill and purity of lifestyle instill confidence in Christians

ness" in mind) is characteristic of Paul's ethical teaching (5:14; 6:1; Tit 2:8, 10; 3:2, 8; compare 1 Thess 4:11-12). The emphasis on observable respectability as that kind of behavior which is acceptable even to the outsider also has the "good witness" of the believer and the church at heart (2:2, 9-15; 5:7-8, 15; 6:1-2, 9-10; Tit 2).

and elicit respect from outsiders to the faith. But the emphasis in this code is often missed. "Irreproachability" does not mean perfection. If Paul meant "without defect" or "in no need of growth," no one would qualify. Rather, as the range of qualities suggests, the code stresses "wholeness" as a measure of development toward maturity. That is, Paul wanted in leadership positions those in whom the Spirit was evidently and actively at work (but not necessarily finished) in the whole of life. Although realistically life is far too complex for anyone to be able to say at any one moment, "The Spirit is now renewing every part of my life" (who could stand the strain, anyway?), still from one's demeanor and attitudes and from evidence that the renovation is already under way, this kind of thoroughgoing commitment to God is possible to see.

As a guide to spiritual maturity, this code is applicable to all believers. It may serve as a map to chart for us a course to those areas in our life that need attention, while along the way we can receive encouragement at the signs of progress already made. And if we lose our way, the map can get us back on the right road. A thoughtful look at this map from time to time will keep our attention on thorough and balanced growth in Christ, with no area of our life escaping notice.

Deacons: A Blameless Reputation (3:8-13) Candidates for the office of deacon come under the same careful scrutiny. The qualifications they are to meet are closely similar to the overseer's. As verse 10 indicates, "blamelessness" (the practical equivalent of *above reproach* in v. 2; compare Tit 1:6-7) represents the acceptable standard (the NIV *there is nothing against them* obscures this point). Verses 8 and 9 explain what is meant by "blameless," and again the concern for wholeness of development emerges. The qualities listed in verse 8 fall into familiar categories of observable conduct. *Worthy of respect* (or "serious"—2:2; Tit 2:2) implies a bearing or deportment that is obviously respectable. Following closely on this is *sincere,* the positive rendering of the literal negative "not double-tongued" (or "two-faced"). That is, the deacon's word must be reliable. The deacon must also have control over drinking and not be allured by *dishonest gain.* Plainly, the same kinds of qualities

---

3:9 On *clear conscience* see the notes at 1:5.
3:11 For the view that "wives" is meant, see Hanson 1982:81, Houlden 1976:80, Easton

expected of the overseer are to be apparent in the deacon.

Paul next (v. 9) inserts what appears to be a "spiritual" requirement—namely, that the deacon *keep hold of the deep truths of the faith with a clear conscience* (compare 1:19). He means they must prove themselves to be unconnected with the false teachers. The latter, whose consciences were seared (4:2), rejected the faith and destroyed their spiritual lives (1:19). Very likely some had been deacons in the church. In Paul's thinking the *clear conscience* is the organ of decision. With it one can cross the distance from *the faith,* embraced with mind and heart, to godly conduct. Adherence to correct doctrine is also a matter of decision and, above all for the church leader, an aspect of godly conduct.

According to the criteria laid down in verses 8 and 9 (and also v. 12), the candidate's fitness to serve is to be *tested.* Both the term "blameless" (NIV *nothing against them*) and the notion of testing imply the public dimension of the candidate's life. The deacon's reputation among believers and unbelievers must be demonstrably acceptable.

Qualities enumerated in verses 11-12 clarify the meaning of "blamelessness" still further. However, at verse 11 a new sentence begins, and Paul issues instructions that refer to either the *wives* of deacons (so NIV) or women deacons ("deaconesses"; NIV margin). It is difficult to be certain which meaning Paul intended. Those who favor the meaning *wives* point out that requirements concerning the women are surrounded by those related to deacons. Furthermore, "women" is too common a term to designate an office. In defense of the meaning "deaconesses" others explain that (1) the introductory phrase *in the same way* (NIV; one word in the original; see *likewise,* 3:8), which is characteristic of exhortation to distinct groups, (2) the exact replication of verse 8's sentence structure in verse 11 and (3) the dependence of each verse on the initial *must* verb of the passage, verse 2, make a reference to women deacons equally possible. The question remains open; but it is well to keep in mind that in the absence of a technical term ("deaconess"), a reference to "women" in a code listing requirements for the office of deacon would have sufficed to direct attention to those candi-

---

1948:134, NIV and NEB. For the view that "women deacons" or "deaconesses" is meant, see Fee 1988:88, Kelly 1963:83-84, Barrett 1963:61-62 and Hurley 1981.

dates who were in fact women (compare Rom 16:1).

The actual qualities expected of these women parallel those expected of men (vv. 8-9). They are to lead lives that command *respect*, no doubt because they speak prudently with control (NIV *not malicious talkers)*, do not drink in excess and generally are *trustworthy* in all things (5:10). The patterns of behavior that characterize overseers and deacons are also to be obvious in the lives of these women. Furthermore, as in the case of the deacons, these women represent the antithesis of certain other women who had come under the influence of the false teachers (5:15; compare 2 Tim 3:6-7).

A final word reminds deacons of responsibilities toward wife and family (3:12). Like the overseer, the deacon must be a faithful husband. He must also have proved himself a capable manager of his household. As we saw, this was a quality greatly admired in (and also expected of) the householder by that society. If the householder clearly lacked this ability he was quickly criticized. Paul's point is again that one who would lead in the church must first know how to lead in the family in a way that promotes harmony among its members and loyalty to its leader. It is a safe assumption that one who manages his home haphazardly, whether he is a heavy-handed tyrant and slow to listen or simply irresponsible and unconcerned for his family, is likely to leave a similar stamp on the church. To be a leader requires having leadership skills that are tried and tested in the most practical of situations, the home.

Verse 13 concludes the list of requirements for office with an encouragement to those who serve well. It parallels the "faithful saying" that heads the list (see on 3:1) and is probably similar in purpose. The apostasy of some elders and deacons in Ephesus almost certainly lowered opinions about leaders and leadership in the church and in the minds of outsiders. So confidence in the office and in the people filling that office needed to be restored. Today this same confidence needs to

3:13 It is possible that the *excellent standing (bathmos kalos)* means "standing with God" (see the discussion in Guthrie 1957:85-86); but this would make the following reference to *assurance in their faith in Christ Jesus* rather superfluous. The latter has been taken as a reference to boldness in speaking or preaching (GNB; Hanson 1982:81); *assurance (parrēsia)* often carries this meaning (2 Cor 3:12; 7:4; Phil 1:20). But the final phrase, *in their faith in Christ Jesus* (rightly interpreted by the NIV), indicates personal faith in Christ rather than the message about Christ, and *assurance* describes an attitude of confidence

be maintained. Thus Paul reminds us that deacons who serve well will receive a twofold reward. Among people faithful deacons will *gain an excellent standing,* a good reputation. They will also grow closer to Christ in *faith* and *assurance.*

The Motivation and Mystery of Godly Behavior (3:14-16) These days my youngest daughter responds to most commands or corrections with the one-word question "Why?" Although this particular question tends to drive parents "around the bend," it is reasonable enough, given that children need to make sense of their life. Instructions concerning behavior, apart from some kind of rationale, do not automatically make sense.

Paul knew only too well that teaching about specific aspects of Christian behavior could fall on deaf ears if it came across as impersonal or irrelevant, if its relation to basic spiritual realities and importance for spiritual life and witness were not clear. Therefore, in this summary of the larger section (2:1—3:13) the apostle infuses his teaching with life and purpose. First, he returns to the personal tone with which he began the letter. Second, he relates godly behavior to the very nature of the church God formed. Finally, he inserts a piece of a hymn celebrating Christ's incarnation and redemptive ministry, a hymn that was well known by this church.

The Reason Paul Wrote (3:14-15) Paul wrote out of personal concern for Timothy and the church's well-being; hoping to return to Ephesus soon, he foresaw the possibility of delay and knew that the church in its predicament could not afford to wait for his teaching. *These instructions* refers to the whole letter, though 2:1—3:13 is uppermost in mind. And Paul's purpose for writing was to explain Christian conduct *(conduct . . . in God's household).*

The term "Christian conduct" may bring to mind different thoughts in

here (compare Eph 3:12; Heb 3:6; 4:16; 10:19, 35; see Fee 1988:89; Guthrie 1957:86). The view that *excellent standing* has promotion to the office of overseer in mind (Spicq 1969:461-63) is doubtful.

3:14-15 The NIV translation smoothes out Paul's rather awkward syntax in these two verses: the concessive *although* is implied by the participle *hope,* and the "purpose indicator" *so that* (v. 14), moved up from verse 15, accurately emphasizes that Paul's purpose in writing is to teach about *conduct.*

different people. Paul's term is holistic, describing a manner of life in all of its aspects from personal to interpersonal, and relationships are very much in view. We might look to the preceding section and the rest of the epistle to fill out Paul's meaning of "conduct."

The Church That Requires Godly Behavior (3:15) When the secular teachers of Paul's day made this kind of ethical exhortation, in similar terms they appealed to reason and the responsibility of each citizen to promote the stability of society. Paul's appeal is based on God and the higher claims that he and life in communion with him make upon the believer—that is, life *in God's household.* The specifics of Christian conduct are treated elsewhere, but the nature of the church that calls them forth is illustrated here. The very nature of the church legitimates and demands godly conduct. Three phrases describe this unique community of faith.

1. The church is God's household. The first and most dominant phrase depicts God's people as a *household* whose Master is God (compare 2 Tim 2:21; see on 2:1). The Greco-Roman household consisted of different groups, duties and responsibilities, and in the larger ones stewards were given authority to see that each did her or his share so that the master's purposes might be achieved. The concept of household with its associated notions of interdependence, acceptable conduct and responsibility was so strong that Paul could borrow it to illustrate the nature of the church. It too, both then and now, is made of different groups (men and women from every level of society, parents and children, employers and employees) who must depend upon and, in love, serve one another, and it is the task of the stewards (bishops/elders, deacons) to ensure that the household accomplishes the Master's goals.

Perhaps today our idea of household is not so central to our view of

---

3:15 Some regard *household of God (oikos theou)* as equivalent to the idea "temple of God" *(naos theou),* thus denoting a spiritual building rather than a household (Hendriksen 1965:136). However, in contrast to Paul's development of the New Temple theme (1 Cor 3:16; 6:19; 2 Cor 6:16; Eph 2:21-22), the thought of the Spirit's indwelling is lacking here. God's presence is implied in the subsequent phrase *church of the living God.* In Galatians 6:10 and Ephesians 2:19 Paul draws an analogy between believers and members of a household to stress the notion of membership and its accompanying responsibilities (notably, in the case of Eph 2:19 the idea of household is placed alongside the temple imagery of verse 20, showing how Paul can blend such concepts in the effort to describe as fully

life. Yet there remains another side to this concept that we can appreciate. Membership in God's household means refuge. We enjoy our Master's protection and find our identity in our relationship with him and with other believers, as we seek to carry out our responsibilities within his household. In fact, if by our commitment to one another we can even approximate the ideal of unity and cooperation traditionally connected with the household, we will present to the unbelieving world an attractive alternative lifestyle.

2. *The church consists of people called out from the pagan world.* With the second phrase, *church of the living God,* Paul reminds the readers how God has called them out from a pagan world. This "assembly" of Christian people is distinct from the other assemblies of the world because the *living God* dwells within it (2 Cor 6:16). The privilege of being called out to live in God's presence carries with it, however, the responsibility to live a life worthy of the One who has called. God's calling of the Hebrews out of Egypt into association with himself required them to be holy (Lev 11:45); and membership in the church of the living God makes the same demand (compare 1 Pet 1:15-16).

3. *The church exists to protect and promote the truth.* Paul employs building imagery in the last descriptive phrase to characterize the church in terms of one of its major functions: *the pillar and foundation of the truth.* As the "supporting foundation" (one idea is expressed rather than two) of the truth, the believing church is the guardian and communicator of the gospel in the world. This aspect of the church also demands from believers appropriate conduct: godly leadership, that the message might not be discredited, and corporate prayer for the missionary enterprise, that the message might be spread.

As Paul's description of the church reveals, the distinctive identity and

---

as possible the nature of the church). The suggestion that the meeting place of Christians is meant (Dibelius and Conzelmann 1972:60) is extremely unlikely in view of the analogy drawn between the church *(ekklēsia)* and the overseer's household *(oikos)* in 3:5.

A description similar to *the pillar and foundation of the truth* has been found in the Qumran literature. In 1QS 5:6 the Qumran community claimed to be "the foundation of the truth" and "the house of the truth." This parallel helps to confirm the idea of "unshakability" intended in the connection of *foundation (hedraiōma)* with *the truth;* see Stauffer 1964:362-64.

---

responsibility of God's people require an equally distinctive manner of conduct. The success of the church's evangelistic mission rests not solely upon the preservation of the gospel but also upon the lifestyle of mutual commitment that "adorns" this message (see Tit 2:10; compare 1 Tim 3:7).

The Mystery Behind Christianity (3:16) Often in our times of corporate worship the cue to respond to God's Word comes in the singing of a hymn. Through chanting or singing in unison, the congregation signals its acceptance of the message and commitment to perform God's will now revealed by the Spirit. In essence, Paul has placed a hymn (or a piece of one) at the end of this section of teaching to elicit the readers' response. Especially in churches associated with Paul, songs were one of the basic components of worship (see 1 Cor 14:26; Eph 5:18-20; Col 3:16-17). They were regarded as expressions of praise and adoration which the Holy Spirit produced in the heart of a human being. Colossians 3:16 draws a close connection between "the word of Christ" and these spiritual songs, which, with their point of origin in the Holy Spirit, may explain their deeply theological nature (Phil 2:6-11; Col 1:15-20). It was by the singing of such hymns that the believing community made the word of Christ live in its midst; in concrete expression, the sung word edified and admonished believers.

Now Paul's citing of part of what was surely a well-known hymn in the

3:16 Fee suggests (1988:95) that Paul had a dual purpose for including this hymn fragment—(1) to correct the heretics' Christology and (2) to state boldly what *the truth* entails in contrast to the false teachers' "demonic errors" alluded to in 4:1-3. The purpose of all the traditional formulations in the letters can be reasonably assumed to represent the apostolic doctrine that Timothy and Titus (and the church) are to guard. It is more difficult to use fragments such as this one as negatives to "develop" the false teachers' beliefs. An important aspect of the purpose in citing the hymn at this point is seen, as shown, in the connections it draws between faith and conduct and the historical incarnation and salvation, both significant "counter punches" to the opponents' tendencies.

For the use of hymns in the New Testament see Hengel 1983:78-96.

The KJV (and NKJV) rendering of line 1, "*God* was manifested in the flesh," is based on an inferior textual tradition. The original relative pronoun *hos,* translated "who" or "he who," was probably either mistaken in its capitalized form *OC* for *O-C* (an abbreviation for God) or deliberately replaced by *theos* to provide a subject for the fragment (see Metzger 1971:641).

Three explanations of the form of the hymn are generally offered. (1) Barrett (1963:64-66) takes a strict chronological approach, treating the six lines as declarations of successive events in the salvation drama. (2) Fee (1988:95-96) and Lock (1924:45) regard the hymn

course of writing instructions for behavior in the church is to bring his readers to the point of corporate response. The hymn itself, like many in the New Testament, celebrates Christ's appearance and ministry on earth. The introductory phrase is a call to consider the implications of this grand event, to evaluate our conduct on the basis of what we confess.

The introductory words, *Beyond all question, the mystery of godliness is great,* remind the readers of their common acceptance of the statement. And both the Greek term behind the NIV's *beyond all question* (*homologoumenōs;* literally, "confessedly") and the hymn piece that follows suggest that the idea of "confession"—that is, public, solemn agreement—may also be present.

But what is this great *mystery of godliness?* "Mystery," as often used by Paul, denotes the appearance of Christ in history as the hidden salvation plan of God which, conceived before time, has been revealed and fulfilled in the cross and resurrection (compare 3:9). The content of the Christ-hymn in 3:16 confirms the deep theological meaning of "the mystery."

The whole phrase *the mystery of godliness* needs some unpacking. It is commonly taken as the equivalent of the phrase in 3:9, "the mystery of the faith." This would make *godliness,* like "the faith," a reference to the objective content of Christianity—that is, "what" one believes. As such, the word here rendered *godliness* is often translated "religion." But

---

as consisting of two three-line stanzas. Approach 1 falters on line 6, which is taken as a reference to the return of Christ but seems a more obvious reference to the ascension. This being the case, either lines 4 and 5 must be interpreted in a less than obvious sense or the chronological approach must be abandoned. The question with 2 is whether it does justice to the apparent pairing of nouns in antithesis (see the thorough critique in Gundry 1970:203-6). (3) The approach followed here and in the work of most modern exegetes (among whom are Gundry [1970:203-6], Kelly [1963:92] and Martin [1977:236, 238]) is to understand the piece as having three two-line strophes, determined mainly by the antithetical pairs of nouns which all describe the *mystery* in some sense: lines 1-2 locate the *mystery* in the spheres of "flesh" and "spirit"; lines 3-4 view the *mystery's* communication to *angels* and *nations;* lines 5-6 perhaps focus on "conclusions" or "results," that is, belief in the *world* and Christ's *glory* (or glorification).

The flesh-spirit antithesis is well attested in the New Testament: Matthew 26:41; Mark 14:38; John 3:6; 6:63; Romans 1:4; 8:4, 5, 6, 9, 13; 1 Corinthians 5:5; 2 Corinthians 7:1; Galatians 3:3; 4:29; 5:16, 17 (twice), 19; 6:8; Colossians 2:5; 1 Timothy 3:16; Hebrews 12:9; 1 Peter 3:18. Against the background of the Old Testament, the pairing is probably a contrast of the natural (human) and supernatural spheres (France 1977:267; see also Ladd 1975:111-29).

---

although "the faith" does often bear this meaning in the Pastorals, "godliness" is a more expansive, less static idea. It includes "the faith" but goes a decisive step further to link a certain Christian manner of life to it (see notes on 2:2). The context, with its focus on conduct (v. 15), supports the broader meaning of "godliness."

Consequently, this phrase *the mystery of godliness* forms a connection between the appearance of Christ, which the hymn celebrates, and Christian living: *the mystery* is the essence of *godliness*. It was critical for Paul to remind the readers of this principle, for the false teachers were successfully driving a wedge between belief and behavior with damaging results. In our day of institutionalized atheism and the popular heresy of humanism, the church faces the same danger. Even if dangers of this sort seem remote, we easily forget the practical implications of what we believe and profess to be true.

The mystery is now explained in the six lines of the hymn, given in three couplets. We must remember that Paul included only part of a longer hymn and that its poetic nature prevented the making of a precise theological statement. Nevertheless, the thrust of this excerpt, to sketch a panoramic view of the outworking of God's salvation plan, is easily seen.

1. The conception of the mystery (lines 1-2). *He appeared in a body* (literally, "he was manifested in flesh") affirms the incarnation of Christ. The original term "flesh" and the passive form of the verb indicate the "mode" in which God revealed Christ to the world—in human form. Historically, the line of demarcation between the events recalled in lines 1 and 2 is the crucifixion/resurrection.

The meaning of *was vindicated by the Spirit* is more problematic, but the juxtaposing of "flesh" (line 1) and "spirit" (line 2), seen elsewhere

Gundry's interpretation (1970:213) of "in spirit" as a reference to Christ's human, presurrection spirit is extremely unlikely: it depends on the doubtful argument that "made alive" in 1 Peter 3:18 (the parallel text from which he takes his bearings) is not a reference to Christ's resurrection (in correction of which see France 1977:267-69).

Vindicated or "declared righteous" is the meaning consistently expressed in the Greek Old Testament by the passive form of the verb *(edikaiōthē)*.

The passive verb *was seen (ōphthē)* in line 3, meaning "self-exhibition," came to be used as a technical reference for the manifestation of God in the Greek Old Testament (Gen 12:7; 17:1-3). This, coupled with the strong New Testament tradition of Christ's triumphant "appearance" before angels (Eph 1:21; Phil 2:9-11; Col 2:15; Heb 1:3-4; 1 Pet 3:22; Rev 5:8-

in the New Testament, provides some help. The NIV correctly shows that Christ's "vindication" is in view. But *by the Spirit* is better left "in spirit" according to the original text *(en pneumati)*. In fact, the rather widespread use of the flesh-spirit antithesis in the New Testament suggests that "in spirit" is a reference to the supernatural realm which is characterized by the activity of the Holy Spirit. It is this realm that Christ entered by his resurrection from the dead. Furthermore, as numerous biblical references show, it was this event of resurrection/exaltation that demonstrated Christ's "vindication" before hostile powers, whether human or angelic (Acts 2:22-36; 3:11-15; Rom 1:4; 1 Cor 2:1-9; Eph 1:20-21). Contained in these two lines, then, is the acknowledgment of the truth of the gospel message, that God came among humankind and introduced a new kind of life (compare 2:3-6).

2. *The communication of the mystery* (lines 3-4). *Was seen by angels* depicts a revelation of Christ to angelic beings, rather than the passive observation of angels. In keeping with the panoramic scope of the hymn, line 3 recalls simply the fact that at some point Christ appeared victoriously before angels. The time of this occurrence may have been after or coincident with the resurrection or perhaps coincident with the ascension—chronology is apparently not a dominant feature of the hymn. In contrast to this "appearance" of the victorious Christ in the spirit realm, line 4 tells of the proclamation of this victory, won in behalf of humankind, in the world. Lines 3 and 4 concentrate on the communication of the good news about Christ. Here is acknowledgment of the church's responsibility to reach the world for Christ (2:1-2, 7; 3:15).

3. *The conclusion of the mystery* (lines 5-6). Line 5 *(was believed on in the world)* and line 6 *(was taken up in glory)* refer respectively to the result of the preaching of the gospel (line 4) and the ascension of Jesus.

14) and the dominant New Testament use of "angel" *(angelos)* for spirit beings, rules out a reference to human beings (who witnessed Christ's resurrection) in the term *angels*. For the same reasons, the intention of the line exceeds the references to angels present on the day of Jesus' resurrection (Mt 28:5-7; Mk 16:5-7; Lk 24:4-7; Jn 20:11-13; but see Hendriksen 1965:140-42).

For the use of the verb *was taken up (analambanō)* in line 6 in reference to Christ's ascension, see Mark 16:19; Luke 24:51; Acts 1:2; 11:22.

In glory denotes the glorified state of the resurrected Christ. On the significance of the ascension as indicating the conclusion of Christ's earthly ministry and the inauguration of the age of the Spirit, see Ladd 1975:128.

Of course, this sketch of the history of redemption would be incomplete without reference to the saving effects of the gospel—the church in Ephesus was to see itself as living proof of God's plan to save (compare 1:15-16). To acknowledge this was to accept at the same time the call to godly living (2:2, 8-10; 3:1-13, 15).

Though we might have expected mention of the return of Christ in the closing line of this salvation-hymn (as we find in many contemporary hymns), the purpose of this piece was to ground the reality and presence of salvation in the past, historical appearance of Christ. So the hymn concludes by alluding to the point that marked the close of Christ's earthly ministry (including resurrection appearances) and the beginning of the age of the Spirit.

Consequently, Paul's readers are reminded of their confession that the first advent of Christ introduced a new way of life in the present age. The hymn combines snapshots of important points of that past appearance (lines 1, 2, 3, 6) with references to the salvation introduced by that event (lines 4, 5). The appearance of the God-man is the essence of the new lifestyle *(godliness)* that, Paul urges, must characterize the church as it gathers for worship and when it relates with the world. Our confession of Christ is our acknowledgment of the call to service and godly living.

□ More Instructions to Timothy (4:1—5:2)

The Christian life is certainly not free of tension. If it were, the triumphant note just sounded in 3:16 might have concluded tidily with "and they lived happily ever after." However, though at times we might wish for it, this life is not a fairy tale, and that sort of ending must be left till the end (Rev 21:4). There it is fitting, but now it is a matter of hope. The biblical picture of the Christian life in this present age, confirmed by a long span of church history, is one of struggle and steady opposition. It is not that there is no joy and peace for the Christian, but that until Christ returns, joy and peace are found within the believer and within Christian

---

Notes: 4:1 The New Testament writers generally affirm that "the last days" had begun with the sending of God's Son (Heb 1:2) or with the outpouring of the Spirit (Acts 2:17; compare 1 Cor 10:11; 1 Pet 1:20; 1 Jn 2:18) and would be marked by apostasy (Mk 13:22 par; 2 Thess 2:3; Rev 13) and evil (Gal 1:4). For further discussion see Towner 1989:64-65. For the view that a literal future occurrence is meant, see Guthrie 1957:91.

fellowship, often in stark contrast to the actual circumstances of life.

The change that occurs at 4:1 following the hymn of victory, then, is not unexpected. Opposition to the faith and the struggle to meet it are in Paul's mind as he enlarges upon two themes introduced in chapter 1—the heresy and Christian ministry. In 4:1-5 the apostle reminds Timothy that apostasy from the faith is predictable and that ultimately Satan stands behind it when it occurs.

Concerning Heresy: It's Here to Stay (4:1-5) Through the centuries heresy and apostasy have come and gone, sometimes like a plague, sometimes like a flu virus, but always with damaging results for God's people. If this danger cannot be wiped out before the return of Christ, its patterns and nature can at least be understood, anticipated and thus controlled.

Prophetic Patterns of Apostasy (4:1) Despite the trappings of modern technology and the great gap of years between, our time and Paul's are inextricably bound together. This is evident in the time frame he indicates: *in later times.* Although some have taken this to mean that Timothy is to beware of a threat that is yet to manifest itself, the time in view actually includes the entire period that was initiated by the first appearance of Christ and that will close with his return (more commonly called "the last days"; 2 Tim 3:1). Paul's point is that periodically throughout the age of the church the faithful can expect the defection and active opposition of some who have professed to be Christians. The developments in Ephesus were to be recognized as "signs of the times," part and parcel of this evil, last age.

This unfortunate aspect of the present age was foretold by the Holy Spirit. The phrase Paul uses, *the Spirit clearly says,* may indicate a fresh prophetic message or (despite the present tense *says*) the restatement of a word given at an earlier time (compare Acts 20:28-31 and more generally Mk 13:22-23; 2 Thess 2:3; Rev 13). In either case, it lends

---

The Spirit clearly says, which is not a formula used elsewhere by Paul, is similar to the formula in Acts 21:11 and Revelation 2:1, 8, 12, 18; 3:1, 7, 14 (and frequently in the Greek Old Testament), introducing a prophetic word from the Spirit or the risen Christ ("Thus says . . ."), and to the formula that closes the prophetic messages to the seven churches in Revelation 2:7, 11, 17, 29; 3:6, 13, 22 (see also Aune 1983:289-90, 292).

authority to the explanation of heresy and implies that the conditions in Ephesus were not to be considered as a surprising development or as evidence that the church would ultimately fail in its task (compare 2 Tim 2:19-21). Since the *some* that are mentioned had evidently professed the faith, and in the Ephesian situation may have been leaders, one of Paul's concerns here is almost certainly to arrest any doubts about the permanence of God's church.

The driving force behind opposition to the church is Satan. Paul describes the heretics in Ephesus as those who *follow deceiving spirits and things taught by demons.* The apostle's ministry was marked by encounters with such movements, and he knew well their point of origin (2 Cor 11:15: "his [Satan's] servants"; see also 2 Cor 4:4; 11:3).

In our era the believing church cannot afford to be ignorant of the evil nature of this last age. Terms such as "heresy" and "apostasy" have fallen on hard times, due largely to the "witch-hunt" connotations associated with them. And indeed through the years (and in the present day) a great deal of injustice has been done to believers in the name of orthodoxy. Nevertheless, the presence of the cults alone recommends that we heed Paul's instruction here. A clear understanding of these "last days" and of the aims of the Enemy will prevent our being taken by surprise and may aid in maintaining a healthy church.

Behavior Patterns of Apostasy (4:2-3) Although the apostle clearly underlines the demonic element in apostasy, he does not minimize the accountability of the apostates themselves. Their own part in denying the faith *(some will abandon the faith)* and thus providing the outlet for the demonic deception *(such teachings come through hypocritical liars;* v. 2) left them "seared in conscience." The latter phrase, by no means mere rhetoric, is vital to Paul's understanding of the nature of heresy.

First, as noted previously (1:5), Paul makes a connection between adherence to the faith and the "good conscience." Here, the reverse operation is seen: rejection of the faith leaves the conscience *seared as with a hot iron.* Behind this image is the practice of branding slaves with a hot iron. Rejection of the faith enslaves one to sin and falsehood, by hobbling the faculty of discernment and making it an ineffective guide to right and wrong.

Second, just as the "good conscience" is related to Christian conduct, here the "seared" conscience issues in perverted conduct (v. 3). For Paul the conscience is the faculty of decision. It enables the believer to proceed from the faith, the vertical dimension of belief and knowledge, to the corresponding horizontal activity of godly behavior (see on 1:5). The false teachers had lost the ability to make such decisions effectively—since their concept of the faith was distorted, their ideas about godly living were equally distorted.

The signal Paul sends is clear. If genuine Christian conduct flows from a vital relationship with Christ, then an imitation that is fanatically forced on others is at best human in origin, at worst demonic. Observable conduct may not be the litmus test of orthodoxy or salvation, but negative results here ought to raise questions, whether one is examining one's own faith (2 Cor 13:5) or the claims of a "Christian" movement (Gal 5:6).

In verse 3 Paul identifies two aspects of the false teachers' misguided behavior: forbidding marriage and commanding abstinence from certain foods. These aberrations probably stemmed from the false teachers' mistaken notion that the resurrection (of believers) had already occurred (2 Tim 2:18). Their view of the resurrection involved a misunderstanding of the times and led to a too-realized concept of the spiritual life.

As parallel situations in Corinth and in later Gnostic circles confirm, this kind of "overrealized" outlook was (paradoxically) accompanied by a negative view of the temporal world. They insisted that the End had come and that salvation was fully obtainable "now," but the world around them remained stubbornly unchanged. Bizarre (to the uninitiated) patterns of behavior (asceticism or libertinism) represented either an attempt to cope with the paradox or an attempt to implement belief. The false teachers in Ephesus evidently favored asceticism. It is possible that both marriage and the eating of certain foods were considered part of the old order (the order of things that they believed had passed away with the resurrection of Christ and the outpouring of the Holy Spirit) and therefore to be avoided. The asceticism alluded to in Colossians 2:16-23 bears a striking resemblance, especially where foods are concerned. But it is also possible that this behavior reflected the attempt to enact the life of resurrection paradise by following the model given in Genesis

1 and 2, before the fall into sin—after all, Jesus taught that there would be no marriage in the resurrection (Mt 22:30), and vegetarianism seems to have been the rule in Eden/paradise (see discussion at 2:11-15). The negative view of marriage seems quite similar to sentiments held by some in Corinth (1 Cor 7:1-7). In any case, whether to cope with the evil material world or to implement the new theology, the heretics enforced a regimen of denial.

The Divine Pattern: Thanksgiving (4:3-5) Paul refutes only the food asceticism (his endorsement of marriage is implied elsewhere in the letter—2:15; 3:2, 12; 5:11). To do this he draws on what had become traditional logic in the church—all food is clean because of its Creator (Lk 11:40-41; Mk 7:15; Acts 10:15; 11:9; 1 Cor 10:25-31). The foods they reject *God created to be received. . . . For everything God created is good* (vv. 3-4). The only stipulation is that these foods be *received with thanksgiving* (v. 4)—that is, with a response of genuine gratitude as (probably) expressed in prayer. This was the custom of Jesus (Mk 6:41; 8:6; 14:22-23; Lk 24:30) and in Judaism in general. In the expression of gratitude to God came also the believer's acknowledgment of the *created* status of the food. Verse 5's additional rationale for the use of all foods *(because it is consecrated by the word of God and prayer)* suggests that all a believer need do to sanctify any food is to make a prayer of thanksgiving to recognize the One who has provided the gift. In this context *the word of God* probably implies the use of biblical expressions in the saying of grace, as was common in Judaism.

It does not take much imagination to see that the Creator's act of giving and the believer's act of receiving (and enjoying) the gifts of creation are both part of a conscious communication process meant to strengthen the bond between Father and child. Furthermore, the communication is intimate, for only believers (v. 3) can enter fully into it. There are undoubtedly implications here that go beyond the dinner table to include the Christian's appreciation of the environment in gener-

---

4:3-4 Some have understood Paul's emphasis on the Creator as an indication that the heretics were Gnostics who held that the world and all matter were created by the evil demiurge (Guthrie 1957:92-93; compare Hendriksen 1965:147). But the closer resemblance to the Corinthian situation and lack of clear Gnostic elements in the Pastorals support the explanation presented here (see Towner 1989:33-42).

al, but the starting point for developing this kind of understanding is the recognition through prayers of thanksgiving of God's gracious provisions. Neither the true gospel nor the life of salvation in this present age calls for ascetic denial. Rather, they encourage responsible use and enjoyment of God's creation.

The Good Minister of Christ Jesus (4:6-16) Just as a skillful coach will often return to the basics of the sport to pull the team or a player out of a slump, Paul returns to the basics to keep this church on track. As he seeks to counteract the influences of the false teaching here, he emphasizes one of the most important practical lessons of the Pastoral Epistles: the soundness of a church depends on ministers and leaders who are sound in their faith and practice.

But wait! This teaching applies to all Christians. Yes, in this section Paul focuses on Timothy, the paradigm of the good minister or Christian leader, who must pursue spiritual priorities and pay attention to his lifestyle and calling. But we shouldn't be fooled by the term *minister*—the principles apply to all believers, just as all believers are to be vitally involved in ministry. The leader or minister is to be a model. In the leader's ministry and life God's Word and its application must be central. Attention to these basics will make a critical difference. As we saw in chapter 1 of this letter, the minister and ministry that accord with God's will are exact opposites of the "enthusiasts" and their version of the faith.

Spiritual Priorities (4:6-10) Of course, there are many things that could rightly be identified as "spiritual priorities." Here Paul selects three that are most essential for the development and maintenance of a sound spiritual life.

1. Nourishment from God's Word (4:6). Perhaps the most basic of all is the first, spiritual nourishment. The good minister, the one who will faithfully and ably confront false teachers, will have been *brought up in* the Christian faith. This might be mistaken as limiting the ministry to

---

4:5 Other interpretations of *the word of God* are possible. Fee (1988:101) suggests the meaning of the gospel message or God's declaration in Genesis 1 that the creation is good. Hanson (1982:88-89) sees a reference to the consecrated elements in the Eucharist. For the view adopted here, see Dibelius and Conzelmann 1972:64.

---

those reared in a Christian family, but that is not the meaning. The image is of taking nourishment, and the present tense emphasizes continual action or lifestyle. However, this lifestyle is rooted in firm decisions made in the past, for the good minister has *followed* the teaching of the faith into the present. Both *the faith* and *the good teaching* identify the true gospel or faith in contrast to the perverted doctrines current in that church. This includes not just doctrine but also the practical principles for godly living.

The implication is clear: the Christian leader must be one who has habitually taken nourishment from God's Word and continues to do so. Yet reports from an alarming percentage of pastors and missionaries, among other Christian workers, show that under the weight of ministry responsibilities time spent in the Word of God (and in prayer) becomes irregular and haphazard. This passage makes the dangers of this neglect clear; God's servants must reverse this trend to maintain spiritual health. At the same time, the mature leader must choose carefully the spiritual food to be taken. *Godless myths and old wives' tales* (v. 7), a certain reference to the false teaching identified in 4:1-3, must be avoided. This does not mean that the minister should be unaware of the competing claims of other popular movements and religions. In fact, Christians ought to understand clearly the trends of thought that are influencing society and its values. But it must be an understanding arrived at and

Notes: 4:6 *These things* refers to 4:1-5 and 7-10.

The word *minister* translates the Greek *diakonos,* which in 1 Timothy 3:8 and 12 refers to an office but in 1 Corinthians 3:5 and 2 Corinthians 11:23 refers to a servant of Christ. The latter nontechnical sense is meant here.

The good teaching (didaskalia), more often described as "sound" (1 Tim 1:10; 2 Tim 4:3; Tit 1:9; 2:1), envisages proclamation directed to the believing community (1 Tim 4:13, 16; 5:17; Tit 2:1, 7, 10). Distinctions between *preaching* and *teaching* (see 1 Tim 5:17) have more to do with audience and emphasis than with content.

Brought up in [entrephomenos] the truths of the faith employs a metaphor connected with the raising and nurturing or nourishing of children. With it Paul characterizes *the faith* and *the good teaching* as spiritual nourishment (compare 1 Cor 3:2).

4:7 The phrase *godless myths and old wives' tales* actually describes the false teaching alluded to in 4:1-3 from two perspectives (literally "godless and old wives' myths," or "myths that are godless and characteristic of old women"). *Godless (bebēlos)* can mean "secular" but here stresses the false doctrine's unholiness or distance from God (1 Tim 6:20; 2 Tim 2:16). *Old wives' (graōdeis)* is a pejorative term drawn from philosophical polemic, which, like the modern epithet, described a story or teaching as beyond belief because its source (the proverbial gullible and superstitious "old wife") would believe anything. Whatever the

constantly examined through a careful weighing of these trends against God's values. In order to carry out this evaluation, the minister and all believers must be absorbed daily in the good teaching of the faith.

2. Training in godliness (4:7-9). The second priority is that of spiritual training—that is, training in godliness (4:7). The heretics' false teaching (the myths and wives' tales) supported a system of asceticism (the abstinence from certain foods and disparagement of marriage, 4:3). *Godliness* for them apparently had mainly to do with knowledge of "spiritual" things. The body, they held, could be controlled by rigorous self-denial *(physical training,* 4:8). But genuine *godliness* is the life of faith strengthened by training in the Word of God (4:7)—that is, a lifestyle lived in obedience to *the good teaching.* Paul admits that physical training does have a certain limited value; by means of it one can learn to control physical urges. *Godliness,* on the other hand, has unlimited value, for it is that life in the power of the Spirit (compare Gal 5:16-24) in which the "whole" believer, in body and spirit, comes to experience the resurrection life of Christ (compare Phil 3:10). Through it the physical passions and propensity to sin can be brought under control, and the reality of the Holy Spirit's operation in the life of the believer becomes evident.

This genuine *godliness* holds *promise for both the present life and the life to come* (4:8). So strong was the emphasis on the pursuit of this life in the Spirit in the early church that verse 8 had become a widely ac-

---

term's origins, it had ossified into a common saying that conveyed no intentional chauvinism.

4:7-8 The training imagery is drawn from athletics. *Physical training (sōmatikē gymnasia;* 4:8) refers to the asceticism of the heretics, which, lacking any spiritual benefit, is of minimal value (see Kelly 1963:100; Pfitzner 1967:171-77). The saying of verse 8, which contrasts physical training with godliness, was probably quoted to underscore the advice to *train . . . to be godly (gymnaze . . . pros eusebeian)* in verse 7. For an example of this sentiment in the secular (Cynic) context, see *The Epistles of Crates* 3: "Take care of your soul, but take care of the body only to the degree that necessity requires."

4:9 Some interpreters understand the *trustworthy saying* to be verse 10 (in whole or part), because of its theological content (Guthrie 1957:95-96; NIV; NEB). Others consider the saying to be verse 8 in its entirety (Knight 1992:198; Barrett 1963:69-70) or the second half of verse 8, because it is more clearly aphoristic in tone (Fee 1988:104-5; Kelly 1963:101). The contrast between *physical training* and *godliness* and the double reference to "profit" suggest that the original saying consists at least of the first two clauses of verse 8; the explanation *holding promise for both the present life and the life to come* may be Paul's own addition, for the language is characteristic of the Pastorals (1 Tim 6:17; 2 Tim 4:10; Tit 2:12).

cepted saying: the *trustworthy saying* referred to in verse 9 is verse 8.

3. Mission (4:10). It is the reality of this life-changing salvation that forms the third priority of the good minister and every faithful Christian—the spiritual goal of mission. Spiritual nourishment and spiritual training draw meaning from the hope of salvation. All of the minister's efforts *(for this we labor and strive,* v. 10) are to be tied to the certain hope in the God who saves. *Labor and strive* ought not to be placed in parentheses in verse 10 (as in the NIV); these Greek terms together express the idea of "making every possible effort," which suggests a very urgent goal. And, just as in 2:3-4, it is the universal scope of God's plan of salvation *(Savior of all men)* that compels participation in the mission. Again, as in the earlier passage, the salvation of *all* is not automatic or unconditional. The qualification that follows *(and especially of those who believe)* links the execution and success of the mission to the preaching *and* specifically belief in the gospel (see notes as well as 2:4 commentary). An undertaking of this magnitude urgently requires the participation of every Christian. Why "urgently"? Because *all* people must be given the opportunity to respond to God. As Paul wrote elsewhere, "How, then, can they call on the one they have not believed in? And how can they believe in the one of whom they have not heard? And how can they hear without someone preaching to them? And how can they preach unless they are sent?" (Rom 10:14-15).

The protection of the church from dangers such as heresy, as well as its return to order, has much to do with the soundness of its leaders. Paul advises his readers to concentrate on the basics: steady nourishment from the Word of God, pursuit of the godly life in the Spirit and the priority of mission. The false teachers in Ephesus had established different priorities as they pushed the church to the brink of destruction.

Effective Ministry (4:11-15) Timothy remains in view as the instructions address other aspects of the leader's life and the essentials of worship in relation to the effectiveness of ministry.

4:10 *The living God* is a designation that sets God off from dead idols (Acts 14:15; Rom 9:26; 1 Thess 1:9).

On *Savior* see notes on 1:1.

The qualifying term *especially (malista),* which occurs here and in 5:17 and 2 Timothy 4:13, is absolute, providing specific definition for a more general statement. It is better

1. Exemplary Christian lifestyle (4:11-12). After the principles above are considered, the first requirement for an effective ministry is an exemplary Christian lifestyle. On one level this holds true particularly for those who, like Timothy, find themselves in leadership positions in ministry among those who are older and (perhaps) wiser. Nothing bridges the generation gap in the church like the spiritual maturity of the younger. At a more important level, nothing proves the veracity of the gospel as well as evidence of its life-changing power. The example Paul calls for here is that very proof: *an example for the believers in speech, in life, in love, in faith and in purity* (v. 12).

Speech and *life* (better, "conduct") encompass most of the observable life—the visible dimension of godliness. In fact, James places first importance on control of the tongue, which will then provide for control of the rest of one's behavior (Jas 3:2). Through what a Christian says and does the truth of the Christian faith will be either demonstrated or denied, for true spirituality *(godliness)* is the composite of faith or knowledge of God and its outworking in the believer's life.

Love and *faith* summarize the Christian life. Paul frequently aligns these two qualities, *faith* referring to the relationship with Christ and *love* to activity generated by the indwelling Holy Spirit. Galatians 5:6 explains that genuine Christianity is "faith working through love": a proper knowledge of and commitment to Christ which controls the life of the believer (see 2:15 notes).

Purity alludes to sexual conduct (compare 5:2). Paul singles out this concern undoubtedly because questionable conduct here will ruin the Christian leader's reputation and ministry.

As the list suggests, effective ministry and godliness are inseparable. Remember, as Paul gives these instructions he warns the readers away from the heretics' one-sided, totally subjective concept of spirituality and encourages leaders to be models of the true life in the Spirit that involves the whole person.

---

translated "in other words," "I mean" or "to be precise"; see Skeat 1979:173-77. The qualification limits the scope of the preceding statement in a way similar to the limits implied by the phrase *and to come to a knowledge of the truth,* which follows the affirmation of God's desire to save all people in 2:4. See 2:4 commentary.

2. God-centered worship (4:13). The second requirement for effective ministry is God-centered worship. Under the false teachers' influence, gatherings for worship were degenerating into speculation about "myths" and strange doctrines (1:3-4) and debate about their meaning (1:4; 6:4-5). Paul responds by refocusing attention on God's Word as the source of knowledge about him and the life of faith.

First, he urges consistent practice of *the public reading of Scripture* (v. 13). This is by no means an innovation; it was already part of Christian worship, having been adopted naturally from Jewish synagogue worship (Lk 4:16; Acts 15:21; 2 Cor 3:14). Its import lies in the way it centers attention on God, who, communicating with his people, initiates and sustains a covenant relationship. Practically, the reading of the lesson also prepares the people for the exposition and application of Scripture.

Second, proper Christian worship will include *preaching.* The term used here could mean exhortation, encouragement, comfort or an appeal, and it is linked to the Scriptures in Romans 15:4 and Hebrews 12:5. Romans 12:8 reveals that preaching is a Spirit-directed activity (that is, a *charisma*) of communicating God's message to the people (compare 1 Cor 12:8). The starting point is the conviction that Scripture is always relevant to God's people (2 Tim 3:16-17).

Teaching is the third activity to be consistently practiced in the worship assembly. As with preaching, a special gift is associated with this activity (Rom 12:7).

But how do these two activities differ? Passages such as this one and 1 Timothy 5:17 and Romans 12:7-8 (see also 1 Tim 2:7; 2 Tim 1:11) seem to make a distinction between *preaching* and *teaching,* though the Greek terms may vary. But the precise distinction is difficult to pin down. The term used here for *preaching (paraklēsis)* refers to appeals made to believers (Rom 15:4; Heb 13:22) and unbelievers (see 2 Cor 5:20). *Teaching,* however, is usually linked to the church. Knight may be correct to see the distinction in terms of purpose, *preaching* being the call

---

4:13 For more on the distinction between *preaching* and *teaching* see McDonald 1980:1-2.

4:14 *Through a prophetic message when the body of elders laid their hands on you* is probably a reference back to the same event recalled in 1:18. Rather than understanding the prophetic pronouncement and laying on of hands as the instrument of mediating the

to respond to God's Word (which would fit an audience of believers or unbelievers), *teaching* being the more intellectually oriented communication of Scripture's principles (1992:208). It may be also that the two activities differed in style and tone of delivery. But distinctions based on content (for example, limiting *teaching* to Christian ethics and *preaching* to theology) do not seem to be in mind (see Tit 2:10-14). Yet often the two activities must have overlapped considerably: it is hard to imagine teaching without leading the people to response, or preaching without providing a reasoned exposition of a text's principles. Nevertheless, as long as we make room for overlap and avoid distinctions that are too rigid, it seems safe to think of *preaching* and *teaching* as two applications of God's Word in the church: (1) the call to response, whether that entails confession, receiving God's encouragement or appropriating his promise, and (2) the building of a solid foundation for living through the systematic teaching of biblical principles that coherently and practically express God's will.

Certainly a worship service includes a good deal more than these three activities, especially elements that are response-oriented: prayer, the singing of hymns, testimony and practical ministering of one to another, observance of the Lord's Supper. Paul was here correcting tendencies introduced by the enthusiasts, and he focuses on the primary tasks of the minister. God's Word, through its reading, preaching and teaching, initiates and sustains spiritual life, and its place in Christian worship is central. Without it there can be no effective ministry.

3. Exercise of spiritual gifts and calling (4:14). A third requirement for effective ministry is the faithful exercise of spiritual gifts. Paul's instruction to Timothy in verse 14 is logically connected with the reference to preaching and teaching.

First, the fact: Timothy has a gift *(charisma)* for ministry. We know that God has chosen to build and maintain his church by empowering believers to carry out this ministry. The source of power is the Holy Spirit,

---

"gift" (the conferring of special gifts, or office, through the sacrament of ordination; see Dibelius and Conzelmann 1972:70-71), we should probably interpret them as a prophetic confirmation of Timothy's "gift" accompanied by the public recognition of his calling by laying on of hands (see above on 1:18 and notes; Fee forthcoming: chap. 11; Knight 1992:208-9).

who manifests himself and releases his power through the spiritual gifts and abilities he distributes to believers (thus the passive *was given* probably refers to the Spirit's act of giving; see 1 Cor 12:7, 11). It is probably not possible to specify a particular gift here (such as teaching, preaching or leadership—Rom 12:7-8), though we are at least to understand a reference to Timothy's Spirit-given abilities for ministry.

But with the gift comes the responsibility to exercise it for the church (1 Cor 12:14-20). Paul's admonition to Timothy in 2 Timothy 1:6-7 (whether or not the "gifts" and situations are identical—see 2 Tim 1:6-7) underlines the personal responsibility that rests with the "gifted" individual. The gift does not operate independently but finds its release into the church and into the lives of other people through the obedient Christian's decision to serve. And failure to use one's gifts does not affect just the individual, for the ministry of the church as a whole depends on the responsible use of each believer's gift.

Furthermore, the one called to leadership in the church has received God's special appointment. God's choice of Timothy was announced or verified through prophecy and then publicly recognized as the elders laid hands on him (compare 1:18; Acts 13:2-3). Thus both the servant and the congregation were bound to one another in the acknowledgment of God's selection. Ordination in most Christian churches today functions similarly, to recognize God's binding choice and publicly bless the minister for service. The gift makes ministry possible. The calling makes ministry obligatory.

4. Diligence and growth (4:15). Finally, effective ministry requires diligence and progress. Paul describes diligence in two ways: *be diligent in these matters; give yourself wholly to them.* He is referring to the pattern of lifestyle and ministry just outlined. The first verb means to practice with diligence and carries similar connotations to the "training" metaphor in 4:7. The second phrase means, literally, to *"be* in these things"—that is, to be absorbed in them. In modern idiom, the minister must "live and breathe" these things.

One reward for dedication like this is *progress. Progress* in the faith

---

Notes: 5:1-2 The sentiment here duplicates that of traditional Hellenistic society: "He will

(compare Phil 1:25) would close the mouths of Timothy's older critics. But more important, progress of this kind is evidence of a vital and deepening relationship with the Lord. If the leadership of a church pays diligent attention to personal spiritual priorities and sound worship principles, its ministry is bound to bear fruit.

The Fruit of Effective Ministry (4:16) Following a summary reminder that takes in all of 4:6-15 (*Watch your life and your doctrine closely. Persevere in them*), Paul describes the end result of the good minister's efforts in Christ as salvation: *you will save both yourself and your hearers.*

But isn't this rather shortsighted? Not at all. Salvation is indeed the goal, but it must be properly understood. In biblical parlance it signifies a process of development that begins with belief in Christ (conversion) and the gift of new life in the Spirit (regeneration) and will end (our glorification) with the return of Christ. In this life we experience the process of salvation as stages of growth in "Christlikeness," "putting on the new self" (Col 3:11), working out our salvation (Phil 2:12); and many things can impede growth. Essential to growth, however, is the ministry of God's Word in preaching and teaching in the church, from which we draw spiritual nourishment, as well as the modeling of godliness by the more mature for those younger in the faith. Important, too, for the salvation process (especially for the Christian leader) is faithfulness in carrying out the calling of God. Effective ministry is ministry in which the Word of God is applied to individual lives and to all situations in life.

The Christian Leader and Relationships (5:1-2) As with an article of clothing, the church has its seams, created naturally by age differences, gender differences, economic differences and so on. These seams, where these various groups come together, often show visible signs of stress. It falls to the Christian leader to cross all these lines from time to time in order to minister effectively. But crossing these lines requires sensitivity and care.

---

regard everyone he meets as either brother or sister, father or mother, son or daughter, grandchild or grandparent" (Plato *Republic* 5. 463).

This section is loosely connected with the preceding passage. Timothy, the minister, is still in view, but the topic changes here to ministry in a more general sense. On the one hand, the minister must carry out the task of ministry at every level of the church. The harsh rebuke that Timothy is to avoid using is the depersonalizing "tongue-lashing." This method of correction relies on fear and authority and is often applied when feelings of anger and insecurity are running high. Exhortation is a far more effective method of ministry. It includes correcting, admonishing, encouraging and comforting. This kind of ministry values the relationship between believers far above any need to assert or prove lines of authority. It seeks to promote unity at (almost) all costs.

But more than a caring style of ministry is required to cross with sensitivity the social lines indicated in these verses. In Timothy's day, role relationships within and across social boundaries were well defined. Respectability was determined by one's adherence to such rules of behavior. Becoming a Christian by no means meant that these social rules ceased to apply. On the contrary, all believers were to obey them (compare Tit 2:1-10). As models, Christian leaders, far from being above the rules, were all the more bound by them.

These rules come clearly into play in these instructions. First, in the course of ministry to older men, even if it be correction (such as the Ephesian situation might have required), the minister must treat them with the respect due a father (v. 1). Exhortation will therefore be gentle and respectful.

Ministry to younger men (the same verb, "to exhort," rather than the NIV *treat,* controls the passage)—or, in Timothy's case, to peers—must similarly not lean on authority, but stress the common bond in Christ.

Paul stresses equally that the rules governing communication and interaction across gender lines must be observed. Ministry here calls for sensitivity and caution. Older women are to be treated with the respect due a mother (v. 2). In ministering to younger women, the male leader

---

5:1 The verb *rebuke harshly (epiplēssō)* carries overtones of violent treatment (the related noun, *a violent man [plēktēs],* is used to denote a person unfit for the office of bishop/elder in 3:3; Tit 1:7).

Exhort (parakaleō), the approved style of ministry, is listed among ministry gifts in Romans 12:8 and appears elsewhere in reference to spiritual encouragement and admoni-

has added need to make every effort to avoid giving the impression of unseemly behavior: [exhort] *younger women as sisters, with absolute purity* (compare 4:12). Incidents of actual moral lapse under such circumstances warn that the utmost care must be exercised here.

Paul urges an approach to ministry that values relationships and personal involvement and applies to all cultures. Yet the rules of respect in social relationships may vary somewhat from culture to culture, and the church and its leaders must be sensitive to obey them. Sensitive ministry will promote the church's unity and guard its witness to those outside.

☐ Instructions Concerning Widows (5:3-16)

Here is a scene that is played out far too often in our churches today. A woman (or man) loses a mate to death. After a few weeks' flurry of attention, she finds it more and more awkward to fit into relationships that had once been natural. Friends, feeling uncomfortable or embarrassed around her, do not know how to relate, and she finds it difficult to relate to them. Her grown children have their own lives to get on with. Gradually, she eases toward the periphery of the church.

Yes, I am aware that this is not always the case, and it is certainly not a problem limited to the church. But when it happens in the church, the heads of even unbelievers shake in amazement and scorn. And they will ask, whether hypocritically or not, the questions that our behavior was supposed to have answered, and answered well. Where is Christian compassion? Where is Christian love for one another?

From the time of Israel's inception, God has been known as the defender of widows (Deut 10:18; 24:17). "Justice" among God's people was measured in part by the treatment of widows (Is 1:17). God's compassion for the widow became the covenant community's responsibility, which the early church naturally took up (Acts 6:1; Jas 1:27).

The present passage is the Bible's most extensive treatment of the subject. Through instructions to Timothy, Paul addresses the issue of

---

tion (see 1 Cor 14:3; 2 Cor 10:1; Phil 2:1; Heb 3:13). It seems to imply genuine concern and personal involvement; the related noun *comforter (paraklētos)* is applied to the Holy Spirit.

An older man (presbyteros) is not here a technical reference to the office of elders (as in 5:17; compare Tit 2:2).

community support for widows. At the same time, the widow is encouraged to make positive contributions to the church's ministry.

The passage reflects a fairly advanced system of care—a "roll" or "list" of widows eligible for support (v. 9). But the system was being abused; families of widows were not shouldering their responsibility, thus placing financial strain on the church. Then certain younger widows, who may have managed to get on the list, were threatening the church's reputation by involvement with the false teaching and scandalous behavior. The instructions address three related topics: the identification of the honorable widow, family responsibility for widows, young widows.

Proper Recognition of Widows in Need (5:3-10) The opening instruction (v. 3) controls the thought of the whole passage. The church must properly recognize its needy widows (literally, "real widows"). Proper recognition ("honor") was to be expressed in practical support. But good stewardship of the church's limited resources and protection of its reputation required the leadership to decide who the "real" widows in the church were, and whether other means of support were available.

The Honorable Widow (5:5, 9-10) If a widow was to qualify for care from the church, her practical circumstances and Christian witness were to be examined. On practical grounds she must be all alone (v. 5), having no family and consequently no one to take up the support formerly provided by a husband. Furthermore, she must be at least sixty years of age (v. 9). This age was the culturally recognized age of retirement, as well as, practically, an age at which remarriage was unlikely. Presumably, at this age the temptations that faced the younger widow (vv. 11-15) would have ceased to be a serious concern.

But practical need alone was insufficient grounds for receiving financial help from the church. In order to guard its testimony in society (vv. 7, 14), the church could, as a church, subsidize only the activities of widows with exemplary lives of faith. Therefore, to qualify for support

Notes: 5:3 Some understand the Greek word behind the command *(timaō)* to indicate that payment for an office or some other kind of "official" recognition is in mind (Kelly 1963:112-13). But apart from 1 Timothy 5:17, where "double honor" gives this sense, support must be drawn from documents dating to the third and fourth centuries. The

the widow had to lead a life that testified to a genuine relationship with God.

Paul emphasizes first the personal dimension of this relationship. In verse 5 it is characterized by her posture of *hope in God*. While hope, that determined expectancy and trust in God's sufficiency, is to mark all believers, the believing widow with no one else to turn to learns to excel in this discipline. The discipline of hope finds expression in personal communication in prayer to God for help. Together hope and prayer characterize the godly widow's personal relationship with God, the vertical dimension of her true faith.

The mention of the *widow who lives for pleasure* in verse 6, an allusion to the younger widows of verses 11-15, provides a graphic contrast. This description calls to mind the fantasy of "living life to its fullest" that the media constantly parade before us. "Life" is defined as a wild (and always fashionable) ride from one new experience to the next. But Paul calls this "living death," for the ride takes one away from the true source of meaningful and eternal life; this "life" is only a crude imitation, a mask on the face of death. The one who pursues God in prayer and hope discovers life out of death.

But Paul also stresses that this relationship with God must have visible and practical results in the form of *good deeds* (v. 10). Many modern Christians tend to view this concept with skepticism, primarily because it brings to mind thoughts of earning merit with God or behaving in a way that brings attention to oneself. However, what Paul means is "doing" that proceeds from genuine faith, fruit produced by the Spirit. The "real" widow will have a reputation for *good deeds.* Yet she may not rest on a past record, but must be generally devoted to this kind of life. The guidelines given here (to determine qualification for inclusion on a list) are very similar in tone, content and purpose to those that appear in 3:2-7 in reference to the overseer; they begin within the home and move outward (vv. 9-10).

For the one who is or has been married, the results of faith must first

meaning is that of 6:1: financial support for the needy widow is an expression of honor or recognition.

5:6 *Lives for pleasure (spatalaō)* describes someone who lives only to satisfy fleshly lusts; compare James 5:5.

be evident in the marriage relationship. The Greek phrase in verse 9, literally, "one-man woman," is the counterpart to the "one-woman man" which describes the overseer and deacon (3:2, 12; Tit 1:6). The NIV translates it accurately as referring to faithfulness in marriage. For it is this, and not a commitment to remain single after one's spouse has died, that is probably in view.

Next (v. 10), since typically the widow's sphere of activity would have been the home, Paul inquires about her skills as a parent (this begins the enumeration of the *good deeds*). Raising children successfully was one of the marks of the ideal woman in the Greco-Roman and Jewish world (compare 2:15; Tit 2:4). Yet in that day, as, sadly, in ours, child abandonment and abuse were common. The proof of the life-changing power of the gospel in the home was to be seen in exemplary marriages and responsible child care. Beyond meeting basic physical and emotional needs, Christian parenting means also training children in the faith (Deut 6:7; Eph 6:4).

A third item related to the home is the practice of hospitality, a highly regarded practice in the ancient world. Hospitality's warmth and sharing made it essential to the Christian mission and to church unity (Rom 12:13; 1 Pet 4:9). It also met urgent needs and required sacrificial sharing (see on Tit 1:8). Help of this sort among Christians is uppermost in Paul's mind, but given the notorious condition of inns in that day, it is easy to see how strategic an open home might have been for the spread of the gospel as well. Such sharing has proved effective over and over again in modern times.

The list mentions two final specific activities that the widow is to be known for. "Foot washing" among the saints and providing "help" to those in trouble were to be characteristic of believers in general (Jn 13:14; Rom 12:10-16; Gal 5:13; 6:2; Phil 2:1-4). Christian widows were to exemplify this kind of service. "Foot washing" on the literal level was

---

5:7-8 B. W. Winter (1988:83-99) may shed some interesting light on the legal background to the widows' dilemma. Ordinarily, custody of the widow's dowry passed to a new lord, perhaps a son or grandson, whose household the widow would then enter. Possibly some in the church were failing to take up this responsibility. The needy widows whose support the church provided were those who had no one to take up this responsibility, or who had no dowry.

These instructions refers to the whole passage; compare 3:14; 4:6.

a service to visitors, an act of kindness that was central to hospitality. But Paul's meaning goes beyond the literal level. Figuratively, the term includes the sense of performing all manner of humble tasks for the benefit of others. The language used here makes certain contact with the pattern of life that Jesus laid down for his disciples (Jn 13:14).

Helping fellow Christians under various sorts of stress is a responsibility that goes with the bond of fellowship in Christ (Mt 25:35-40; Gal 6:10; Jas 1:27). Paul asks that the "qualified" widow be especially known for this good deed.

Clearly, the widow eligible for financial support was the one who manifested the Spirit in every part of her life. Genuine Christianity can mean nothing less.

Family Responsibility (5:4, 7-8) Among Paul's readers were those who were believing children or grandchildren of a widow. For them, making provision for the widow was an essential expression of genuine faith. In fact, that key word in the Pastorals, *godliness* (NIV *put their religion into practice*), occurs here in such a way that the home is envisioned as the initial "test tube" of faith.

What is actually at stake here is obedience to the fifth commandment: "Honor your father and your mother" (Ex 20:12; Eph 6:2). Not only is care for the widowed mother or grandmother a logical recompense for her faithful service to children and grandchildren, but in the obedience to God's will that it reflects, this care is *pleasing to God.* Disobedience amounts to rejection of the faith; the judgment that such a one *is worse than an unbeliever* (v. 8) is harsh, because that one has consciously broken God's law.

Paul's vivid language suggests that actual instances of neglect needed to be corrected. Furthermore, it is very possible that the heretical movement, which took a dim view of marriage (4:3), was also undermining traditional family values (compare 2 Tim 3:6; Tit 1:11); Paul's description

---

5:9 Some find a new topic, that of enrollment into the office of widows, as distinct from that of support for the real widow of 5:3-8, to begin at this point (so Verner 1983:161; Jeremias 1975:36-39). But the evidence for the alleged office is quite late (third and fourth century), and the repetition of the same word for widow *(chēra,* 5:3 [twice], 4, 5, 9, 11, 16 [twice]) and the similar opening and closing (5:3 and 16) hold the passage tightly together.

in verse 8 matches his description of the false teachers (those who had *denied the faith;* 1:6; 4:1; 6:21; 2 Tim 2:18; 3:5; Tit 1:16).

But there was another danger. Just as surely as the loose-living widow of verse 6 (see vv. 11-15) would attract criticism, failure to provide for the financial support of the widow would leave the family and, by association, the church open to criticism (v. 7). The whole passage is under the category of conduct that affects witness. The reference to *blame* (literally, "blameless," as in 3:2 in the case of the overseer) is an allusion to the observant outsider. Additionally, the sentiment of verse 8 would have been shared by the respectable unbeliever, whose civil structure included laws providing for the protection of the widow.

For both the widow and the family of the widow, these instructions express the need to keep one's confession of the faith and one's conduct in harmony. In contrast to the false teaching that had been circulating, spirituality was to have practical, respectable and observable results.

The Young Widow (5:11-16) To the modern ear, Paul comes off sounding very unfair here. Certainly it is not true that "as a rule" young widows would succumb to sensual desires. Paul generalizes. But he does so because he is aware of the stereotypes that existed in his society, because a very serious pattern of behavior had developed among some young widows, and because he wants to avoid the damage to the church's reputation that would surely result from its young widows' being so "typed." Consequently, *the general rule* is that young widows were not to be considered for enrollment in the team of widows alluded to here that was supported by the church (v. 11). But what is meant by the difficult rationale that follows?

Habits to Avoid (5:11-13, 15) First comes the causal sequence of *sensual desires* that *overcome their dedication to Christ,* which results in a desire *to marry.* Younger widows would be more subject to physical desires. Similar advice, directed to men and women, appears in 1 Corinthians 7:8-9. The fact of the matter is that physical desires are a current factor for younger people, and the strength of these desires often makes

---

Notes: 5:12 "The faith" *(hē pistis)* is a technical term in the Pastorals which denotes the

(re)marriage a wise course.

But verse 11 as rendered in the NIV is not graphic enough: it is more literally "sensual impulses that alienate them from Christ." It is not clear whether these widows engaged in immoral behavior (though it is possible that they did). In any case, the desire to remarry is connected with alienation from Christ—not because remarriage is prohibited (compare 1 Cor 7:8-9), but probably either because it was considered a hasty alternative to genuine repentance for immoral behavior or because they were seeking to marry unbelievers (compare 1 Cor 7:39).

The fact that Paul goes on in verse 12 to say that in this case remarriage leads to *judgment,* because they have rejected the first (that is, "foremost") faith (NIV *they have broken their first pledge)* does seem to indicate remarriage outside of the guidelines of God's will. Some have taken this as a reference to a vow of chastity, which would imply that an office of widows existed in the church at this time. But the more likely meaning of the actual term is "the faith" (the same term occurs in v. 8), which in these letters refers technically to Christianity and implies the need to believe. Given the Pauline background on teaching regarding remarriage and the positive teaching about it in verse 14, it is more likely that unsanctioned remarriage to unbelievers or precipitate remarriage in general is in mind.

A second reason not to include young widows on the list may seem like another unfair generalization: the tendency to become idle, to flit from house to house and, worse yet, to become gossips and busybodies, saying things that are inappropriate (v. 13). It may mean that young widows, their financial burden lifted, lacking the spiritual maturity to apply themselves to prayer and other tasks of ministry associated with the *list,* became lazy and even counterproductive. But a glance down to verse 15 *(some have in fact already turned away to follow Satan)* suggests that Paul already has those young widows who had fallen prey to the false teachers in view. If so, then the gossip and other foolishness belong to the category of meaningless, paradoxical chatter (1:6; 4:7; 6:20) spread by the heretics, which Paul calls "false." It is also well to

whole matrix of the Christian religion (1 Tim 1:9; 3:9; 4:1, 6; 5:8; 6:10, 12, 21). Rejection of the faith here is equivalent to denial of the faith in 5:8.

keep in mind that the false teachers were particularly effective in the homes of believers (2 Tim 3:6; Tit 1:11).

A Lifestyle to Pursue (5:14) What Paul has just laid down as reasons for excluding young widows from church support now leads to the logical conclusion: So they should marry. A comparison with the approved credentials of the older widow (vv. 9-10) shows that he calls young widows to pursue that same domestic lifestyle. The three phrases *to marry, to have children, to manage their homes* describe the responsible and socially normative role of the homemaker, which the apostle elsewhere endorses (2:11-15; Eph 5:22-23; Col 3:18; Tit 2:5; compare also 1 Pet 3:1-7).

That the critic outside is again in mind emerges in the fourth phrase, *to give the enemy no opportunity for slander.* The *enemy* is probably the non-Christian and not Satan in this instance (3:7). It is because the wanton behavior of verse 11 and the foolish talk of verse 13 occur where the church meets with the world that the outside critic is a concern. It is doubly of concern if this disrespectful behavior be seen as financially subsidized by the church.

Christian Women and Widowed Relatives (5:16) In the conclusion to this section the apostle repeats the instruction to care for widows with some refinement. The reference to the *woman* of the family is not necessarily surprising, since within the household it would have fallen to a wife to perform this task anyway. Narrowing the focus to the *woman* also reinforces the teaching to the young widows, for care of older widowed relatives (vv. 4, 8) falls within the scope of the appropriate activities described in verse 10. In any case, the purpose of this last instruction, as also of the whole passage, is to allow the church to concentrate its limited resources on helping those widows who, alone, trusting only in God and committed to service, are really in need (v. 3).

Yet this passage, which addresses a very specific situation, springs from a truth about God that compels us to ask some very penetrating questions regarding the focus of our compassion today: God is committed to helping those who cannot help themselves. As already pointed out, the Old Testament announces clearly God's special concern for widows,

Notes: 5:16 Fee suggests the possibility that the problem alluded to in verses 4 and 8

alongside of whom are often named the fatherless. The directions of Jesus' ministry developed the theme of God's compassion with even greater clarity to encompass the poor, the sick, the outcasts of society, the disfranchised, the marginalized. It was to these that Jesus reached out. The need for the church to minister to widows and the accompanying concern for the church's testimony in the world evident in 5:1-16 are an application of God's care for those unable to care for themselves.

Widows presented that church at that time with a specific need, and in our churches this same basic need is common. But our technological age is creating some problems (or at least raising them to proportions never before known) that belong to this category. What about our poor—the homeless, the jobless? What about our disfranchised—the single mothers, the elderly, the convicts and ex-convicts, the divorced? While the questions come easier than the answers, I think we will all agree that the church is to be God's channel of compassion as he seeks to include the excluded. Paul's treatment suggests that there is far more involved than simply handing out money. The pattern presented here is a carefully structured ministry to the whole person which encourages and facilitates godliness and a productive life while it also guards against misuse and abuse that might endanger the church's witness. It remains for us to implement this teaching creatively in our particular situations.

□ Instructions Concerning Elders (5:17-25)

Leaders can make or break a church. What makes leadership so solemn a responsibility? One part of the answer is implicit in this passage: the importance of the church community's trust in its leadership. A member's mistakes may affect only the member, but a leader's mistakes affect the whole church. But if a church is to continue to exist and to carry out its God-given task, it must support and trust its leaders. For God has ordained that the fellowship of believers be led by people called to that task (1 Cor 12:28; Eph 4:11).

The church that Paul addresses had been torn apart by the false teachers, and much of this letter is aimed at putting the pieces back together. It is essential that he restore the church's confidence in its

---

was that of a young widow who neglected to care for a widowed relative (1988:124).

leadership, and he has already begun in chapter 3. The faithful elders needed to be distinguished from the unfaithful. The unfaithful needed to be disciplined, but in fairness. And some of the leadership had to be replaced. This task must have been first on Timothy's list of things to do (1:3-4), for the unity and mission of the church depended upon it. The passage before us contains practical principles for the regulation and maintenance of a church's leadership.

Proper Regard for Faithful Elders (5:17-18) Paul's esteem for those called to leadership is evident from the way he begins his instructions with those who had remained faithful. The church was to honor them doubly. On the one hand, believers were to give them all the honor and respect due them as leaders appointed by God. In practice this means submitting to their authority and following their leadership (compare 1 Cor 16:16; 1 Pet 5:5). Not only had God chosen them, but they had proved themselves to be devoted to the work. On the other hand, as verse 18 indicates, those called *elders* were to be supported financially (or perhaps "materially," since we do not know what form this support would have taken) by the church for their service. *Double honor,* therefore, brings together respectful submission to authority and remuneration.

What characterizes the faithful elder? First, this leader must have an established record of skillful management. Perhaps those appointed to the *presbyterion* ("the body of elders"—4:14) did not initially receive support. This management (3:4-5) included the whole range of pastoral activities, from preaching and teaching to administration and oversight of the church's entire ministry and life. In the Ephesian house churches, management also meant upholding the Word of God in the face of false teaching, turning back the verbal attacks of the heretics and making every effort to hold the people together.

However, the second characteristic is that the elder be involved in

---

Notes: 5:17 The NIV *who direct the affairs of the church well* fails to capture the "from past into present" time element of the perfect tense *(proestōtes).*

On the qualification *especially* see 1 Timothy 4:10 notes.

Paul's term for these ministers is a technical one—literally, "those who labor" *(kopiōntes;* see 4:10; Rom 16:12; 1 Cor 15:10; Gal 4:11; Phil 2:16; Col 12:29).

preaching and teaching. *Especially those whose work is preaching and teaching* should probably be read "in other words, those who preach and teach." It is possible that these full-time ministers of the Word represent a subgroup of all the elders. But it is more likely that the task of managing the church was generally associated with those selected for full-time ministry. In modern terms, Paul has in mind the pastoral staff, whose members, in obedience to God's calling, have devoted their lives to service in the church. The "overseer" of 1 Timothy 3:1-7 is the same as the elder in this passage.

The full-time minister's right to remuneration was not an innovation but a well-established tradition in the early church. Paul supports his teaching by appealing to the Scriptures. First comes a citation of Deuteronomy 25:4, which originally provided that threshing oxen be allowed to eat from the field in which they were working. Paul had applied this text earlier, in 1 Corinthians 9:9, to argue for the right to material support from that community.

A second citation applied the teaching of the Lord to the matter; in Jesus' opinion those working for the kingdom of God deserve to be supplied by those benefiting from their ministry (Mt 10:10; Lk 10:7). This principle probably derives from God's regulations for provision for the priests and Levites, who had no lands to till and whose responsibilities as ministers of God occupied their whole time (Num 18).

God's choice of the elder and the work of ministry are to be specially honored by God's people. Those who labor faithfully in this ministry deserve and need to be supported both by the congregation's respect and submission and by its financial contribution.

Discipline of Elders (5:19-21) When a leader errs, the rest of the leadership must discipline the offender. Given the situation that existed in Ephesus, it is easy to imagine that tempers would have run high. A purge mentality may have set in among those who had resisted the false

---

5:18 *For the Scripture says* introduces supporting or illustrative material from the Old Testament (Rom 4:3; 9:17; 10:11; 11:2; Gal 4:30) and refers to the first quote. The reference to Jesus' words is equally authoritative, though the concept of New Testament Scripture had not yet developed. See also on 2 Timothy 3:16.

teachers, leading them to make every effort to root out any elders even remotely associated with the opposition. Then again, pockets of adherents to the false teaching may have brought false accusations against the faithful leaders. In any case, while discipline of the leadership was not to be avoided, it was to be executed carefully and fairly.

Admissible Evidence (5:19) In order to protect a person from false accusation, the law of Moses stipulated that the testimony of two or three witnesses was necessary to establish the matter (Deut 19:15). This became a part of the early church's procedure of discipline (Mt 18:16; 2 Cor 13:1). Paul's readers are probably already embroiled in controversy surrounding accused elders, and when he invokes the well-known regulation it is to protect the accused and instill some order into the process. Thus the protective device is not lacking; but in the church there continue to be strong-willed, self-seeking individuals who would use their influence and even underhanded means to shape others' opinions about one person or another. It falls to the leadership to ensure that as far as possible this injustice is avoided.

Actual Sin (5:20) Discipline must be meted out to those elders whose sin is properly confirmed. But what constitutes sin? First, Paul uses the present tense, which implies that some elders are presently sinning, perhaps refusing to acknowledge their sin and repent.

Second, primarily in view in this context would be the sin of participating in the false teaching, such as Hymenaeus, Alexander (1:20) and Philetus (2 Tim 2:17) were charged with. This would have included actual teaching (1:3; 4:1-3; 6:3) and more generally promoting the strife and dissension that went with the movement (1:4-5; 6:4-5).

Of course, these rules would apply in any case in which an elder willfully transgressed the revealed will of God in matters of faith and practice. But the standard for determining sin must be Scripture, and areas of faith and practice in which opinions differ because the teaching of Scripture is not clear or is capable of more than one reasonable interpretation ought not to be so categorized. The purpose of this proc-

Notes: 5:19 The present-tense prohibition *do not entertain* may imply that inadequate evidence was being accepted as sufficient.

5:20 "Rebuke" *(elenchō),* which can express various shades of meaning (bringing something to light, reproof, correction), is associated with ecclesiastical discipline (Mt 18:15) and

ess was to deal with actual, identifiable sin.

This raises a serious question for us: Granted that divergent views on certain issues (separation from the world, eschatology, gifts of the Spirit, the role of women in the church) may ill-suit one to ministry in one church or denomination or another, ought such divergence to be met with disciplinary measures? Or was Martin Luther, whom the Catholic Church branded a heretic, right to attribute to the devil Zwingli's interpretation of the Lord's Supper (that Christ meant that the bread and the wine are only symbols of his body and blood) and label the Swiss reformer a fanatic? To bring this kind of debate into the context of these instructions about discipline is a dangerous thing. It is equally dangerous to fail to discipline Christians known to be involved in actual sin: sexual immorality, marital infidelity, dishonesty, spreading rumors, promulgating false doctrine.

Appropriate Discipline (5:20) Once sin is established, discipline by the leadership is to follow. The approved method is public rebuke. A look at Matthew 18:15-17 suggests that discipline of the elder here is comparatively harsh; but then the leader's sin affects the whole congregation. Yet it is not as harsh as it might be—a rebuke is not "excommunication" (compare 1:20), nor is it necessarily dismissal from office. Public rebuke is meant to produce repentance in the sinning elder (2 Tim 2:25). Another purpose *(so that)* is to remind the rest of the church's leadership, and indeed the whole congregation, of the gravity of sin and its consequences.

Absolute Impartiality (5:21) Finally, the matter must be judged and (if warranted) discipline must be administered with absolute impartiality. This is meant to ensure both a just evaluation and the consistent application of discipline in actual cases of sin. And this is no casual footnote to the guidelines Paul has already issued. First, he uses the strongest terms to bind Timothy and the church leadership to this principle: an apostolic command, with God, Christ Jesus and the elect angels acting as witnesses. An awareness of the presence of God in the believing

---

authoritative correction (2 Tim 3:16; Tit 1:9).

The others refers to the rest of the elders; but the public nature of the event would naturally include the entire congregation (see Fee 1988:130).

community is a strong inducement to obedient Christian living (5:4; 6:13; 2 Tim 2:14; 4:1). It was precisely this awareness—of "the LORD your God, who is among you" (Deut 6:15)—that motivated the newborn community of Israel to obedience.

Second, the two phrases that command impartiality take up a dominant theme in Scripture. The judgment of God is said to be completely impartial (2 Chron 19:7; Rom 2:11; Eph 6:9; Col 3:25; Jas 2:1; 1 Pet 1:17; compare Sirach 35:12). So strong was this belief in God's impartiality that it became a requirement that God's people reflect it as they discharged leadership duties. This applied doubly to leaders of the community, such as the judges whom Jehoshaphat appointed (2 Chron 19:7), whose role was to represent God among the people. It is quite possible that Paul had this Old Testament story in mind, since the two verbs that appear in the Greek Old Testament, "keep" and "do," also occur here. In any case, impartiality is a requirement in the discharge of church leadership duties, because church leaders are God's representatives among the people.

The gravity of the situation addressed here certainly calls for immediate action. But Timothy is not to allow the pressures of the moment to force him to conclude that expediency alone is the objective. On the one hand, the reputations and feelings of people are at stake, and expediency, which might suggest the need to take shortcuts, often does not take them into account. On the other hand, sometimes expediency forces real problems to be swept under the carpet. The instructions envision a process designed to aid the church's leadership in making responsible decisions about discipline. The process emphasizes attention to the problem, justice and appropriate disciplinary measures. No matter how urgent the moment might seem, church unity and witness will be better served if the procedures outlined here are followed.

Careful Selection of Elders (5:22-25) The recent defection of some elders in the church certainly underlined the need for care in selecting replacements. But frankly, whether defection is involved or not, in the

---

5:21 In 2 Chronicles 19:7 and here the Greek verbs are *phylassō* ("to keep" or "guard") and *poieō* ("to do"). There the command is prefaced by a reference to "the fear of the LORD," which is parallel to the reminder here of God's presence *(in the sight of God)*. The strikingly

best of circumstances this process involves risks. The apostle urges thoroughness so that the risks might be minimized. Prior to the laying on of hands, the ceremony in which the elders signaled before the congregation God's choice of a new elder (4:14; compare Acts 13:3), the leadership of the church must thoroughly examine the candidate. To judge from the bishop/elder code in chapter 3, which Paul gave for this purpose, evidence of Christian lifestyle, not just correct doctrine, was essential.

The issue in verse 22 is sin or tendencies that lead to sin, and a sloppy assessment will implicate the examiner or examining committee in the leader's sin. Consequently, if the well-being of the church is not enough to ensure careful attention to the process, the thought of personally sharing in the sin of another is added. This concept of sharing in the sin of another (whether by tacit approval or by apathetic failure to take a stand) rests on an important theological premise. We might call this a "theology of separation," though we must develop it with balance. God called his people to be separate from the sinful nations, where separation had geographical and religious implications (Is 52:11; Jer 51:45; Rev 18:4), and that call was fundamental to the formation of Israel (Gen 12:1). In the New Testament the concept of separation develops into the dialectical call to be "in the world but not of the world" (Jn 17:15-18; 1 Cor 5:9-11). Separation now calls the believer and the church to resist conformity with the world not by a physical withdrawal from it, which would make mission impossible, but rather by a spiritual transformation that brings an understanding of God's will and prepares one for critical evaluation of the world's thoughts and ways (Rom 12:2; 1 Jn 2:15-17). The implications of conformity are serious not simply for the church's well-being but for its standing before God. Revelation 18:4 suggests that conformity with the world is not only unfortunate but culpable, for it will lead to judgment. Equally grave is the careless appointment to the church's leadership of one whose sin ought to have meant disqualification, or turning a blind eye or tolerating sin that is later discovered in a leader.

similar contexts and verbal parallels suggest that the Old Testament story may have had a part in Paul's thought.

In view of this theological background, it should be unthinkable that the leadership of a church would be indifferent to sin among its leaders. It is also not possible for the leaders to wash their hands of the sins of one they have placed into office. By laying on hands, they willingly identify with that one's sin. In the concluding exhortation to purity, Paul rephrases and abbreviates this theology of separation that underlies the verse.

But in the Ephesian church *pure*, as a description of Christian living, had various connotations. To the false teachers it meant asceticism, including abstinence from certain foods (4:3). Whatever benefits abstinence might have for the believer, the heretics had taken it to a sinful extreme. Not only is Timothy to distance himself from these false views, but he is, for the sake of his health, to demonstrate Christian freedom and drink wine instead of exclusively water (5:23).

Paul's conclusion to this passage on the selection of elders has a proverbial ring, appealing to common sense. This popular wisdom emphasizes the two advantages of a thorough examination of leader candidates. First, some who are unfit to lead the church disqualify themselves from the start with obvious sins. But the disqualifying sins of others, who are equally unfit, come to light only after extensive scrutiny (v. 24)—thus Paul's instructions.

Second, the marks of genuine faith *(good deeds;* compare 3:2-7) that point toward eligibility may be immediately evident in some people. But in the case of other qualified people, perhaps of quieter temperament, careful searching will be needed to recognize their potential (v. 25)— yet another reason for heeding Paul's advice.

The importance of the church's leadership has already been well illustrated in this letter. A leader's influence in the community is inevitable. But will it be for good or for ill? Clearly both possibilities exist. Some of the risks can be minimized when leaders are selected. Quick decisions based on cursory evaluations have no place in this process.

□ Instructions Concerning Slaves (6:1-2)

Somewhere inside most of us is the desire to be free. We feel it most

---

5:23 The medicinal use of wine was widely known (for example, Hippocrates *Ancient*

when we are constrained to do someone else's bidding. And if the demands of those in authority are onerous enough, the longing for freedom will eventually become a mobilizing force. Whole peoples have fought for it. Individuals, like my father, have left the relative security of large companies for the freedom to be found in running one's own business. Yet many discover that the road to freedom is a hard one, and that freedom carries with it new constraints and responsibilities that are often more frustrating than any previously endured.

Slaves were one group in the early church that had been especially drawn by the freedom that Paul's gospel promised. The apostle announced: "It is for freedom that Christ has set us free" (Gal 5:1). And he said that in Christ the distinction between slave and free had (in some sense) ceased to exist (Gal 3:28).

In the first century, slaves formed a distinct group within the society of the Roman Empire. Although they were the property of their masters, in practice this did not prevent many of them from experiencing a good deal of freedom and social mobility. Many earned a living or worked in partnership with their owners. Some actually held positions of authority within businesses or administrative posts in lower levels of the government. It was also not unusual for a slave to receive a good education. On the whole, the slaves in the churches of Asia Minor who heard Paul's message lived in a time when conditions were improving. Nevertheless, the desire to be free of slavery was always present. It might be won by outstanding service. But some saw in the gospel a more direct route.

What they failed to see was that freedom in Christ does not release the Christian from obligations to those in rightful authority. This is a lesson I began to learn shortly after becoming a Christian, while serving in the military in England. There were several of us who had just set out on the Christian adventure. In our enthusiasm to serve Christ we somehow concluded that we didn't need to concern ourselves with mundane rules about shined boots and clean, pressed uniforms. Our superiors quickly made the connection between our new faith and our sloppy appearance. And in that small corner of the world, Christianity was in danger of being linked with insubordination.

Medicine 13; see Spicq 1969:549).

Some Christian slaves in Ephesus suffered from a similar kind of confusion. The promise of freedom and equality in Paul's gospel had set them expectantly on the edge. Here they met with a new frustration, for they discovered that salvation, and with it freedom and equality, is a progressive thing, often more principle than practice. Its consummation remained a promise to be fulfilled completely only when Christ appeared (6:14). Neither their masters nor their masters' expectations disappeared. Life on that edge must have been frustrating indeed. Very likely, the false teaching of a completed salvation (see introduction) pushed them right over that edge into insubordination. Both the misunderstanding and its consequences in the church were serious enough to call forth Paul's corrective teaching: Christians must respect the authority of their masters, whether they be superior officers, employers, managers or supervisors, whether they happen to be fellow believers or not. The reputation of the church is unavoidably at stake.

Christian Slaves of Unbelievers (6:1) In Paul's churches there were two categories of slave. The first had come to Christ independent of their masters. From what we have seen of their mobility, this is not at all surprising. But normally the religion of the master determined the religion of the whole household. Any deviation in this pattern would probably not escape notice.

Apparently certain Christian slaves were taking home with them some rather radical ideas. Instead of finding contentment in the hope that God would reward their humble diligence (Eph 6:5-8; Col 3:22-24; compare 1 Pet 2:18-20), they began to treat their masters with disrespect. The masters could not help but think that this insubordination had something to do with the new religion and the one called Christ. What possible good could come from a religion that encouraged such revolution-

Notes: 6:1 For additional background on ancient slavery, see Bartchy (1973:72-82).

It was a general belief among pagan slaveowners that foreign religions corrupted slaves (Cicero *Laws* 2. 7. 19-27).

The yoke of slavery suggests the harsh and difficult nature of this life.

Concern that God's name might be mocked takes up an Old Testament theme (Is 52:5; Ezek 36:20-23; Rom 2:24; compare Cairo *Damascus Document* 12:7-8). It coincides with the concern for the Christian community's witness to the world in other ethical passages (Jas 2:7; 1 Pet 2:11-12; 4:4, 14; 2 Pet 2:2).

6:2 The original word order makes perfect sense: "because they [the masters] are believers and beloved [brothers] who do good deeds." Dibelius and Conzelmann (1972:82)

ary behavior? The insubordinate behavior of slaves posed a definite threat to the church's reputation.

Consequently, Paul issues corrective instructions. Although the relationship between Christian slaves *under the yoke* and pagan masters is difficult, they are to continue to live by the rules of slavery. The fact that they have a higher Lord (Col 3:22-25) does not release them from this obligation. It obligates them all the more to be models of obedience, for this service to human masters is simultaneously service to the Lord.

Yet Paul's chief concern and chief rationale in issuing these instructions is mission. The purpose *(so that)* of the slaves' respectable conduct is protection of *God's name* and the Christian message (compare Tit 2:10). The danger of disrespectful attitudes toward social institutions is that the intention of the gospel will be totally misunderstood and the church's evangelistic mission incapacitated.

Christian Slaves of Believers (6:2) It was also common to find Christian slaves and their believing masters within the same house church (Eph 6:9; Col 4:1; Philem). To imagine the pressures this might have involved, think how in our day the conflicting secular interests of managers and union members or military officers and enlisted personnel might affect ministry and worship in one church. If even under ordinary circumstances slaves and masters in the church struggled with this relationship, it is not surprising that the situation in Ephesus reached critical mass with the added influence of triumphalistic false teaching.

The slaves based their claim to freedom on the common bond in Christ *(because they are brothers)*. But while this common bond, and a common Lord, does indeed have implications for the masters' treatment

---

insist that "beloved" *(agapētoi)* must mean "beloved by God," since "slaves who must be admonished to serve . . . cannot be expected to act out of love." However, a glance at a parallel, Philemon 16, suggests that it is the common bond in Christ (which ideally produces mutual love among slaves and masters) that the term describes.

"Who benefit from good deeds" is a possible translation of the final phrase, which views the masters as the recipients of the slaves' service (NIV; RSV; GNB; Fee 1988:139), but the verb *(antilambanō)* more frequently means "to devote oneself to" than "to benefit from," and the Greek term that the NIV translates *service (euergesia)* ordinarily denotes service performed by a superior (see further Hanson 1982:105).

of slaves (Eph 6:9; Col 4:1), it also has implications for the slaves' service to masters. Paul actually turns the slaves' slogan back upon them (though the NIV does not bring this out). Slaves ought to serve with excellence *because those who benefit from their service* (the masters) *are believers and dear to them* (the slaves). The relationship of believers in Christ demands mutual respect (Gal 5:13), which in this case slaves were to express in obedient service. Notably, the same reasoning would be applicable if the problem were reversed (compare Philem 16).

An additional part of the reason for the slaves' good conduct is the benefits to the church's ministry to be derived from the masters' service (the NIV turns this around). It is quite likely that some of the elders were householders who owned slaves (3:4-5, 12). While insubordinate slaves would be a liability to the ministry and witness of the church, respectful slaves would be an asset.

Respect for authority even in time- and culture-bound institutions continues to be a necessary part of Christian witness. The common bond in Christ certainly bears upon such institutions within the church, but it does not necessarily make the institution or its authority structure obsolete.

□ Final Orders to Timothy (6:2-16)

How quickly and completely credibility disappears when Christian leaders are found to have financial motives! The temptation of financial profit may characterize false teachers, but it also poses a threat to unwary believers, particularly if they are financially well-to-do and in positions of leadership. The dangers are probably even greater today. For one thing, large churches will pay well for those with outstanding gifts of ministry. How does this affect one's outlook on ministry and life?

In this epistle's closing section, which is very similar in tone and content to the opening section (1:3-20), Paul's final instructions concerning the errorists, the Christian leader and the wealthy of the community center on the matter of godliness and money and emphasize responsible Christian behavior.

Notes: 6:3-5 For other examples of Paul's use of the vice list, see Romans 13:13; 1 Corinthians 5:10-11; 6:9-10; 2 Corinthians 12:20-21; Galatians 5:19-21; Ephesians 4:31; 5:3-5. Together vice and virtue lists set forth the two ways of life.

Opposing False Teachers (6:2-5) The Christian leader must not forget the responsibility to protect the faith. Those of Paul's readers who fell into this category, including Timothy, were to discharge this duty by teaching and urging the true faith (v. 2). The command that sets Timothy in this mode again (see also 3:14; 4:6, 11; 5:7, 21) also reminds them that in this operation the Christian leader is not unarmed. Paul has given specific teaching *(these . . . things)* for confrontation with the false teachers.

Having repeated the command, Paul issues a kind of "wanted poster." It is the counterpart to the "job description" given in chapter 3. Notably, each begins with the general *if anyone* (compare 5:4, 16; Tit 1:6). Here, verses 3-6 consist of one long sentence in the Greek, beginning with the "criminal" and the "crime" and going on to give identifying characteristics in a list of vices. By using the list (compare 1:9-10; 2 Tim 3:2-4; Tit 3:3) Paul meant to create a strong stereotype or caricature of the false teacher that would communicate primarily two things: an authoritative denunciation and a solemn warning. Readers, after seeing this "poster," would not be likely to form or maintain casual attitudes about the false teachers or their doctrine.

False Doctrine (6:3) Paul first categorizes their ministry. As in 1:3, he charges them with, literally, "teaching different doctrine." *False doctrines* were determined on the basis of divergence from the approved teaching of the church. The remainder of verse 3 defines the approved canon or standard. *Sound instruction of our Lord Jesus Christ* is a reference to the gospel about Christ which Paul himself introduced. It produces soundness or spiritual health in those that receive it (see 1:10). The approved *teaching* is that which can be measured by "godliness" (the NIV *godly teaching* is too vague; compare Tit 1:2). The true gospel announces and produces a genuinely transformed lifestyle.

Corrupt Behavior (6:4-5) What characterized the opponents? First, verse 4 tells us they were *conceited.* They felt that they had special knowledge of God, better knowledge than the apostle had. In fact, they did not, and the arrogant air about them betrayed their unregenerate

---

6:5 Although the vice list was meant to give a general impression rather than to detail the faults of the heresy (see on 1:9-10), Paul's treatment of greed suggests that here the actual situation is in view.

nature; gentleness, a quality of true spirituality in the Pastorals (6:11; 2 Tim 2:25; compare 2 Cor 10:1), was totally absent.

Second, they were ignorant. Paul's phrase (literally, "understanding or knowing nothing") recalls the tone of 1:7. These teachers were not simply misguided, they were totally ignorant. This was apparent as their doctrine was measured against the apostle's and as their conduct was measured against true godliness. Moreover, from the context it seems that this condition was a culpable one, for it came about as the result of decisions made about the apostolic gospel which they knew (compare 1:13).

Third, they took perverse pleasure in controversy and quarreling. This so marked their behavior that Paul describes them as "sick with" (having *an unhealthy interest in)* disputes. As this dangerous sickness spreads, it produces poisons that destroy relationships and church unity.

Paul lists several. *Envy* is a discontented thirst for advantage and position that breeds distrust. In Galatians 5:21 it stands in opposition to the joy and peace that the Spirit produces. *Strife* refers to an atmosphere of constant struggle. *Malicious talk* and *evil suspicions,* rumor-spreading and distrust, are the offspring of *envy* and *strife.* This list closes in verse 5 with the graphic summary *constant friction.*

Ultimately, the disease spread by the heretics would result in a kind of spiritual mental illness. Paul makes the same connection in verse 5 between corrupt behavior and rejection of God that he did in Romans 1. There, rejection of the knowledge of God is seen to spawn a corrupt life (Rom 1:28-32). Here, the *corrupt mind* and being *robbed of the truth* amount to the same thing. The heretics could no longer apprehend God's truth because their mind, that organ of rational discernment, had been corrupted by false teaching (2 Tim 3:8; Tit 1:15).

It is little wonder, then, that missionaries of the cults are so resistant to the gospel and so easily angered in theological discussions. Corrupt minds and argumentative dispositions go hand in hand with opposition

---

Notes: 6:6-10 Some commentators maintain that the heretics are no longer in view after 6:5 (Dibelius and Conzelmann 1972:84; Verner 1983:174). But the description in verse 10, *wandered from the faith,* suggests that they are in mind as the negative model (as elsewhere) all along, even though Paul's teaching has general application to all believers (see Kelly 1963:135-38; Fee 1988:143-46).

to the gospel.

Financial Motives (6:5) This poster caricature of the heretics concludes with the main point Paul wishes to develop. These false teachers were "selling" their teaching. People in that day were often suspicious of the motives of teachers of religion and philosophy. Paul apparently had to deal with similar allegations himself (1 Thess 2:5), and Christians were warned about peddlers of the gospel (Rom 16:17-18; 2 Pet 2:2; 1 Pet 5:2). Here *godliness* may refer to one of the errorists' own catchwords (see 2 Tim 3:5), their special knowledge of the divine (6:20). As they taught certain things that people wanted to hear (2 Tim 4:3) and offered initiation into an elite club, the false teachers discovered a lucrative business (compare Tit 1:11). In reality, this was the result of corrupted minds that had broken from the truth of the gospel.

As much as we would prefer to avoid this warning, we must not allow Paul's concentration on the motives of false teachers to deflect this word's relevance for those in Christian vocations today. While there is no easy rule to apply, we must constantly evaluate the influence of "financial packages" and "fee structures" on our motives, and be willing before the Lord to make radical adjustments.

The Christian View of Money (6:6-8) It is clear from the transition at verse 6 that Paul has intended all along to teach a Christian view of money. The false teachers have provided a vivid contrast for instruction. If Paul felt his first readers needed to be taught concerning their outlook on material possessions and contentment, how much more do we modern servants of God need to gain his insight!

Detachment (6:6) Paul tells us that the Christian's goal with respect to material things is *godliness with contentment*. *Godliness* in Paul's vocabulary means the genuine Christian life, a faith-relationship with God and a new way of life. *Contentment* is a Pauline word in the New Testament (2 Cor 9:8; compare Phil 4:11). It had a prominent place in Stoic

---

6:6 The similarities to secular philosophy in Paul's concept of *contentment (autarkeia;* see the references in Dibelius and Conzelmann 1972:84) stop short of aloofness and indifference, as his positive teaching on responsible use of wealth shows (2 Cor 8—9; 1 Tim 6:18).

philosophy, where it defined an attitude of "self-sufficiency," meaning detachment or independence from things or possessions. Contentment came from within. Paul approved of this idea but naturally supplied a Christian basis for it: "I have learned to be content whatever the circumstances. . . . I can do everything through him who gives me strength" (Phil 4:11, 13). Thus for Paul the Christian goal is a genuine relationship with God, our source of contentment, and a healthy detachment from material things. This combination is *great gain.* In contrast to 6:5, *gain* here is measured according to spiritual rather than material value. Eternal benefits are surely promised, but the focus is on how the believer with this healthy perspective can avoid the many pitfalls of greed in the present life.

The Eternal Perspective (6:7) To ground his view of contentment, Paul draws on Old Testament wisdom. Both Job 1:21 and Ecclesiastes 5:15 expound the principle that material things belong only to this world. Things have no lasting value and provide no eternal advantage. Therefore one's contentment cannot stem from things. Human contact with the material world begins at birth and terminates at death. But Christian hope takes the believer beyond the material limit to a boundless eternity, and logically, then, eternal values must shape our view of temporal things. To put it simply, Job and Paul mean that "things," their value and usefulness, pertain to this world, which is but a temporary home (compare Heb 11:10).

Material Sufficiency (6:8) This leads to a question: For the Christian how much is enough? Paul's principle implies a standard of material sufficiency that is minimal indeed. *Food and clothing* ought to be enough. While Paul may be quoting popular philosophy, it is far more likely that he is drawing from the model of Christ (Mt 6:25-34; Lk 12:16-21). He does not say anything negative about living above this minimum standard, though he will teach that life at a higher material level carries with it heavy obligations. But he does say that real *contentment* and material prosperity have nothing to do with one another. And acquisitiveness has nothing to do with godliness.

6:8 Paul's choice of vocabulary, *food and clothing (diatrophē, skepasma),* reflects his sensitivity to the culture and vernacular, not the secularization of his ethics.

6:10 A contemporary of Christ, Ovid the Roman poet, wrote of "the criminal love of

How can the Christian learn to be content with simple living? Certainly not by accepting the standards set by this world. Paul suggests that an eternal perspective and an attitude of detachment toward things are prerequisites. As an eternal perspective develops, dependence on things material will decline.

Greed: A Love That Consumes (6:9-10) But the reverse is also true. An obsession with acquiring wealth is a self-feeding fire. It consumes not only time and energy but also values. Strangely, this panacea, money, leads more to ruin than to wealth. People will do anything necessary to obtain it. As St. John Chrysostom said, "Riches are not forbidden, but the price of them is." Nowadays it is difficult to decide which is more dangerous—the love of money in a materialistic society or the Christian's rationalization for joining in the chase.

The Dangers (6:9) Paul sets out for his readers the dangers of *the love of money* in both general and specific terms. First, the pursuit of wealth leads down a road filled with every variety of pitfall. The words *temptation* and *trap* may well be used with Satan's manipulations in mind (3:7), and the Enemy is certainly capable of using the hope of wealth to blur the moral distinctions of believers. *Foolish and harmful desires* not only are for wealth itself but are probably also immoral cravings unleashed by access to wealth. Wealth leads people into circles where the rules are different, the peer pressure is tremendous, and the values are totally distorted. What, for the believer, might have been unthinkable from the outside becomes quite natural once on the inside. And the end of this is utter devastation, which Paul emphasizes with a verb that means to *plunge* (as if to drown) and two nouns that combine to describe complete *destruction.* Let the reader beware, for there are no such warning signs along the path to riches.

Love of Money (6:10) The then-current proverb, *for the love of money is a root of all kinds of evil,* is meant to give to the warning a kind of popular authority. Beyond this, however, the *root* metaphor contains an important truth. The hidden root is the source of life. If one is

riches." For further secular use see Fee 1988:147.

In the Greek sentence *root* comes first for emphasis. The NIV interpretation *the root* captures Paul's meaning well. See further Fee 1988:147.

to rid a garden of weeds, the roots must come out. Similarly, Paul's hearers must not simply treat the problems caused by greed. They must tear out the root that produces the problems.

But how? We know from the story of the rich young man (Mk 10:17-31) how hard it is to loosen this particular root. Jesus' own assessment which follows is no easier: "How hard it is for the rich to enter the kingdom of God. It is easier for a camel to go through the eye of a needle" (10:24-25). But the same passage points to our only hope: "all things are possible with God" (10:27). The answer must lie in seeking God for the strength and determination to do what is impossible for us— to somehow take control of the lust for money and things, to somehow bring about the paradigm shift that will allow God and others to occupy the places of priority in life (Mt 6:33; see below on 6:17).

The Destruction (6:10) Paul's readers knew that financial motives and greed had helped destroy the testimony of some who turned (perhaps) from positions of leadership in the church to become teachers of heresy. If it is difficult for the rich to enter the kingdom of God, it is relatively easy for those who strive to be rich to turn away from it. *Wandering from the faith* describes the apostasy of these false teachers, whose avarice Paul denounced in 6:5 (1:19; 6:21; 2 Tim 2:18). Fueled by greed, the opponents "lost their way," a sobering illustration of how the desire for riches drives a wedge between the believer and God (Mt 6:21, 24; 13:22; Lk 12:16-21). Paul describes the toll taken in spiritual loss, broken relationships and damaged reputations as *griefs* that pierce like thorns.

Timothy: Man of God (6:11-16) God has placed an incredible weight of responsibility onto the Christian leader's shoulders. The leader must not only faithfully nurture and direct the church but also pay careful attention to personal piety. A healthy church depends on healthy ministers whose ministry and personal life reflect equally the power of God.

Paul emphasizes the weight of this dual responsibility by closing the letter as he opened it, with a solemn charge to Timothy in the presence

---

Notes: 6:11 The *flee-pursue* formula *(pheugō-diōkō)* has immediate roots in the Greek Old Testament and intertestamental Judaism, where readers were commanded to "flee from sin" (Sirach 21:2; Tobit 4:21) and "pursue righteousness" (Deut 16:20; Prov 15:9; Is 51:1; Testament of Reuben 5:5). This language is basically Pauline in the New Testament: see

of God. The dangers of unfaithfulness, both to the leader and to the church, have been graphically spelled out in the interplay between descriptions of false teacher and faithful minister throughout the letter. Now, as the final contrast is made, the clarion call to faithful service resounds. The shape and tone of the text suggest that Paul may have adapted a formal ordination or baptismal charge for emphasis. But again, although the focus in this passage is on leaders, the instructions Paul gives apply to us all.

Personal Holiness (6:11) The calling to serve God is a calling to a position of special honor. Paul designates Timothy (and equally all faithful ministers) as *man of God,* a title given to Moses (Deut 33:1), David (Neh 12:24), Elijah (1 Kings 17:18) and Elisha (2 Kings 4:7) in the Old Testament. In so doing, he sets the minister apart as one having a special relationship with and an origin in God. The minister is God's special representative, one whom God has personally chosen and sent.

And God's expectations of those with a high calling are great. There can be no compromise in the Christian leader's lifestyle. Against the backdrop of spiritual defection, Paul makes this clear in the *flee . . . pursue* command that he issues. This traditional formula of exhortation (2 Tim 2:22) compels the readers to "escape" from the dangers of sin (in this case, the way of the false teachers in 6:3-5, 9-10—*all this*) to pursue a righteous life (compare 2 Tim 2:22). The tone is that of an emergency. Both flight and pursuit, however, require not only a conscious decision but also a sustained, lifelong effort; the emergency ends only with the appearance of Christ (6:14).

The object of pursuit is a balanced spiritual life. It is described with a list of virtues that throughout these letters stand for marks of genuine faith (4:12; 2 Tim 2:22; 3:10; compare Gal 5:22-23; Phil 4:8). The purpose of this list is to provide poetic impact more than precise description. Nevertheless, the items included give ample direction for the Christian life.

The first four terms, *righteousness, godliness, faith* and *love,* depict the

Romans 9:30; 12:13; 1 Corinthians 6:18; 10:14; 14:1; 1 Thessalonians 5:15. The force of the present-tense verbs of command is to stress continual action.

Galatians 5:22 links these kinds of Christian virtues to the Holy Spirit (love, faith and gentleness occur in each list). Thus Paul's command here is to pursue life in the Spirit.

new life of faith in contrast to the perverse behavior of the false teachers (6:4-5). *Righteousness* means observable "uprightness," a life in accordance with God's values. *Godliness* is Paul's term for the whole of the Christian experience, the vertical posture of faith and its horizontal, visible outworking in life (see notes on 2:2). It appears in this list (it is not in the others) because the heretics' false notions about it were mentioned in 6:5. *Faith* and *love* (see 4:12; notes on 2:15) depict these two dimensions of genuine Christianity, a balance of personal faith and correct doctrine and works done in the power of the Spirit.

The final two items anticipate the charge to ministry (v. 12). *Endurance* is the "won't quit" determination of God's servants in the face of opposition to the gospel (2 Tim 3:10; compare 2:10, 12). *Gentleness* is an attitude of patient, gentle composure that encourages the repentance of the unbeliever and the apostate (2 Tim 2:25; Tit 3:2).

The six virtues together describe the lifestyle of balanced spirituality that ought to characterize the Christian. A Christian leader must be a model of these things. A holistic portrait, it encompasses one's walk with God and disposition toward unbelievers. Are these standards impossibly high? If we think in terms of human effort, yes; but with the high calling to ministry also go vast resources for godly living.

Timothy, Fight the Good Fight (6:12-15) The servant of God must also fulfill the calling of ministry. The charge issued in 1:18 is repeated here. Paul has changed the metaphor, however, from ministry in terms of a military struggle to ministry in terms of an athletic contest (see also 2 Tim 4:7). Thus the need for perseverance, sustained effort and training dominate in this charge (compare 1 Cor 9:24-27; 2 Tim 2:5). Like a skillful coach, Paul supplies ample motivation for maintaining the struggle.

1. Eternal reward (6:12). Especially for the minister, to "finish the race" is no mere option. The command tone *(take hold)* reminds us of the real element of human responsibility in the salvation process, as it

---

6:12 *Fight the good fight* here translates *agonizou ton kalon agōna* (perhaps "compete in the contest"; compare 1:18, *strateue tēn kalēn strateian*—literally, "fight [as a soldier] the warfare"). The two phrases are basically interchangeable, though some difference in nuance may be implied (see Pfitzner 1967:177-80).

God's "calling" *(kaleō)* is an important theme in Paul's thought (Rom 8:30; 11:29; 1 Cor

also implies the real possibility of success. Though the cost is great, the Christian leader can arrive at the goal of personal salvation, *eternal life.*

But while the athletic imagery emphasizes the human side, it is the prior action of "calling" that establishes the believer's future success. In the passive, the verb refers clearly to God's call to eternal life. Yet as we have just seen, divine sovereignty does not preclude human responsibility. Timothy had an obligation to participate in his salvation. We too must view faithful Christian living and service, in whatever context God places us, as our necessary responsibility to God.

2. Past promises (6:12). The Greek sentence continues without a break, and attention shifts to Timothy's past commitment to God. It may be (as the NIV interprets it) that the phrase *good confession in the presence of many witnesses* relates directly to God's calling (to eternal life), indicating the time when realization of this occurred. In this case, the event in mind would probably be Timothy's baptism. However, the phrase may be linked more directly to the parallel commands to *fight* and to *take hold,* making the event grounds for obedience to those ministerial commands. In this case, the allusion would be to a commissioning ceremony of some sort. The two ceremonies would have been similar in tone, each including a confession of faith, a charge and a vow of commitment.

To judge from the ministry context here and probable allusions to the event elsewhere (1:18; 4:14), Paul may have had in mind Timothy's commissioning (similar to the more modern ordination). Then his reasoning is that the two commands of verse 12 are in keeping with the promises of God's selection of one for ministry. The ceremony that bound the congregation to acknowledge the authority of the new minister also bound the minister to faithful service.

Today the binding force of one's word is often questioned, but before God that is not so. The minister's pledge to serve must not be taken lightly. But it takes discipline as well as forceful reminders from co-

1:9; Eph 1:18; 2 Thess 2:14; 2 Tim 1:9). It is that sovereign action by which God brings to himself those he has chosen for salvation.

Representatives of the baptism interpretation are Fee (1988:150) and Kelly (1963:142). Favoring ordination is Hanson (1982:111); compare Barrett 1963:86-87.

workers or from God's Spirit to bring us back to first promises that bind. Yet what the servant must recall are not only human commitments to God but also God's commitments to his servants.

3. Present promises (6:13). This comes more clearly into view as Paul reminds Timothy of his present situation. Christian service is not something God initiates, like the christening of a ship, then leaves to run its own course. It begins with God's choice and continues in his presence and fellowship. So when Paul repeats the solemn charge, which begins in verse 13 and ends in verse 14, he emphasizes Timothy's continuing fellowship with God and Christ.

In this fellowship, too, obligation and promise are combined. To be *in the sight of God* (5:21; 2 Tim 4:1) is cause for reverent fear. The Hebrews were terrified of God's presence, which, as Moses explained, was to keep them from sinning (Ex 20:20). But God's presence meant for them also his faithful care—guidance, food, clothing (Deut 8:1-5). And the description of God as life-giver means the same for Paul's readers. God's constant presence should spur the Christian on to excellent service. Equally, this truth provides encouragement and strength, for the ever-present God is the one who gives and sustains life.

At the same time Timothy is reminded of his fellowship with Christ. He is our ever-present Lord (compare Mt 28:20). This comforting promise of continual fellowship, however, ought to compel us to the heights of faithfulness, for our Lord is also our judge (2 Tim 4:8; Rev 3:15-16).

Christian leaders in difficult situations have always found encouragement in Christ's experience. In fact, God has called us to participate in the very ministry Christ initiated. He *made the good confession* first, *before Pontius Pilate.* Paul's allusion is difficult to ascertain. Probably the reference is to Jesus' trial and to the supreme testimony he gave in his death. He authenticated his calling and commitment to serve God before

---

6:13 The NIV adds the verb *made* in its translation. The verb in the material Paul selects that describes Christ's *good confession* is "testify" *(martyreō).* It denotes a solemn testimony and came to be used in reference to testimony about Christ or the gospel (Acts 23:11). The noun "testimony" may refer to the gospel—that is, the testimony of God's grace in Christ (Acts 4:33; 1 Cor 1:6; 2:1; 1 Tim 2:6; 2 Tim 1:8). In this confessional setting, the theological meaning is intended.

Before Pontius Pilate is a possible reference to "the time of" Pontius Pilate (Kelly 1963:143-44), which might make Christ's *good confession* a reference to his entire life and

the representative of this world, despite great danger and temptations to denial (see Jn 18:28-37). The one called to serve God makes a confession and commitment to continue Christ's own mission at any personal cost. Christ's commitment to his servants is continual fellowship.

4. Future promises (6:14). It is equally important for Timothy to concentrate on the promise of Christ's return, for two reasons. First is the promise of relief. The term Paul chose to describe the Second Coming here *(the appearing)* pictures the event as a glorious intervention to bring help. In fact, Paul uses the same term to refer to Christ's first advent (2 Tim 1:10; Tit 2:11; 3:4); this shows how the present age is to be understood in relation to Christ's two "appearances"—what began with Christ will end with Christ. When God's appointed time arrives, relief will come to the minister. A Christian's earthly duties will cease.

Second is a note of urgency. The obligations connected with the call to service *(the command,* vv. 11-12, to lead an exemplary Christian life) must be kept, the course must be finished in all faithfulness *(without spot or blame),* for Christ comes to judge (2 Tim 4:1, 8). In light of the certainty of this future event, *without spot or blame* stresses the need for a life that expresses godliness consistently and in all respects. The early Christians lived as if Christ's return would occur during their lifetime. We for the most part do not, and we are the weaker for it. This confident hope of consummation and evaluation can sustain us when days are long, bodies grow weary and results seem few.

5. Sovereign God (6:15-16). Last of all in the charge to Timothy, Paul calls to mind the sovereign and majestic God. A clear vision of the true nature of God is a strong motivation for holy living and service for all Christians. Paul declares that God has ordered all events (v. 15), including the appearance of Christ. But what a God! The Greek makes it clear that Paul has actually inserted a doxology, which celebrates the majesty

---

ministry.

6:14 For the meaning of *without . . . blame (anepilēmptos),* see the discussion (at 1 Tim 3:2, 7 commentary) of the implications of the term *above reproach.*

The appearing is *epiphaneia,* a term with a significant religious history in the Hellenistic era. First used of kings (or gods) in a military context, in Hellenistic Judaism through the influence of the Old Testament tradition it came to be used in reference to the one God of the Jews who intervened in history in behalf of his people (2 Macc 3:24; 5:24; 12:22; 14:15; 15:27; 3 Macc 2:9; 5:8, 51). See further Towner 1989:66-71.

and mystery of God, to describe the subject of the verb of execution *(bring about)* in verse 15. The force of Paul's artistry is to close the charge to God's servant in adoration and worship (compare 1:17).

The God whom Christians serve is *the blessed and only Ruler.* This description comes out of intertestamental Judaism. God's oneness and sovereignty (*Ruler* means "sovereign"), which might suggest transcendence and "otherness," are balanced by the blessing he intimately bestows on his people. The phrases *King of kings* and *Lord of lords* ascribe to God absolute sovereignty. This powerful combination appears in Revelation 17:14 and 19:16 in reference to Christ.

Majesty gives way to mystery in verse 16 as the doxology next declares God to be "the only one having immortality" (1:17). The meaning is that God is the source of eternal life, that life which is proper to him alone, which he has chosen to bestow on others. His dwelling place is *unapproachable light* (Ex 24:15-17; 34:29-35; 1 Jn 1:5-7), which speaks symbolically of his absolute holiness. The mystery becomes complete in the reference to his "invisibility" (1:17). The actual phrase, *whom no one has seen or can see,* recalls God's response to Moses, who in preparation for leading God's people requested to see God: "no one may see me and live" (Ex 33:20). Still, enough was shown to Moses to carry him through in confidence.

Finally, the doxology closes in praise, ascribing *honor and might forever* to the sovereign God (Rev 5:13). In the end, God's servants must set their concentration upon the invincible God. Turning the thought to praise, Paul reminds his readers that Christian life and ministry together form the appropriate response to the blessing of God.

□ Instructions Concerning the Wealthy (6:17-19)

Never has the disparity in the distribution of wealth in the world been so evident as in modern times. It is not simply that most of the wealth is in the hands of a few. In the Western world salaries and disposable income have escalated across the board. The sad truth is that the relative wealth of Christians in the West does not seem to have affected the

---

6:15 For *only Ruler* see Sirach 46:5; 2 Maccabees 12:15. For *blessed* see 1 Timothy 1:11; Philo *Special Laws* 1. 209; Josephus *Antiquities* 10. 278.

6:16 *Light* implies the absence of sin (1 Jn 1:5-7).

conditions of needy Christians in other parts of the world.

Paul's readers also knew economic disparity. The Ephesian church consisted of slaves, poor widows, well-to-do women and householders, and some of these could be categorized as "the rich." To the latter Paul has left important instructions. They come at the end of the letter because of the preceding discussion about the false teachers' greed. He has written already of the dangers of wealth. Now his concern is for the spiritual state of wealthy believers. He focuses on the responsibility and proper attitude toward wealth that comes from a proper understanding of God.

Object of Hope (6:17) Christians must not put their hope in this world's wealth. Money in this world means power and security. Those who have it often rely upon it. Arrogance or pride is a warning sign that one is taking oneself or one's wealth too seriously. With the way the world looks up to the affluent, it is easy to believe the illusion it projects and trust in one's accomplishments or acquisitions. But there is great danger in this. First, *hope in wealth* undermines trust in God. There is no clearer statement of this truth than Jesus' words: "You cannot serve both God and Money" (Mt 6:24). Reliance on material goods or worldly status is antithetical to reliance on God.

Second, the wealth of this world is *uncertain.* Today's gains are tomorrow's losses. Even on the best of days, the value of this world's wealth is extremely limited; it pertains only to *this present world* (v. 19).

We can avoid this danger only by being properly oriented to God. Paul defines this orientation as *hope in God.* How can the rich believer hold on to God in this way? It can only be done by recognizing that one's wealth has come from God (2 Cor 8:15). Gifts from God are things to be "enjoyed," for Paul states clearly that God gives *richly* for this reason. But the gift is not to be confused with the Giver; it is rather to point the recipient back again to hope in God. Hope, which acknowledges the Giver, releases the recipient of the gift to "enjoy" or make use of it in ways that mirror the divine Giver.

Responsibilities to Others (6:18) The sentence continues in the

---

Paul uses four forms of the word "wealth" (the *rich [plousios], wealth [ploutos], richly [plousiōs], to be rich [plouteō])* in these two verses to define true wealth as that which has eternal value.

Greek as the thought now turns to the observable lifestyle of the wealthy. First Paul calls them to service, much as he does any believer. *To do good,* as Paul quickly translates into their vernacular, is to be *rich in good deeds.* The two expressions are equivalent, each describing the observable out-working of genuine faith (2:10; 5:10). The readers are to strive to amass spiritual wealth, and as the command continues, it is clear that they are to put their material wealth to use in this effort.

Their material blessing involves a special responsibility. For them, the normal Christian life of good works must include practical expressions of generosity and the willingness to share. The principle of economic equality in the Christian community that Paul enunciated explicitly in 2 Corinthians 8:13-15 implicitly undergirds this instruction. Since all they possess has come from God (v. 17), the rich are to assume a healthy attitude of detachment toward their wealth and use it to help the needy. Paul envisions a stewardship of the world's goods, and those blessed with this wealth are to be responsible administrators of it (Lk 16:8-9).

Spiritual Benefits (6:19) This responsible use of wealth promises tremendous benefits. Paul first draws on Jesus' similar teaching in Matthew 6:20. But he goes a step further to incorporate into Jesus' teaching the actual use of material wealth in the process of "storing up treasure in heaven." For the continuation of the Greek sentence in verse 19 links the "laying up of treasure" immediately to generosity and willingness to share. Rather than evidence that Paul was more moderate than Jesus in this matter, we probably see instead Paul's practical application of the earlier principle.

When rich believers share, what they actually *lay up* (as if it were a treasure) is *a firm foundation for the coming age.* The building metaphor with the time reference communicates an important truth. Responsible living in this life is a necessary building block or stepping-stone to *the coming age.* For the rich, responsible use of wealth (sharing, giving) is evidence of genuine faith. In this way they "work out their salvation" in this age. This practical evidence of new life provides unshakable certainty that one's future hope is secure. Thus it becomes

---

6:19 Verner (1983:175; see also Hanson 1982:114) labors to show that "the author" regarded the wealthy as a privileged class. But the commands to the rich are just as sharp

possible for them to *take hold of the life that is truly life,* which is the same possibility held out to Timothy (the faithful minister, the faithful believer) in 6:12. It is true of each that responsible behavior is closely tied to realization of the Christian hope of eternal life. In the case of wealthy Christians, by exchanging temporary material wealth for spiritual wealth, they may exchange this fleeting life for eternal life.

□ Final Charge to Timothy (6:20-21)

At the close of the letter, Paul summarizes his instructions to Timothy in this personal appeal (which begins, literally, "O Timothy"). The language Paul uses sheds some additional light on the nature of Timothy's mission and the gravity of the situation.

Guard the Deposit (6:20) Paul has used special terminology to describe Timothy's task. First, what the NIV translates as *guard what has been entrusted to your care* is literally "guard the deposit." This phrase, which in the New Testament is limited to 1 and 2 Timothy, comes from a rather formal procedure (a "sacred trust") that was current in Greek, Roman and Jewish societies. One could securely pass some commodity to another party by entrusting it to an authorized agent. Some commentators interpret the "commodity" in this case to be Timothy's ministry as a whole. But as the contrast with the false teaching here and in 2 Timothy 1:13-14 suggests, it is more likely that Paul means "the faith" or "the gospel" that was under attack by false teachers.

Second, Paul's language emphasizes continuity. Timothy was to carry on with a mission given by Christ to the apostles much earlier (compare 1 Cor 15:1-3; 2 Tim 2:2). The gospel ministry is a single (though multifaceted) task with a single message, which is to be transmitted through the generations by servants whom God chooses (2 Tim 2:2).

Third, this task is a sacred one, as Paul's choice of "deposit" terminology confirms. God has planned that the evangelistic mission be executed by the proclamation of the gospel. The mission depends on the gospel message. Consequently, God's servants in each generation must *guard* it—that is, faithfully proclaim and protect it. The threat to the message

as those addressed to other groups in the church, and the sentiment parallels Paul's teaching in 2 Corinthians 8.

and the church's mission posed by the false teachers in Ephesus was Paul's main reason for writing.

The Danger of False Doctrine (6:20-21) The closing description of the heresy also sheds some additional light. Because of the dangers involved in the heresy, aptly illustrated in the lives of some prominent Christians who destroyed their faith (1:20; 2 Tim 2:17), Timothy must avoid it. *Turn away,* however, does not mean refrain from confrontation. Rather, this action represents the conscious decision not to become involved in or even contemplate the false doctrine.

Paul denounces it as *godless chatter*. Not only does it have nothing to do with God or godliness, but it is also foolish nonsense (1:6; 4:7). It may have been systematic, but in comparison with the "standard" gospel, and given the results it brought—argument, speculation, inconsistent behavior and so on—it was no more than profane nonsense.

But Paul's description reveals another clue to its nature. *Falsely called knowledge* is a reference to one of the errorists' catchwords, *gnōsis*. This was indeed a misnomer, for its message contradicted the gospel. One specific point of contradiction presents itself in their belief concerning the resurrection of believers (2 Tim 2:18). Their choice of the word *knowledge* to describe their doctrine is no sure connection to later Gnosticism. It does reveal, however, that what one "knew" rather than what one did determined one's spiritual status. From this came their negative view of the physical world (4:3) and other perversions of behavior. In correction Paul used another form of the word knowledge, *epignōsis*, in

---

6:20 The technical terms for the formal procedure are those that occur here: "guard" (*phylassō*), "the deposit" (*hē parathēkē*). See further Barclay 1975:160-61 and Towner 1989:124-26. More common terminology related to the passing on of Christian tradition occurs in 1 Corinthians 11:2; Galatians 1:14; 2 Thessalonians 2:15; 3:6. The earlier Pauline emphasis on "accepting" and "maintaining" the tradition (as reflected in the verbs in 1 Cor 11:2; 1 Cor 15:1; 2 Thess 2:15) changed, with the encroachment of the apostates and the apostle's imminent departure, to the concern to "transmit" the tradition "safely" to future generations.

See Fee 1988:161 for the view that "the deposit" is Timothy's whole ministry. But see also Guthrie 1957:118, Kelly 1963:150 and Dibelius and Conzelmann 1972:92.

For other examples in which the term *knowledge (gnōsis)* is linked to misconceived, enthusiastic doctrines, see 1 Corinthians 8:1, 7, 10, 11; 13:2, 8; compare 2 Corinthians 10:5; 11:6 (where Paul may adopt the term from the pneumatics' vocabulary). He also seems to have employed the compound word for *knowledge (epignōsis)* to counter a gnosis-concept of some sort in Colossians 2:3; 1:9-10; 2:12; 3:10 (see O'Brien 1982:21-22).

reference to "the" knowledge of God that affects all dimensions of human life (2:4; 4:3; 2 Tim 2:25; 3:7; Tit 1:1).

Finally, the false doctrine was also destructive. Paul alludes to *some* (1:20; 5:15) in the community who *professed* the new teaching and *wandered from the faith.* Paul's concern was not only for the church's mission but also for the salvation of individuals. Cults have always had various ways to attract new members. Those cults that make any use of the Bible inevitably twist its message, and Christians who are not well grounded in the faith can be taken in by an atmosphere of camaraderie or promises to give meaning to life. Whatever the trap, the victim is set to wandering off course, farther and farther into uncharted waters. This is a warning to all of God's servants, and for Christian leaders it is a motivation to more urgent service.

Closing Wish (6:21) In an abrupt closing, *grace be with you [all],* the apostle places Timothy and the entire community in God's loving care. As in the letter's opening greeting (1:2), *grace* signifies the whole of God's love and care for his people, coming to those who cannot earn it—an encouraging reminder that despite the awesome responsibility to pursue godliness in all parts of life, the Christian stands by *grace* alone. What Paul has said to Timothy and the Christian leaders he has said to all.

Outline of 2 Timothy

COMMENTARY

2 Timothy

□ Greeting (1:1-2)

The will of God and eternal life are concepts that seem to take on much more meaning during periods of struggle. C. S. Lewis put it this way (1961:43):

> Bridge-players tell me that there must be some money on the game, "or else people won't take it seriously." Apparently, it's like that. Your bid—for God or no God, for a good God or the Cosmic Sadist, for eternal life or non-entity—will not be serious if nothing much is staked on it. And you will never discover how serious it was until the stakes are raised horribly high; until you find that you are not playing for counters or for sixpences but for every penny you have in the world. Nothing less will shake a man—or at any rate a man like me— out of his merely verbal thinking and his merely notional beliefs. He has to be knocked silly before he comes to his senses. Only torture will bring out the truth. Only under torture does he discover it himself.

The Christian will concentrate most on the mystery of God's will when life seems least to make sense. We cling to the promise of eternal life hardest when the life in our bodies can no longer be taken for granted.

The apostle Paul was not very much different from us. Second Timothy 4 reflects hard thought about these matters. When the stakes were at their highest, the personal importance for Paul of these eternal realities found very clear expression. Even if he had received answers to his hard questions about life and death, they did not come without struggle. The

apostle's eternal outlook, which culminates in chapter 4, has its beginning in the greeting of verses 1-2, which is very close in form to
1 Timothy 1:1-2.

The circumstances that Paul faced as he wrote this second letter to
Timothy have changed from those of the first. He was mobile when he
wrote 1 Timothy and apparently expected to continue to be so (1 Tim
3:14-15). However, 2 Timothy has a Roman orientation (1:17): Paul is
in prison, resigned to the end of his ministry and life there (see introduction).

The different purposes of 1 and 2 Timothy may also reflect changes
in the circumstances of Timothy. First Timothy is almost wholly devoted
to opposing the false teachers in Ephesus and to organizing the church
to that end. Second Timothy remains interested in the false teachers and
their influence, but this interest is registered in a more general way, and
the context is now the church in a broader sense (2:19-20; 3:1-4), even
though the heretics mentioned (2:17) are those associated with the
Ephesian church. The greater interest is in Timothy's own spiritual condition, which needs attention. As we will see, the battle with heresy
provides a background that helps to illuminate Timothy's present condition, and here the contact with 1 Timothy (in the individual heretics
who are named) may allow the explanation that 1 Timothy is the background of 2 Timothy.

On the assumption that Timothy was still in Ephesus, it may be that
1 Timothy failed to achieve its purpose, that Timothy and the church
there took an awful beating and were still under the same attack. However, since the only reference to Ephesus in 2 Timothy (1:18) is a rem-
iniscence (which does not necessarily place Timothy there but does—
in view of 2:17—at least suggest a connection), it may be instead that
Timothy has moved on to other parts of Asia Minor. If we assume that
the excommunication of the key figures in the heresy (1 Tim 1:20)
removed them from Ephesus, but that this measure failed to produce
their repentance (2 Tim 2:17), then perhaps we might also assume that
2 Timothy records something of the spread of their poisonous influence
(2:17) to churches beyond Ephesus.

The Sender (1:1) Paul addresses Timothy again as *an apostle of
Christ Jesus.* This is a reminder to Timothy (and other readers; see on

4:22) of Paul's authority in view of the instructions to come. Moreover, this is no self-styled designation, for Paul's position and authority were conferred *by the will of God* (see 1 Cor 1:1; 2 Cor 1:1; Eph 1:1; Col 1:1). The next phrase introduces the purpose or goal of Paul's apostolic ministry: *the promise of life that is in Christ Jesus.* It is the good news of that promise that he has sought to bring to the world through preaching. At the moment of writing, Paul in his circumstances probably thinks of "life" (eternal) as something yet to be fully obtained—thus the reference to a *promise* (compare 1 Tim 6:19). Elsewhere he focuses more on the Christian's present experience of eternal life (1 Tim 4:8). The main purpose of the gospel is to introduce people to the possibility of new life. Such a possibility is a compelling reason to persevere in ministry and a powerful source of personal encouragement and hope.

The Recipient (1:2) As suggested above, in one respect Timothy's circumstances have also changed; in another, unfortunately, they remain stubbornly unchanged or have worsened. I have proposed as a reasonable scenario that at this point he is no longer located specifically in Ephesus and is working more widely in Asia Minor. But the local heretical movement he was first left to deal with in Ephesus has not been stopped. After expulsion from the Ephesian church, certain ringleaders have perhaps taken their show on the road. To judge from the exhortation that follows, it is possible that Timothy has decided this has become a futile fight; he may have chosen to assume a lower profile in his ministry or even to step out of it altogether.

But these developments are already in mind as Paul addresses Timothy in a very personal tone as "my beloved child." There is no concern here to emphasize Timothy's approved status (as in 1 Tim 1:2). Rather, Paul addresses Timothy intimately in a way that creates an atmosphere of mutual devotion and love for the encouragement and instructions that will follow (see notes on 1 Tim 1:2).

The Blessing (1:2) The blessing is an exact replica of 1 Timothy 1:2. It amounts to a promise or prayer that all Timothy or any believer needs to accomplish God's work is fully available in God (see on 1 Tim 1:2).

☐ Opening Charge to Timothy (1:3-18)

Second Timothy takes the form of a personal letter of admonition. At points its purpose and tone give it the feeling of a last will and testament. Paul bequeaths to Timothy a ministry, Paul's own. His protégé is now to summon up courage and commitment to complete the task, and Paul attempts this encouragement from several important angles. Second Timothy is intensely personal, more so than 1 Timothy, even though some of the subject matter overlaps. First Timothy's structure moves back and forth between instructions to Timothy, teaching to the whole church and denunciation of the false teachers. Here the focus is almost entirely on Timothy, though we will see that his approach to false teachers is again no small matter. Of course, teaching to Timothy is teaching to be applied by the congregations in which he works, just as it is teaching to be applied by us today in our own situations.

Thanksgiving (1:3-5) It was typical of letters in Paul's day to include a section in the beginning which expressed hopes of blessing and welfare for the recipient. Paul put this into the form of prayers of thanksgiving for the churches to whom he wrote. A careful look at these sections of his letters (including this one) reveals that Paul's point was to call his readers to remembrance of their unique mutual relationship and to certain spiritual realities in the lives of those Christians. Why? Later in the letters he develops these realities into themes. He encourages believers (1) to take stock of what they have received in Christ (things for which Paul is thankful in their behalf) and therefore (2) to implement these things in their individual and corporate lives. It is Paul's method of encouraging Christians to "become what you are," as well as a subtle reminder that it is the Christian's obligation to respond to God's grace in this way.

We have all at one time or another felt the influence of important people in our lives. We have also felt a sense of responsibility to act according to that influence. Influence of this kind might be misused to manipulate, but it also has a positive use. Paul's recollection of the

---

Notes: 1:3-18 The popular modern argument that 2 Timothy belongs to the category of ancient "testamentary" literature, and so should be regarded as pseudo-Pauline, is not very likely. The contents and literary devices found in 2 Timothy indicate closer kinship to a personal letter of admonition (see Johnson 1987:13-14; Prior 1989:13-24).

1:3 As Paul insists on his "clear conscience," the issue uppermost in his mind may be

relationship he shares with Timothy is meant first to signal his confidence in Timothy, despite setbacks and perhaps even the withdrawal of Timothy from the ministry. But once that confidence is communicated, Timothy is to respond to certain obligations connected with his call to join the apostle's work.

Paul is interested here in heritage. Verse 3 describes his service to God as the proper outgrowth of the service of God's people (his *forefathers;* compare Acts 22:3-5; Phil 3:5-7) before Christ came. This and the insistence on his *clear conscience* (see on 1 Tim 1:5; 4:2) are aimed at contrasting his apostleship and message with the claims of the false teachers, who badly misinterpreted the Old Testament and perverted the gospel, and whose consciences were ineffective guides to behavior. It is to Paul's heritage that Timothy (and all Christians) can and must lay claim.

Verses 4 and 5 provide a glimpse of special relationships that influenced Timothy and truly bound him to continued service. Paul drew real joy from Timothy, as Timothy undoubtedly did from Paul. This intimate relationship with the apostle was one of the instruments by which Timothy gained a place in the line of redemption just mentioned. The *tears* shed by Timothy may well have been tears of frustration and fear caused by his inability to resolve the problems created by the opponents in Ephesus. Timothy's *faith* also stemmed in part from the faith of his family members (Lois and Eunice). Their faith was not contaminated by the false teaching (see on 1 Tim 1:5). The heritage of genuine faith and the special relationships through which it was transmitted to Timothy were recalled to restore his confidence. But they also called to mind a responsibility (to continue in the faith, to persevere in ministry) that he could not walk away from. No matter how bitter the opposition, he could not deny his heritage.

When times are tough we may almost wish we could deny the people and events that brought us to genuine faith in Christ. In fact, we may be tempted in the face of hard circumstances to view it all as some psycho-

---

his adherence to the orthodox teaching of resurrection, which in the Acts accounts he links to the biblical tradition or redemptive history (23:1; 24:16), and which was being denied by opponents in Ephesus (and Asia Minor) as it had been in Corinth (2 Tim 2:18; 1 Cor 15:12; see further introduction).

logical fantasy. At such times a look back at the godly people who have influenced us and at the duties that go with our spiritual heritage may provide a stabilizing perspective.

The Gift of the Spirit (1:6-14) The reminder to Timothy which follows begins and ends with the Spirit. It is this fundamental gift from God that Paul associates with Timothy's ministry. But we must pause to ask what called forth this reminder.

Misunderstandings About the Spirit and Resurrection Verse 18 of chapter 2 identifies clearly what was probably the central doctrine of the false teaching—the belief *that the resurrection has already taken place*—and it almost certainly implies a related view about the Holy Spirit. This belief in a "realized" resurrection could conceivably have grown out of a misunderstanding of Paul's own teaching about the believer's present participation in Christ's death and resurrection (Rom 6:1-11; see introduction), in which the role of the Spirit was central. Apparently the gift of the Holy Spirit came to be viewed as proof of one's resurrection, just as in Corinth (see introduction), rather than as the down payment guaranteeing future resurrection (Eph 1:13-14). And also similar to the Corinthian misunderstanding (1 Cor 15:12), the resurrection itself was held to pertain only to the spiritual side of humanity (the "flesh" and "body" belong to the material sphere, which is temporary), because of a dualistic understanding (current in their pagan religious environment) that accorded more importance to the spiritual dimension of life. A committed adherent's approach to life in this world tended to one of two extremes. Either life in the body became irrelevant in view of the attainment of spiritual perfection (apparently the Corinthian response—1 Cor 4:8; 5:1-2), or it was something to be severely restricted through ascetic practices so that the spiritual side could be kept pure (1 Tim 4:1-2; compare Tit 1:15).

In this context, Paul's teaching to Timothy about the importance of the Spirit for ministry introduces a challenge to the opponents' views about the Spirit. The crucial matter here is the effect of their view of the Spirit

---

1:6-7 View 1 is held by most; see Knight 1992:209, 370 and Fee 1988:226. For view 2 (p. 160), see especially the discussion in Fee forthcoming: chap. 11. For the view that the

on the church's understanding of Christian life and ministry in this world. For them (1) "Spirit" meant power in the sense of the completion of their spiritual life; (2) the gift of the Spirit at conversion meant transfer (resurrection) from this fallen world to a spiritual dimension of final triumph; and consequently (3) the Holy Spirit had very little to do with suffering and struggling, things that pertain to the physical, bodily existence. Suffering and struggling may have been viewed as indications of unspirituality.

The current teaching was much the same as what in our times has come to be called "triumphalism" and the "health and wealth gospel," the idea that faith in Christ promises immediate solutions to life's problems. These views are tough to overcome—it is much easier to hear that the gospel brings peace and rest than it is to be reminded of the "sword" and the opposition of the world that Jesus promised. Timothy had grown tired and discouraged at the resistance of the false teachers to a balanced biblical message and at the church's willingness to receive a sugar-coated message (4:3). He had grown weary of the struggle. The solution comes in the form of a reminder that the gift of the Holy Spirit means power for the Christian struggle, not removal from it.

Relying on the Holy Spirit (1:6-7) To have a gift and to put it to use are two different things. In verses 6 and 7 Paul continues (*for this reason*, v. 6) his encouragement of Timothy now in relation to *the gift of God*. This description of the gift and the means by which it came to Timothy (*through the laying on of my hands*) have led to different interpretations.

A first view takes this passage in close connection with 1 Timothy 4:14, which also mentions a gift related to the laying on of hands—in that instance, the elders' hands. The gift in each case is understood as a special gift for ministry, and the laying on of hands as a reference back to the time of Timothy's commissioning, at which time the elders and Paul, by laying on hands and prophesying, acknowledged Timothy to be one set apart (and appropriately gifted) by God (see on 1 Tim 1:18; 4:14). Paul's more personal recollection of the same event in 2 Timothy

---

passage witnesses to a post-Pauline understanding of ordination, through which the minister receives the gift necessary to minister, see Hanson 1982:121.

simply reflects the tone of the letter.

While this is certainly a possible explanation, a second view seems more probable in view of the immediate context and the background of the letter. In this case, *the gift of God* in verse 6, which Timothy is to rekindle, is the Holy Spirit himself, and this passage and 1 Timothy 4:14 do not necessarily reflect on the same event. First, if verse 7 is explaining verse 6 as the connecting *for* suggests, it is the Spirit to which Paul refers (see below). Second, a reference to the Spirit at the outset of this exhortation balances well with the closing emphasis on *the help of the Holy Spirit who lives in us* (v. 14). Third, to judge from 1 Thessalonians 5:19, Paul was apt to employ the imagery of fire to describe the Holy Spirit: there the Spirit could be "put out"; here he is to be "fanned into flame" (compare Mt 3:11 par; Acts 2:3). Finally, given what were the false teachers' probable misconceptions about the Holy Spirit, a reference to this fundamental gift as the source of courage and stamina for continuing the messy struggle of the faith would serve as an encouraging reminder to Timothy and a correction of the false doctrine. It is also in keeping with this context for Paul to follow a reference to Timothy's genuine faith with a reminder about the corollary gift of the Spirit (and his role) in his life. If the statement that the Holy Spirit came to Timothy via Paul's hands sounds strange, we might recall that Timothy came to faith during the apostolic ministry through which (at least in certain cases) this very thing occurred (see Acts 8:17-18; 9:12, 17; 19:6).

Discouragement and withdrawal from the struggle of ministry marked a failure to rely on the Holy Spirit's enabling power. A fresh look at the resources he brings to the believer is meant to encourage daily dependence on him. What God has given, according to verse 7, is not to be understood in the sense of contrasting attitudes, dispositions or abilities (so the NIV's *a spirit*). Rather, as a comparison with Romans 8:15 suggests, the "not-but" contrast underlines the marks of possession of the Holy Spirit.

First, the Spirit supplies *power*. On the one hand, this means the undoing of *timidity* (though "cowardice in battle" is the more likely

---

1:7 On *self-discipline* see the discussion at 1 Timothy 3:2.
1:8 The best study on crucifixion is Hengel 1977. On the concept of shame in the early

meaning). One important application of the Spirit's *power,* as in the case of Timothy, is in preaching the gospel (see 1 Cor 2:4-5; 4:19-21) in the face of immense opposition. But it is the same *power* in the life of the believer that enables holy living (Rom 14:17-18).

Second, the Spirit produces *love.* Primarily in view here is the observable counterpart to personal faith in Christ. In the New Testament *love,* much more than a feeling, takes the tangible form of service done to others in the power of the Spirit (Gal 5:6, 22-23; see notes on 1 Tim 2:15). This mark of the Spirit was indispensable for Timothy's ministry, since it would lead some to repentance (2:22-26).

Third, the Spirit produces *self-discipline.* The Greek word-group to which this term belongs plays a significant part in Paul's description of genuine Christianity in the Pastorals, and it was dominant in secular ethical teaching of that time. It is a hard term to pin down, for its meaning covers a range including prudence, moderation, discretion and self-discipline. While Titus 2:12 declares that this aspect of the life of faith was made possible by the appearance of Christ, 2 Timothy 1:7 completes the thought by linking it to the gift of the Spirit. Paul has in mind a measure of control over one's thinking and actions that allows a balanced outlook on any situation. When everything is coming unglued, this quality of "levelheadedness" will keep the Christian focused calmly on the power and love that the Spirit provides, and so it makes perseverance in life and ministry possible.

Timothy was in need of recalling and appropriating all that the Holy Spirit makes available to believers. The human part in this involves the decision to submit to the Spirit, to live in reliance on his power (Gal 5:16, 18, 25). Circumstances often succeed at diverting the Christian's attention from this truth. We would do well, like Timothy, to recall it daily.

The Holy Spirit and the Gospel (1:8-12) Paul now applies his teaching on the Holy Spirit to one specific aspect of the Christian life, ministry. And it is absolutely vital that we hear the note he sounds.

The call to suffering (1:8). Verse 8 contains a prohibition and a pos-

church see Malina 1981:44-47.

itive instruction which cannot be separated. On the one hand, the temptation Timothy faces is to take the course of least resistance, which means in the face of opposition to keep quiet about the gospel. This in Paul's mind is to *be ashamed*, which in that culture meant to regard someone (or the message about someone) as scandalous, having a dishonorable reputation. It might seem incredible that anyone would view Jesus in this way. But for both Jews and Gentiles, crucifixion (a penalty reserved for the worst criminals) was the supreme emblem of shame and dishonor. So failure to identify fully with the crucified One and the message about him was to *be ashamed* of him (compare Rom 1:16). Failure to identify openly with Paul, who suffered imprisonment in Rome for his faithfulness to the message about Christ, also amounted to shame for the gospel. However, the added dimension of opposition by false teachers suggests that the issue here is not simply Timothy's reluctance to proclaim the crucifixion of Christ but his reluctance to preach the gospel Paul endorsed, because its "limited," traditional notions about the Holy Spirit and the resurrection of believers were being ridiculed by the opponents as unspiritual, insufficient or outmoded. In any case, to withdraw from battle in this way is simply not consistent with the Spirit Timothy possesses. *So* (because of the power and courage of the Holy Spirit) Paul urges him to continue in bold service. There is no middle ground offered.

Verse 8 describes ministry as *suffering*. First, it may lighten the heart somewhat to recall that Jesus promised this from the start (Mt 5:11-12; Mk 13:5-23; Jn 15:18-20). Then we should also note that suffering for the gospel is not something to be endured in solitude—Timothy is called to "suffer together [with Paul] for the gospel." What is unbearable alone is something to take pride in and draw strength from in fellowship with other believers (Acts 5:41; 1 Cor 12:26). Third, this suffering is to be undergone not in human strength but rather *by the power of God*. This is power provided by the Holy Spirit (1:7).

The connections are clear. The Holy Spirit is the ground of all ministry; therefore this call to renew the struggle begins and ends with the ena-

---

1:9-10 See Paul's use of the formula in Romans 16:25; Ephesians 3:4-7, 8-11; Colossians 1:26-27.

1:9 While the New Testament development of God's calling of "the elect" to faith retains

blement and staying power he provides. Second, the gift of the Holy Spirit is linked expressly to suffering, struggling, and what he provides for the believer is what is needed to keep one persevering in the midst of trials that come because of faith—not removal to some higher plane. This view of the Spirit was quite different from that of the enthusiasts that Timothy and Paul faced. It is also an understanding quite different from that held by those in our churches who equate "spiritual" Christianity with the immediate resolution of life's difficulties. Paul's view is the correct one; the other is escapist fantasy covered over with a thin coat of "spiritual" paint.

The gospel that requires suffering (1:9-10). What is this message that demands so much from a Christian? In verses 9 and 10, which continue the sentence begun in verse 8, Paul inserts a piece of a hymn or early creed in explanation of *the gospel* and the God who made its promises (see on 1 Tim 3:16).

First, the gospel is the message about a God *who has saved us and called us* to a new mode of living. The past tense is not incidental. Because of what God accomplished in Christ (see below), salvation, the rescue from the judgment and eternal death we deserve, is a fact. Moreover, God himself has drawn *(called—*Rom 8:28, 30) us to participate personally in this fact. One thing we should not miss in this description is that a relationship is in view. God took the active role because he wants us to be related to himself. Salvation, the fact of rescue, is to find practical expression among God's people *(us)* in the form of *a holy life* (see 2:21 commentary), a lifestyle that is visibly different. It is a life lived in close relationship with God.

Second, the gospel is the message about a gracious gift. Legalism and human effort cannot obtain this gift. God is the initiator *(his own purpose)*, and his grace, mercy and love are fully in view (compare Tit 3:5). This more than anything captures the meaning of the gospel. It is a message declaring that God alone decided to do for us what we can never do—bring us into right relationship with himself.

Third, the gospel is the message about *Christ Jesus*. If the information

the dimension of human response (Mt 22:14; Rom 10:13-15; Eph 1:11-13), it nevertheless places the whole sequence of events (calling/proclamation, hearing with understanding/response) within the domain of God's sovereign will (Rom 8:28-30; 11:29).

that this gift *was given us in Christ Jesus* seems remedial, we should remember that the false teachers had taken their eyes off Christ. It is the gospel about him that saves, not a message of instant release from this life's worries through fullness of the Spirit. It is in Christ's work on the cross that the new life became a possibility for us.

Fourth, the gospel speaks of a salvation that is certain, grounded in God's will and already executed in history. The transition from verse 9 to 10 is a kind of formula: *before the beginning of time, but . . . now* (Tit 1:2-3). Paul uses this formula to emphasize that what had formerly been conceived in the mind of God has *now*—that is, in this age—become reality. The historicity of the cross and resurrection constitutes our guarantee that God has applied his solution to the human dilemma. A corollary of this is that salvation belongs to the present—it must be taken hold of *now* and proclaimed *now* (2 Cor 6:1-2)—even if our full enjoyment must await Christ's return. In fact, the "epiphany" language that Paul uses here to describe Christ's *appearing* in history, as he does elsewhere to refer to the Second Coming (4:1, 8; see on 1 Tim 6:14; Tit 2:11, 14), reminds the readers of the need for his return and of the fact that we now live between these two poles, in an age of unfinished tension.

Fifth, the gospel proclaims the ultimate solution, the end of death and the beginning of eternal life. But in contrast to the false teaching (2 Tim 2:18), the resurrection to which verse 10 refers has so far been experienced only by Christ. His experience is our guarantee of the future inheritance. As for us, Paul has said in 1 Corinthians 15:55-56 that death has yet to be finally vanquished. Our present life in Christ is only a foretaste of what is to come (Phil 3:10). At this point, when thinking about resurrection, our thoughts must be centered on Christ's past, historical resurrection and his future return. We have not yet been released from the world as he has been.

Finally, the gospel is the means of extending salvation to the world today. Paul appends the phrase *through the gospel* to the end of verse 10 to make this point (see on Tit 1:3). The message about God's promises,

---

1:12 Those in favor of the first view include Fee (1988:232), Hendriksen (1965:235), Lock (1924:88), Barclay (1975:175) and Knight (1992:380); those in favor of the second

Christ's history and our certain future hope is the means to save people now.

This piece of tradition cannot possibly describe the whole glory of the gospel. Yet in connection with verse 8, Paul's material has made one thing clear: In light of what God has done for us, complete devotion to his mission, even to the point of suffering, is our only reasonable response.

Paul's model of suffering (1:11-12). As he has done elsewhere (1 Tim 1:11-16; 2:7), Paul verifies his teaching by submitting his own experience as proof. Since his Damascus Road encounter with the Lord, Paul has been commissioned to serve the gospel. Verse 11 uses the same three categories as 1 Timothy 2:7 to describe Paul's commission in relation to the gospel: *herald, apostle, teacher. Herald* and *teacher* probably distinguish between the activities of evangelistic proclaiming and instructing the church (4:2). *Apostle* focuses on authority; Paul was selected and sent by Christ himself (see on 1 Tim 1:1, 11). This appointment, verse 12 continues, is the reason for his imprisonment in Rome.

Despite the scandal of the cross in that society, despite imprisonment, despite bitter opposition from false teachers, Paul is *not ashamed* (see on v. 8). His confidence in God and his gospel is unshaken. But this is not simply due to his strength of character. First, as the context points out, he is convinced of the gospel's power to impart new life (vv. 9-10; Rom 1:16).

Second, in his personal relationship with God (or Christ; the reference to *whom* is uncertain) Paul has come to know One who is fully trustworthy and capable. Verses 9 and 10 provide a glimpse of his understanding of God.

Third, that growing relationship and his ministry experience have taught Paul that God *is able.* This is generally true, but here Paul has one of two things in mind. As the NIV translates it, *he is able to guard what* Paul has *entrusted to him,* either his life or his ministry. Another view understands Paul to be saying that God will guard what he has entrusted to Paul: the authorized gospel or the *sound teaching* (v. 13). The crux

include Guthrie (1957:132), Kelly (1963:165-66), Stott (1973:46-47) and Barrett (1963:97).

of the matter is the Greek word meaning "deposit" (some commodity that has been entrusted into another person's care) with a form of "me" added, which means either "what has been entrusted *to me*" or "what *I* have entrusted [to him]." In verse 14 below and in 1 Timothy 6:20, the *deposit* and the verb *guard* describe Timothy's responsibility to keep the gospel pure. If the same verb and noun in verse 12 have the same meaning, then Paul is probably alluding to the enablement of the Spirit (v. 14) for the task of preserving the gospel, and that will ensure Paul's reward on *that day* (see 4:1-8).

Although certainty is not possible, since Paul is giving a model for Timothy to follow in ministry, a personal testimony about Paul's experience of God's enabling power would be fitting as a lead-in to verse 14's explicit statement (see also the recurring theme of the persistence of God's Word despite attacks on it or on his servants—2:9, 19; 3:10-17; 4:1-8, 16-17). In either case, he has in view the final judgment that will occur on *that day,* the day of Christ's return (see below on 4:1).

Summary Charge to Timothy (1:13-14) Paul closes this section as he began, with an exhortation to Timothy. In these two verses the two commands *(keep, guard),* the two objects of concern *(the pattern of sound teaching, the good deposit that was entrusted to you)* and the source from which these things came to Timothy—namely, Paul (implied in v. 14)—are set out in parallel fashion. When they are set together in this way, we can see Paul's main concerns for Timothy.

First, Timothy is to preserve and transmit (see 2:2) the apostolic message. The phrase *sound teaching* reflects both its purity and its health-producing elements (see on 1 Tim 1:10) and makes an implicit reference to the danger of false teachers. Paul's "guard the deposit" terminology gives to this task critical and sacred dimensions (see on 1 Tim 6:20-21). This and only this commodity gives life, so each generation of God's people must guard it until the mission has been completed.

Second, again with the false teachers' attacks in view, Paul emphasizes the apostolic shape or stamp that the approved message must bear. It is the *pattern* given by Paul, the *deposit* entrusted by Paul.

1:13 The term translated *pattern (hypotypōsis;* 1 Tim 1:16) carries the idea of "standard," "model" or even "outline." The apostle's message, and not that of any competitor, was to

Third, the message is to have a practical effect on the life of the bearer. The phrase *with faith and love [which are] in Christ Jesus* that ends verse 13 is a near replica of 1 Timothy 1:14. It describes the source of genuine Christianity (Christ Jesus) and the invisible and visible dimensions essential to it (see notes on 1 Tim 2:15). The point: the life of the message bearer must reflect a genuine, balanced relationship with Christ.

Fourth, the task must be carried out in full reliance on the Holy Spirit. The starting point in Paul's encouragement of Timothy to rejoin the work (1:6) is also his conclusion. The "indwelling" of the Spirit is not only the mark of true belief (Rom 8:11; 1 Cor 3:16; 6:19; 2 Tim 1:6-7) but also the only source of enablement for the Christian's life and ministry (Rom 14:17; 1 Cor 2:10-16; 2 Cor 10:1-6; Gal 3:3).

What Paul calls Timothy to engage in is not a contest that he will necessarily see won. He will see victories, but only with great and steady opposition. This is what drove the younger worker underground. Continuing the work is essential to God's plan, but so is the suffering of his servants. The message that saves and the grace of God it announces are worth the suffering, and the Spirit has been given to provide strength to persevere.

Examples of Unfaithfulness and Faithfulness (1:15-18) Continuing the opposing themes of desertion and unashamedness, this passage of personal notes and recollections should not be passed over lightly. With them the apostle illustrates very tangibly the two possibilities that face a Christian (see also on 4:9-13).

Desertion: The Way of Unfaithfulness (1:15) The apostasy from the faith that Paul first encountered in Ephesus seems to have spread while he was imprisoned in Rome. The expulsion of certain ringleaders (1 Tim 1:20) apparently did not produce their repentance (2 Tim 2:17). Instead, they may have taken their teaching beyond Ephesus to churches throughout Asia Minor in the time between the writing of 1 and 2 Timothy. Furthermore, given their triumphalist view of the Holy Spirit, the imprisonment of Paul might have been used to demonstrate to their

---

be considered the authoritative "standard" for the church (compare Gal 1:6-9).

listeners the eclipse of Paul's ministry. To continue to side with Paul was to side with a "loser." In any case, Paul's *everyone in the province of Asia has deserted me* indicates how drastically the tide had turned. Two individuals are singled out, as in 2 Timothy 2:18 and 1 Timothy 1:20, which means not only that Timothy knew of them but also probably that they were leaders in the churches. Perhaps it is hard to imagine Timothy joining this movement, but with the church's mission and the gospel at stake, to retreat from this battle when the spiritual resources to persevere were readily available was much the same thing.

The Way of Faithfulness (1:16-18) It was not too long ago that open association with the Christian church in Eastern Europe and the former Soviet Union meant severe persecution. In Islamic countries and provinces this still holds true (while the situation in China is hardly predictable from one day to the next). When the church is under fire, to give aid to an imprisoned pastor becomes a courageous act of faith. At one of the worst, most dangerous times for Christians, this is precisely what Onesiphorus did for Paul. The apostle was in prison in Rome in the time of Nero. By repeatedly visiting him at this time and giving aid, Onesiphorus identified himself closely with this enemy of the state and his illegal religion. It is certainly not exaggerating to say that this friend risked his life in order to help Paul. This is "unashamed" loyalty to the gospel.

Paul apparently had met Onesiphorus during his time in Ephesus. This may have been before or after the period that Timothy ministered alone there (see introduction), but it is clear that he distinguished himself as a faithful servant of the gospel (v. 18). To judge from Paul's blessing/ wish for him (*mercy from the Lord on that day*—v. 18), Onesiphorus may have died by the time Paul wrote, and if so, he may have died because of his association with Paul! One so loyal to the cause of Christ could surely hope to find mercy on the day of Christ's return and a just reward (4:8).

What is "unashamed" loyalty to the gospel today, in our situations? Association with the crucified One as with one rejected by God (the Jewish notion) or as with a despised enemy of the state (the Greco-Roman notion) may no longer bear the stigma it once did. But we learn from this instruction to Timothy that the faithful Christian will not shrink back from speaking up about Christ and his work. Loyalty to the Lord is measured in perseverance in the face of opposition. We also learn that all that is needed to be this kind of Christian is provided in the Holy Spirit. In view of the gift of the Spirit, the gospel record of all that God has done for us and the human models of faithfulness and loyalty, there is no excuse for halfhearted commitment to God. How do we react when challenged by friends, family, classmates, colleagues who ridicule the Christian message as anti-intellectual, old-fashioned, narrow-minded or sheer fantasy? Perhaps the church had more riding on Timothy than it does today on us. But in our personal walk with God, we, like Timothy and Onesiphorus, must decide ourselves to be loyal to Christ or ashamed of him.

☐ The Charge Repeated and Expanded (2:1-7)

In a vast world or a large church, feelings of insignificance are not unusual. We have all felt them from time to time, and we know how they can paralyze us. It may be an encouragement to be reminded that each Christian is meant to play an important role in the unfolding of God's plan of redemption. Second Timothy 2:1-7 is often reduced to a pattern for professional ministers. There is certainly a pattern here to be seen, and the Christian teacher is very much in view, but it applies to us all. Timothy (and all ministers) provides a model for us, not an excuse for lack of participation in spreading the good news.

Now Paul repeats his instructions to Timothy with some enlargement. Verses 1 and 2 explain in very down-to-earth language what "guarding the deposit" (1:14) really means, and both in terms of his "power" source and his ministry we stand in the same direct line to Paul that Timothy does. Verses 3-7 reveal that faithful service entails more than simply understanding and claiming the promises of God, as the focus shifts to personal characteristics of behavior and responsibility.

Links in the Chain of Ministry (2:1-2) Let us begin with Paul's description of this work. First, it involves a commodity, *the things you have heard me say in the presence of many witnesses.* Paul means the gospel, or, more broadly, the apostolic teaching that God charged him to proclaim and teach. This is the same body of material ("the good deposit") that Timothy is instructed to "guard" in 1:14. It is unchanging, yet it is dynamic rather than static, for it produces life and must be applied in fresh ways in each generation. Attempts to amend or revise its message, such as Timothy faced, must be resisted, because God's Word is a final word. For this reason God spoke through specially chosen servants (prophets, apostles, his Son) who together form a standard to measure the purity of the message in each generation. Paul himself was part of that standard, and what he taught Timothy had the approval of the apostles (Gal 2:2-10).

Second, Paul envisions a process *(entrust)*. This is the same word that occurs in 1:14, where Paul speaks of the good deposit "entrusted" to Timothy. Here we learn that guarding the deposit does not mean burying it somewhere safe. Rather, it means keeping an eye to its purity (protecting it from false teachers) as it is communicated. We also learn that Timothy, like every other minister and every other believer, is a link in the chain of redemption. Each believer has received the gospel as a stewardship. And it carries the obligation to pass it on similarly to others (1 Thess 1:6-8; 1 Pet 3:15). Through each believer the gospel may be spread far and wide in each generation. This part of the task begins in the home, where children may learn the Bible and how to live according to biblical principles taught and demonstrated by godly parents (Deut 6:7-9; Eph 6:4). It continues as mature Christian friends pass on what they have learned about godly living to friends who are younger in the faith. The church, through its teachers *(qualified to teach others)*, passes the faith from one generation on to the next, continuing the evangelistic mission.

Third, it involves faithful (reliable) people *(you . . . me . . . reliable men . . . others)*. Paul has used the term "faithful" to describe himself (1 Tim 1:12) and Christ (2 Tim 2:13). The term can cover the range of meaning from "believing" to "trustworthy" (1 Tim 1:15; 3:1; 4:9; 2 Tim 2:11) to "reliable"; it characterizes believers as people who have the marks of true faith in Christ. This quality was totally lacking in the false teachers. They could not be trusted with the task Paul speaks of here. What is needed are people who are fully dependable, whose commitment to God will carry them the distance. Such teachers will be able to accomplish the task of communicating and applying the faith in their generation and of preparing the next generation to continue. But "faithful" is what all believers should strive to be, in order that in small or large ways they can take their place in the chain of redemption.

Whether it is as a teacher or in some other capacity that we fit into this chain, we do well to remember how sacred a trust and how important a task is assigned to each link. "A chain is only as strong as its weakest link" applies to the process introduced here. And the Bible is filled with stories of human weakness. How can this process hope to succeed? The solution to our weakness is in verse 1, which repeats some very important advice to one of the links. *The grace that is in Christ Jesus* encompasses all that God freely gives to those who are "in Christ," believers. To *be strong* in this grace is to rely on strength that comes from the indwelling Holy Spirit (1:6-7, 14). This is strength for living the Christian life and for taking our place in the ministry. All that God requires of us he himself plans to accomplish through us.

The Fellowship of Suffering and Reward (2:3-7) But this does not reduce the importance of personal commitment and responsibility. Paul brings these aspects of service to mind through a command and a series of metaphors.

When it comes down to it, the choice to take one's place in the church's ministry is not to be made lightly. Paul returns to the theme of his initial appeal to Timothy (1:8) in verse 3: "join in suffering with us." It is specifically "suffering" for the gospel (the NIV's *endure hardship* is too vague), such as imprisonment in Paul's case, that is in mind, as the earlier identical command (1:8) and the related teaching below (2:8-13) confirm. His choice of language here—"suffer together with"—underlines again that the experience of suffering is a shared one (see on 1:8). Paul envisions a fellowship not just of those called to full-time ministry but of all who are called to be Christians (3:12; 1 Pet 2:20-21; 3:14, 17; 4:12-19).

The Soldier (2:3-4) But to serve Christ with this degree of commitment requires more than a one-time decision. It requires single-minded devotion and discipline. To illustrate this, Paul introduces the image of soldiering. Josephus, the Jewish historian of that time, described the Roman soldier thus:

Each soldier every day throws all his energy into his drill, as though he were in action. Hence that perfect ease with which they sustain the shock of battle: no confusion breaks their customary formation, no panic paralyzes, no fatigue exhausts them. All their camp duties are performed with the same discipline, the same regard for security: the procuring of wood, food-supplies, and water, as required—each party has its allotted task; nothing is done without a word of command. The same precision is maintained on the battlefield; nothing is done unadvisedly or left to chance. This perfect discipline makes the army an ornament of peace-time and in war welds the whole into a single body; so compact are their ranks, so alert their movements, so quick their ears for orders, their eyes for signals, their hands to act upon them. None are slower than they in succumbing to suffering. (*War* 3. 72-108)

Roman troops were a model of discipline, and because of that discipline, they were unbeatable. Such ideas were in Paul's mind when he chose the image of the soldier to describe the servant of Christ. Just as the duties of soldiering required freedom from entanglements of the world, so too does Christian service. And right here we come face to face with the dialectic or dilemma of Christian existence: to be in the world but not of the world. Clearly, the metaphor implies "separation," but this does not mean departure from the world. Attempts to create geographical distance from "the world," however well-intentioned, are neither practical nor biblical (1 Cor 5:10; 7:17-24). And the "separationist" policies of certain Christian groups who want nothing to do with churches outside of their orbit (let alone unbelievers) would seem to be in need of some reevaluation and revision.

What must be avoided is involvement in the world's ways and acceptance of the world's values, all of which subtly or overtly pose a challenge to the ways and values of biblical Christianity. But let us not be fooled into thinking this is an easy task. We face the same danger as the frog in the pan of slowly heating water. Unless we remain sharp in the faith,

---

Notes: 2:4 Dibelius and Conzelmann (1972:108) and Hanson (1982:129) understand *civilian affairs* to be "business affairs," but this is based on the assumption that the passage teaches mainly that ministers ought to be content with support received from the church and refrain from working outside the church.

constantly testing the thoughts and trends of the world about us against the revealed will of God, we too will slowly die. In all walks of life Christ (our *commanding officer*) is the priority. In every context we are to be living expressions of the new life in Christ (1 Thess 4:12). The discipline of a soldier is needed at each point, so that our eyes can remain focused on Christ and our ambitions set on pleasing him. This kind of discipline will lead us past the world's conflicts of interest and hold us firm in the face of the suffering that our nonconformity may well elicit (Rom 12:2).

The Athlete (2:5) Next Paul uses the picture of an athlete to depict the Christian. As in 1 Corinthians 9:25, the metaphor pictures the Christian life as a period of disciplined training in preparation for victory. To qualify to run in the Olympiad or Isthmian games, a contestant had first to complete the required period of training (ten months). *According to the rules* may well have this requirement in mind. If so, the Christian's "training period," the whole of life, includes suffering. As Barclay points out (1975:185), the original phrase behind *competes according to the rules* designated the professional in distinction from the amateur. In modern athletics what often separates the two when basic skills are nearly equal is dedication and determination. Thus again wholehearted, single-minded devotion to service is in mind, the kind that will carry one through times of suffering when the temptation to quit is very strong.

While we may not all be called to suffer to the same degree, this same devotion still has its place: it allows us to give ourselves to other people when we are tired (Mk 6:30-44), to pray when we do not feel like it, to continue to hope in God when the circumstances seem to be impossible.

As with the soldier who may please his commanding officer, the real possibility of victory is held out before us here. In the case of the Christian, *the victor's crown* and "the crown of righteousness" (4:8) are one and the same—Christ's ultimate approval on the day of judgment.

The Farmer (2:6) A third image, *the hardworking farmer,* describes the Christian life of service (v. 6). The point of this picture is to connect the promise of reward with diligent service. The priority of the farmer's

---

2:5 On the use of athletic imagery, see Pfitzner 1967:157-86; see also notes on 1 Timothy 6:12.

2:6 See Hanson 1982:130 for the view that the remuneration of church officials is in mind; see also Dibelius and Conzelmann 1972:108.

interest here *(the hardworking farmer should be the first)* and the *share of the crops* due to him suggest to some the idea of remuneration for the minister (compare 1 Tim 5:17). And Paul did employ similar analogies to address this issue in 1 Corinthians 9:7, 10. However, the dominant eschatological atmosphere in 2 Timothy (1:14, 18; 2:11-12; 4:1, 8, 18) suggests that here he is underlining the certainty of final rewards on "that day" for diligent and faithful service.

Reflection (2:7) Thus the three images reinforce the main command to persevere in suffering (v. 3). But Paul's teaching does not apply only to unusual circumstances. He portrays the normal Christian life. In fact, to judge from the New Testament, it is not the presence of struggle and suffering in the life of the Christian that ought to be questioned, but rather the absence of them. The images remind us that discipline, devotion and diligence all come into play in faithful Christian service. The strength to serve in this way comes from Christ (v. 1), but the images persistently sound the note of personal decision and commitment to the task. This is one of the reasons for the call for reflection in verse 7. The Christian must decide to be a soldier who will suffer, a well-trained athlete who will compete according to the rules, and a farmer who works diligently until potential becomes reality.

Of course, the other reason Timothy is to *reflect* on Paul's teaching is that it represents an adjustment to the false teachers' views, which were quickly gaining ground—they denied the role of suffering in Christian service, and qualities such as discipline, devotion and diligence necessary for prolonged struggle had little to do with their triumphalistic spirituality. Where do such qualities figure in our thinking? Both as to their correctness and as to their necessity, *the Lord will give insight.* So the strength to do and the understanding of what is to be done *will* (a promise, not a wish) come from God, but the decision to serve him rests with us.

□ Hope, Promise and Fulfillment (2:8-13)

Paul brings three things together in this section to close the call to

---

Notes: 2:8 Some regard this as a formula, cited here with no particular emphasis on either fact (Dibelius and Conzelmann 1972:108; Hanson 1982:130-31). Kelly (1963:177) sees the

suffering: a statement of the gospel, more personal testimony and a quotation from what may have been a baptismal liturgy. The section forms a theological basis or conclusion to the summons by establishing a focus on the gospel which places the present Christian experience in proper perspective. In keeping with the summons (all of 1:3—2:7), Paul seeks to reestablish the important place of suffering and struggle in this life and to balance this with a hope that is properly conceived. It is impossible to make sense of this section (or the whole summons) without being aware that it counters and corrects the false doctrine of escape from suffering and struggle by the gift of the Holy Spirit (see on 1:6). Yet the correction is equally important for us today. The "easy life" has long been a Western ideal. This kind of ideal and modern-day misunderstandings about the Holy Spirit leave us in need of a fresh look at the Pauline perspective on life in the Spirit.

Paul's Gospel (2:8) That this section forms a basis for the teaching that precedes is clear from the connecting imperative *remember*. Paul goes back to the basics to ground Timothy's thinking—a fresh statement of the elementary gospel. The first thing to notice is the content of this gospel presentation. It consists of a person, *Jesus Christ,* and two events, resurrection and incarnation or Davidic descent. While we might be surprised at what Paul has left out of this summary of the gospel (forgiveness of sins, salvation, eternal life and so on), what he has included probably spoke directly to Timothy's situation. What he has left implicit was well understood. The content is similar to that of Romans 1:2-4.

At this point only the meaning of *descended from David* calls for attention. Some regard the reference as an affirmation of the humanity of Christ (the Incarnation), included by Paul as a blow aimed at the Gnostic views of the false teachers, which denied Christ's humanity. But there is no evidence in 1 or 2 Timothy that they actually held such views. Fee (1988:246) may be correct that the phrase emphasizes the appearance of Jesus Christ as the fulfillment of God's promises. However, while not to minimize the importance in Paul's gospel of the Incarnation and the thought that the Messiah did come as planned through the Davidic

---

reference to resurrection as implying that, as for Christ, the pathway to glory includes death (suffering).

line, it is likely that in this context the first phrase is the more important one for the argument; the latter one either tagged along as an immovable part of the tradition or was deliberately retained to make the emphasis on resurrection clear.

The order of the sentence rivets the readers' attention on Jesus Christ and on his resurrection from the dead. A comparison with Romans 1:3-4 gives the impression that Paul has indeed inverted the more normal, chronological order of events (Davidic descent = Jesus' entrance into humanity, then resurrection). The reason for this adjustment may lie in the false teaching and in the view of the Christian life that Paul has been expounding and now seeks to ground. Verse 18 of this chapter shows that the high point in the false doctrine was the mistaken notion that believers have (by virtue of their possession of the Holy Spirit) already been resurrected from the dead (see on 1:6 and introduction). Disengagement from the struggles of this life and denial of any need to participate in suffering resulted. Paul calls Christians to set their focus on Jesus Christ. It is he who has been raised from the dead, not believers. He is still the "firstfruits" of the resurrection (1 Cor 15:23), the proof that God's promise is good. And our present-day participation in Christ's death and resurrection (Rom 6:1-11) does not mean removal from the sinful world, but it means power to continue the struggle in its midst with the potential to gain victory over sin. Paul calls Timothy (and all Christians) to reenter this struggle in the power of the Spirit. To concentrate on Jesus and his resurrection is to keep strong our hope in the future victory, so that the necessary present struggles do not overwhelm us.

Paul calls this *my gospel* (Rom 2:16; 16:25; compare 1 Cor 15:1; Gal 1:11; 2:2; 2 Cor 4:3; 1 Thess 1:5; 2 Thess 2:14). In so doing he claims not to be its author but rather one to whom it has been entrusted (an apostle) by Christ. The reminder of apostolic authority here is, however, intentional. Paul's view of things accords with Christ's, while opposing views do not (Gal 1:8).

Paul's Experience (2:9-10) The theological grounds for Christian suffering were more than theory for Paul. His own life experience testified to the reality of the resurrection of Christ and to the availability of resurrection power for engagement in the Christian struggle.

It is a hard thing for us to understand, but the cost of freedom may be a loss of freedom. The cost of discipleship is crucifixion. And it is God's plan that the church in some mysterious way bring to completion the sufferings of Christ (Col 1:24). Those who understand these truths best are those whose freedom or health has been seized from them because of the gospel. Wang Ming Dao, the Chinese Christian leader who died recently, spent more than twenty years in prison, much of it in solitary confinement, because of his stand for the gospel. He walked in the same footprints followed centuries earlier by Paul himself (1 Pet 2:19-21).

Officially, by virtue of his leadership role in an illegal religion (Christianity was not sanctioned by Rome), the apostle was an enemy of the state. It didn't help Paul that the fire which destroyed much of Rome at about that time was blamed on Christians (by Nero, to get out from under the blame himself). Paul knew that the price he was paying was part of his commitment to the gospel. And the message was well worth the price (see on 1:9-10).

But God's word is not chained have to be some of the most inspiring words spoken in history. God's people can be put away or killed, but his *word* cannot be stopped. He is its source; it is his living communication to the world. To imprison it or kill it would require imprisoning or killing God. Ironically, efforts to halt the spread of the message only caused the early church to grow (Acts 8:1, 4). Paul reported, "What has happened to me has really served to advance the gospel. . . . Because of my chains, most of the brothers in the Lord have been encouraged to speak the word of God more courageously and fearlessly" (Phil 1:12, 14). The growth of the church in China from the time of the communist takeover to the present, with even small portions of Scripture scarce, is equal proof of the power of God's Word.

Such truths sustained Paul in the hardest of times, but his compassion for people is what gave meaning to his experience of suffering. It was for *the elect,* those who would respond to God's calling through the gospel as well as those who already had (see on Tit 1:1). Paul's term *the elect* reflects more than anything the belief that God himself is sovereignly active in forming "a people for himself" (see Tit 1:1 [notes]; 2:14). This activity is carried out through the church as it proclaims the gospel and, as Paul did, bears faithful witness to the gospel as *God's word.*

There is another truth here. A Christian's life has an impact on others. That impact is meant to be positive and redemptive. Paul endured suffering that the church's evangelistic mission might continue to completion, that Christians like him, willing to continue the struggle for the sake of the gospel and for others who need to hear it, might come to faith and then maturity in Christ. If Paul, then Timothy; if Timothy, then us. We all have responsibilities to other people. Through the preaching of the gospel, and only through this means (1 Cor 1:21), people may come to know Christ Jesus, in whom alone is *salvation.* This is salvation from sin and its effects, God's rescue that results in eternal life. The final phrase describing salvation, *with eternal glory,* is not superfluous. On the one hand, it is the final goal of the Christian pilgrimage. It is also the hope that can bring the believer through the present necessary experience of struggle for the gospel. Glory, victory, resurrection and removal from troubles are all yet to be fully experienced.

Conditions of Faithfulness (2:11-13) The conditions that follow depict *salvation that is in Christ Jesus* as a life to be lived in a hostile world. This *trustworthy saying* is part of a hymn or baptismal creed that was well known and widely accepted in the church (see on 1 Tim 3:16). Its grave tone and conditional (if—then) form draw us to reflect on the importance of this life in relation to the life to come.

Throughout the saying (vv. 11-13), Paul alternates from the present life of faith to the future (eschatological) reward. The first condition, *if we died with him, we will also live with him,* recalls the words of Romans 6:8. In the earlier setting, the symbolic meaning of baptism is surely in view: through baptism one testifies to identification with Christ in his death and reception of the Spirit, and acknowledges the promise of

---

2:11 *Died with him* suggests to some the thought of martyrdom (Brox 1989:244; Jeremias 1975:55; compare Fee 1988:249), and with the thought of suffering dominant in the context, the baptismal commitment must be regarded as including the possibility of death for the faith. Still, the main thought is of a commitment to Christ that includes the willingness to undergo suffering for him; see Kelly 1963:179-80; Stott 1973:63.

2:12-13 The change in verb from "deny" (NIV *disown;* Greek *arneomai)* to *faithless (apisteō)* may signify that two different situations, the denial of unbelief (the hardened false teacher) and the unfaithfulness of a believer are in view, and verse 13 is thus understood to be a promise (see Knight 1992:405-7; Fee 1988:250-51). But another view is possible,

resurrection. In our passage, Paul probably extends the application of the original saying beyond the event of baptism to the entire Christian life. That is, a believer's life must be the living out of death to self for the sake of Christ and his gospel. *Died with him* depicts a life characterized by sacrifice that may (and must be ready to) end in martyrdom. But neither baptism nor martyrdom is exclusively in mind. The saying functions as an abbreviation of the life described above (1:5—2:7).

The reward for this life is resurrection. Here Paul is focusing mainly on the future promise, though it is equally true that for Paul that future promise has already begun to be fulfilled in the life of faith, in the form of power over sin and power to endure (Rom 6:6-7).

Verse 12 gives a slightly different reflection of the present Christian life and the future reward. Here faithful Christian living is "endurance," the same term Paul used to describe his life in verse 10 and an aspect of the normal life of faith in Titus 2:2. This is a description of the Christian response to struggle, and *endure* is often used when the task of communicating the gospel is in view (1 Tim 6:11; 2 Tim 2:10; 3:10). Thus faithfulness includes the decision to keep on struggling. The reward, which is clearly future and eschatological, is a share in Christ's dominion (1 Cor 4:8; Rev 3:21).

The tone changes dramatically in the last two lines of verse 12: *if we disown him, he will also disown us.* This warning has the treachery of apostasy in view. Both the *we* and the *us,* as well as the language of denial (1 Tim 5:8; 2 Tim 3:5; Tit 1:16), show that Paul is thinking of rejection of the faith by those who profess it. Not only actual false teaching but also a rejection of the call to endure give evidence of a decision to deny Christ. Jesus' own words may lie behind this warning: "whoever disowns me before men, I will disown him before my Father in heaven"

---

that "deny" and *faithless* are parallel, and that the lines *he will disown* and *he will remain faithful* are therefore also parallel, so that verse 13 strengthens the warning of v. 12 *(he will remain faithful* and so punish those who deny him, those who are faithless); see Stott 1973:64-65; Hendriksen 1965:259-60. This is a difficult problem to resolve, and the theological backgrounds of interpreters undoubtedly influence decisions. The question whether one can actually lose the gift of salvation is not so much in mind as is the question of what can happen to those who profess the faith, enjoy the benefits of the believing community and then prove to be false believers: Paul has in mind primarily the sin of apostasy, which for its treachery seems almost to be a special category of sin.

(Mt 10:33). In that context too faithfulness includes a willingness to suffer, struggle and die. Rejection by Christ means exclusion from eternal life.

While Paul does not go into the questions whether such apostates ever really "believed" in Christ or what constitutes unfaithfulness to the point of denial, verse 13 may sound a note of hope intended for the church that has experienced defection and perhaps for the individual who has experienced defeat: *if we are faithless, he will remain faithful.* The change from denial to *faithless* (or "unfaithfulness") marks a change in atmosphere (though the warning issued in verse 12 is no less real). With the corporate *we* still in view, Paul's point may be that no matter what, God's promise to save his people will not fail because some prove to be false. Or from a more personal point of view, it is possible that this is a promise that God will preserve even the weakest believer (Peter's restoration in Jn 21:15-19 comes to mind). God must keep his promises, for they are grounded in his own being and "he cannot deny himself."

This life of decision, sacrifice and struggle is the life of *salvation that is in Christ Jesus.* From the standpoint of our experience this salvation remains at the best of times in progress, unfinished; at the worst of times it is nearly invisible. Its completion involves our response, our commitment to endure what can only be called a struggle. The decision to withdraw from it carries grave consequences. The decision to press on in the power of the Spirit promises eternal glory, complete life and fellowship with Christ forever.

□ God's Worker in a Turbulent and Paradoxical Workplace (2:14—3:17)

Battle plans appear to be very reasonable and "doable" when viewed in the war room. For the Christian, the thought of struggling for God, maybe even to the point of suffering, may seem exciting in the safe environment of a worship gathering. But out there where the enemy may wear a disguise or may be overwhelming and relentless in opposition, where the war drags on, terms such as "struggle," "uncertainty" and "fatigue" take their place in the vocabulary of Christian life and service. This reality lies behind the instructions and encouragement that Paul gives here.

In this section Paul presents a study in contrasts to bring what he has been teaching to bear on Timothy's real-life situation. There is a resemblance with passages in 1 Timothy. First, 2:14-18 describes the false teachers in contrast to the approved workman (notice v. 15; see also 1 Tim 1:3-20; 4:6-16; 6:3-16). Then 2:22-26 completes the contrast with a picture of God's worker. Between these opposing portraits sits the realistic description of the church (2:19-21). It does nothing to resolve the tension created by the two opposing profiles; on the contrary, it heightens the tension even more, by showing that this opposition is an inevitable dimension of the church's existence (compare 1 Tim 4:1-3) and that somehow in spite of it the church will continue to stand (compare 1 Tim 3:15).

The Difference Between False Teachers and God's Worker (2:14-18) False teachers are destructive. As this passage shows, this applies to their methods, their doctrine and the results they cause in the church. With regard to method, they are argumentative. Throughout these letters, it is this trait that most typifies the activities of the false teachers (1 Tim 6:4; Tit 3:9). In fact, the translation *quarreling about words* (v. 14) expresses one side of a single Greek word that can also mean "fighting with words." The one term sums up their activity as a whole, content and method. Their fight with words and disputable doctrines caused strife and division. The outcome of their efforts was negative in two respects. First, because of the spurious nature of the words and their improper motives, their arguments produced nothing of value. Second, the greater danger was that poorly grounded believers might be influenced by personality or cleverness of words to accept some novel view that could "ruin" their faith. Their quarrels about doctrine and "word fighting" did nothing to build up the church or the individual.

In contrast stands God's approved *workman* (v. 15). What makes this worker different from the false teacher? First, this one's life and work must be oriented toward God. The opponents looked to people for approval, but God's servants must seek it from God. This orienting of oneself toward God involves an active *(do your best,* or "make the effort") and conscious *(present yourself)* decision. Avoiding the ways of the false teachers and remaining true to the gospel in teaching and life form the test that faced Timothy. God's approval would rest upon the one who passed this test (1 Cor 11:19; 2 Cor 10:18).

Second, and inseparable from this focus on God, God's worker will demonstrate unashamed commitment to the gospel. Paul's rather traditional views may not have seemed as interesting as the doctrines of the "new" movement, but regardless of popularity Timothy was to make his stand for the apostolic faith (1:8, 12, 16). The NIV translation *correctly handle* expresses well the intention of the Greek term traditionally rendered "rightly divide" (KJV). Attempts to isolate the precise image in mind have varied: (1) cutting a stone to fit into a building (Barrett 1963); (2) a father distributing food at a meal (Calvin); (3) cutting a road through the countryside (Barclay 1975; Stott 1973). But certainty is not possible. Nevertheless, as Paul has employed the metaphor in this context, the broad idea of accurate interpretation and appropriate use of Scripture is at least clear. For Timothy this meant to provide a responsible interpretation of *the word of truth* in the midst of controversy and quarrels about "new-fangled" teaching (see on 1 Tim 1:4).

This certainly applies to the interpretation of the Bible today as well, but in view of the tremendous historical, cultural and social distance that separates us from the Christians of the first century and the Israelites of the Old Testament, our task is more complicated. Our "correct handling" of the biblical text includes first understanding the original message in its original context, which requires knowledge of the biblical languages and the historical-cultural-social setting that the author addressed (or depending on those who do have such knowledge). But the task is not finished until the original message has been brought across the centuries and applied freshly in our own situations. This is not the task of a single person, but is to be carried out in the church in dependence on the Holy Spirit and with a view to the understanding of the church down through the ages and in our present time.

At verse 16 the thought returns, by way of a command to Timothy *(avoid godless chatter),* to the destructiveness of the opponents. *Godless chatter* is Paul's term for the opposing doctrine. It may have been sys-

---

Notes: 2:15 *Present yourself* draws on the image of submitting something (here, a whole life; in Eph 5:27 and Col 1:22, the church) as a finished product for God's evaluation.

On *correctly handle (orthotomeō;* literally, "to cut in a straight direction"), see also Kelly

tematic, but it had nothing to do with God or truth (see on 1 Tim 1:9; 6:20). Timothy is to avoid it, for those who embrace it make a very destructive sort of "progress," progress in ungodliness. Here it is important to note two facts, signaled by two key terms. (1) *Become more and more* (v. 16) is the NIV rendering of Paul's verb "to make progress" (see on 1 Tim 4:15). False teaching bears fruit, but the fruit is rotten. It produces death or separation from God, and a way of life so marked. (2) *Ungodliness* depicts this way of life as the exact opposite of genuine Christianity, which Paul defined with the term "godliness."

Verse 17 finishes the graphic description of this inexorable process. The destructive teaching will *spread* its infection *like gangrene*—hard to stop, deadly. This medical imagery depicts false teaching as utterly unhealthy, unsound, destroying wholeness, in contrast to the health-producing gospel (see on 1 Tim 1:10).

Ultimately, false teaching destroys faith, as the lives and teaching of two of the opponents, Hymenaeus and Philetus, illustrate. The fact that Paul draws attention to them suggests that they were well known and probably leaders of the movement (1 Tim 1:20). The similar description of the false teachers in 1 Timothy 1:6 is given more precision here in verse 18. In both cases Paul describes the false teachers (possibly the same group) as "wandering," moving slowly but surely away from the reference point of *the truth.* And this drift is particularly evident in their teaching *that the resurrection has already taken place.* As we saw (see the discussion at 1:6), this doctrine forced a radical reorientation of the church's view of salvation and the Christian life. The realized resurrection meant the completion of salvation. Since this pertained only to the spirit, life in the flesh and life in the world diminished in importance.

But the saddest side of this story is also the most dangerous—as they wander from the truth, they take other immature or weak believers with them. The promise of our future resurrection is the very foundation of the Christian faith (1 Cor 15:19). Remove the foundation, and faith collapses. Equally, to adopt the realized spiritual resurrection of the heretics

---

1963:183; Fee 1988:255; Lock 1924:99. For more on the task of interpretation, see Osborne 1992.

2:16 The two concepts, *ungodliness (asebeia)* and godliness *(eusebeia)* are set in opposition in Titus 2:12 (see also on 1 Tim 2:2).

means destruction of the faith, for it leads to withdrawal from the world or a disregard for sin connected with the body (see below on 3:6). This false resurrection teaching (which they called "knowledge"—1 Tim 6:21) was the antithesis of the gospel *(the truth,* v. 17; *the faith,* 1 Tim 1:6; 6:21) taught by the apostles.

God's Permanent but Paradoxical Church (2:19-21) Now let us consider the core of this passage. How can all of this go on and God's promises continue to be good? Is not the success of false teachers evidence that God's plan has failed? Unsettling questions like these occurred to Timothy, just as they may occur to us. Paul therefore drops an anchor into this turbulent sea that holds the church in place.

Permanent Foundation (2:19) Paul's reference to a *solid foundation* has been explained in different ways. In 1 Corinthians 3:10-11 Paul uses the terminology of Christ (or the gospel about him), who is "the foundation" of the church. According to Ephesians 2:20, the ministry of the apostles and prophets is "the foundation" of God's household. But here *God's solid foundation* describes God's people, the church. The description is similar to 1 Timothy 3:15's metaphor of the church as "the pillar and foundation of the truth." In each passage the burning issue is the implication of heresy for the permanence of the church. The architectural imagery declares that the church will not fall.

God's Seal of Ownership (2:19) In the ancient world a seal could be affixed to a scroll (Rev 5:2) or inscribed in a stone. It was proof of ownership or authenticity. So the "seal" (guarantee) of genuine faith and of God's promise to save is the presence of the Holy Spirit in the Christian's life (Eph 1:13-14). Here, in the midst of false claims to truth and leadership in the church, Paul identifies the seal that guarantees that God's church is permanent. It might seem a bit surprising in that it combines a promise about God's action and the necessity of human response.

Notes: 2:19 For the view that *God's solid foundation* refers to the church, see Barclay 1975:202-4; Stott 1973:70; Kelly 1963:186; Dibelius and Conzelmann 1972:112-13; Brox 1989:249. Hanson (1982:137) takes it as a reference to Christ, and others (see Fee 1988:257; Guthrie 1957:150) understand it to refer possibly to something more than (but including) the church.

The life to be avoided *(wickedness* or "evil"—*adikia)* is the opposite of the life to be

The Lord knows those who are his is nearly a direct quote of Numbers 16:5 (LXX). The scene in Numbers 16 finds Korah and his companions challenging the authority of Moses and Aaron, God's chosen leaders. Moses claims that God knows those who are his and will make this clear to the people, and ultimately Korah and his followers are removed by God. Paul's point is that in the face of similar competing claims to authority and superior spirituality, God will distinguish between his people and impostors.

But while it is true that God's special knowledge is the prior factor in belonging to God, it is equally true that God's people must verify their membership with the proper response. The second half of the seal represents a combination of Old Testament ideas. The phrase *confesses the name* (literally, "names the name") calls to mind Acts 2:21 and Romans 10:13 (which cite Joel 2:32 [3:5 LXX]) where calling upon the Lord is equivalent to trusting in the Lord for salvation. The demand of an appropriate lifestyle response, *turn away from wickedness,* echoes Job 36:10. The point is, those who claim to belong to God (who name his name in faith) must verify their claim (and faith) with their conduct.

Thus the permanence of the church rests on God's prior and effective knowledge (God's choice), which itself finds visible expression in the life of God's people. Both halves of the seal are intrinsic to Paul's logic. The church is the living interplay between God's will and the response of his people. Perhaps the certainty of the seal flows from the first half—God's perfect knowledge—but the human part of the equation is also a necessary part. God's sovereignty does not negate human responsibility. It is simply a fact that God's knowledge is effective, and he has always reserved some "who have not bowed the knee to Baal."

Paradoxical Church (2:20-21) There is another question—why are there false believers in the church at all?—and the "household" imagery of verses 20-21 suggests an answer. The answer given has two parts, a statement of the facts (v. 20) and a reminder of the importance

---

pursued in verse 22, *righteousness (dikaiosynē).*

Leviticus 24:16 (LXX) shows that "naming the name" of the Lord in a blasphemous way warranted death.

2:20 For the imagery of vessels for noble and common uses elsewhere in Paul, see Romans 9:19-21. The imagery is put to different use here.

of human response (v. 21).

Paul might have cited Jesus' teaching about the wheat and the tares (Mt 13:24-30) to describe the mixed nature of the church, for the point is very much the same. He chose instead the household imagery more familiar to him (see on 1 Tim 2:1; 3:15; compare Eph 2:19-22), probably because of his emphasis on variety among the church's membership. From the household analogy comes the raw truth: the church as a household by definition has implements that can be distinguished on the basis of value and usefulness. The valuable implements are those made of *gold and silver,* while ordinary ones are made of *wood and clay.* The former are reserved for important occasions, the latter for mundane, day-to-day tasks. Guests of honor get the fine china, crystal and silverware, not the everyday dishes. And no one would use the silver punchbowl for scrubbing the floor. But what distinction within the church is Paul making? As with Jesus' teaching, the present context shows (in v. 21 the *instrument* is the one who claims to be a Christian) that the presence of false believers within the church is the issue. God knows who they are, but the point is, they are there, and this fact should not take Christians by surprise. Neither should it cause despair, because the church will not fall.

The fact of a mixed church is no excuse, however, for personal failure, for as verse 21 reminds us, the *master* of this household is not absent. The question rather becomes, How can we be implements destined for noble purposes? And the answer rests very much with us.

By employing the household metaphor in the first place, Paul evokes thoughts of order and faithful service to *the master* (see on 1 Tim 2). But service in God's household requires preparation. First, the human vessel must be "cleansed," just as holy implements would have been cleansed for sacred use. The pollutants in this case are false teachers and their teaching *(the latter),* and God's servants must not be involved with them. But the general principle is that given in verse 19—God's people *must turn away from wickedness*—and there is much besides heretics and heresy that can draw people away from God. The Lord asks for undivided allegiance, and cleansing is a practical enactment of commitment. It is also the Christian's basic step in preparation to become a useful servant. This positive response demonstrates one's place among the implements destined for noble purposes.

Second, once cleansed the true believer is "set apart" (reserved for something special), which is what *made holy* means (compare Rom 12:1). And God, *the master* of this household, determines such a one to be *useful* for service. In the final analysis, this instrument proves to be *prepared to do any good work.* That is, this Christian will be equipped to live a life in which genuine faith continually finds expression in tangible, visible ways (see on 1 Tim 2:10; 5:10; Tit 3:1).

More Marks of the Approved Worker (2:22-26) Addressing a situation dominated by false teachers, Paul instructs Timothy to pursue an entirely opposite style of life and service.

In Pursuit of Genuine Godliness (2:22) Verse 22 resumes the portrait of God's worker, which began at verse 15, by introducing another basic but sweeping area of contrast—lifestyle. "Godliness" does not occur in this listing of the virtues that mark genuine Christianity (see 1 Tim 6:11). But it is godliness, the visible life that proceeds from true faith, that Paul describes here (see on 1 Tim 2:2). As in 1 Timothy 6:11, the demands of God (v. 21) and the presence of spiritual impostors make pursuit of this life something of an emergency. The *flee . . . pursue* formula gives the teaching an urgent tone. Timothy's faith and ministry depend on godliness, and *the evil desires of youth* pose a serious threat. In this context, Paul probably thinks first of the characteristics of youth that open one up to false teaching and prevent effective ministry, everything from impatience with old ways of thinking to love of debate and the tendency to seek human approval. But the flight from this danger cannot be accomplished simply by denial and prohibition. Genuine Christianity is a positive pursuit. A comparison with the similar instructions in 1 Timothy 6:11 shows that the balanced Christian life is again in view: visible "uprightness" (NIV *righteousness),* a genuine relationship with God *(faith)* and a resultant life of service to others *(love).* The characteristic of *peace* is added here no doubt because of the turbulent setting in view and the emphasis on the redemptive (peacemaking) role of God's worker.

The very decision to flee evil and pursue this lifestyle is a mark of belonging to God's people. Those who belong to God turn to God. God's people are often designated as *those who call on the Lord* (Rom

10:12, 13; 1 Cor 1:2; 2 Cor 1:23). They are those who are in communi-cation with him and who respond to him. Of course, the false teachers laid claim to this communication, but Paul excludes them from God's people with the phrase *out of a pure heart.* This term designates genuine believers, who have been cleansed from sin (see on 1 Tim 1:5). God has claimed them, and they desire the life that pleases him.

Compassion for People (2:23-26) Paul's picture of God's worker includes one final contrast. Self-promotion and self-preservation are characteristics of sinful people. These interests lay behind the arguments of the false teachers. It is a mark of genuine faith that the Christian learns to place the needs of others first. For Timothy this new set of priorities even included the needs of the false teachers.

Verse 23 describes the content of the false teaching and perhaps the teachers as well with two harsh terms, *foolish* (see Tit 3:9) and *stupid arguments* (which means "uneducated" or "uninformed"; compare 1 Tim 1:7). Debates about their groundless doctrines led to quarrels which had destructive results (v. 14).

The Lord's servant must take an opposite course, which has at least three dimensions (v. 24). First is kindness and gentleness. *Kind* de-scribes a disposition or attitude toward others that is helpful and peaceful (compare 1 Thess 2:7) and provides a fitting contrast with the quarrel-some behavior to be avoided. Moreover, the Christian should *be kind to everyone,* which suggests that even here the goal of repentance has come into view (see v. 25; compare Tit 3:2).

Second, in contrast to the false teachers (who had nothing of value to teach—v. 23), God's servant must be *able to teach,* the same require-ment that is made of the overseer (1 Tim 3:2). This instruction will be filled out in verse 25. Here it is enough to note that the *kind* attitude of acceptance expressed *to everyone* is to be matched with the ability to lead them into the truth.

Third, the leader must set an example of tolerance and patience with those in error. This particular virtue obviously is cited to address the conflict setting. But conflict or disagreement can occur in all levels of

Notes: 2:22 See further the discussion at 1 Timothy 1:5 (and notes) of the term *pure [cleansed] heart.*

intensity within the church, and the leader, to be a unifying influence, must respond to criticism, opposition and error patiently, without becoming resentful. As the succeeding verses show, to succumb to resentful feelings is to cut oneself off from the very people who need to receive help. These three dimensions set the needs of others ahead of personal desires. In general, God's servant must have compassion for others.

Compassion is spelled out graphically in the conflict setting described in verses 25-26, both in terms of what Timothy is to do and in his reason for doing it. First, Timothy is to respond to his opponents with "gentle instruction." It is not through harsh treatment or loud teaching that the wayward will be won back to the faith. The qualification *gently,* which Paul uses elsewhere of Christ and Christlikeness (2 Cor 10:1; Tit 3:2), by no means precludes forceful instruction or correction. The forbearing spirit it implies, however, intends to ensure that all such teaching will have the genuine good of the hearers in mind. Why? *Those who oppose* the truth (the false teachers and their followers) may yet be brought to repentance and be saved.

Here several things become clear about the battle that Timothy is to fight. First, it is a battle for the minds of people. Repentance is seen as an aspect of God's grace, but it involves a human change of mind, a human response. The importance of the mind is seen too in *come to their senses* (a return to clarity of thinking) in verse 26. The false teaching has captivated minds and hearts to do the will of Satan; God's teaching clears these channels so that a decision for him may be made.

Second, it is a battle against Satan, not simply against a human opponent (compare Eph 6:11-12). All opposition to God and God's servants is ultimately engineered by the devil (see on 1 Tim 3:7; 4:1). God's enemy is actively and consciously behind the false teaching *(the devil, who has taken them captive to do his will;* compare 2 Cor 4:4). The Christian who forgets this takes a great risk.

Third, the stakes in this battle are very high. To put it simply, eternal salvation is at stake. The goal of repentance is *the knowledge of the truth,* salvation, which from our perspective involves a rational decision about

---

2:23-25 Timothy, *the Lord's servant,* must be *able to teach (didaktikos,* v. 24; *paideuō,* v. 25); the false doctrine is useless for teaching *(apaideutos,* v. 23).

the gospel. Minds muddled by false teaching cannot make this decision (see on 1 Tim 2:4). This passage underlines again the depth of God's love as he relentlessly pursues even those who trade the gospel they have known for an opposing message. It also underlines the responsibility of God's people, who must embody his patient love in this pursuit. The alternative is enslavement to the devil. There is no neutral ground.

So the one who would serve God must be committed wholeheartedly to God, to his Word and to reaching people in need. While we would agree unreservedly to the first two conditions, we might be tempted to place some limits on the last one. But the passage before us takes compassion to the very limit, even as far as those who actively oppose the gospel, who have defected from the faith. When we consider the defection and reinstatement of the early disciples and our own experiences of God's mercy, compassion even to this extent is not unreasonable, no matter what must be endured.

Warning of Apostasy (3:1-9) In a passage somewhat reminiscent of 1 Timothy 4:1-3, Paul places the problem of heresy into a prophetic framework. The main difference to be seen here is the focus on the lifestyle of false belief (their *form of godliness*—3:5) rather than the fact of "falling away" and demonic influence (compare 1 Tim 4:1-2). Nevertheless, the same phenomenon is in view, and Paul draws on a well-established prophetic tradition, going back to Jesus, to explain the problem of heresy and false teachers (see on 1 Tim 4:1 and notes).

Terrible Times in the Last Days (3:1) In the back of Paul's mind as he wrote was the understanding that the world, as an opposing force led by Satan, is waging a war against God and his people. Jesus spoke of this war plainly (Jn 14-17; 16:33; Mk 13), and so did Paul (2 Cor 10:3-6; Eph 6:10-18). The war would take many shapes, and God's people were to be ready for the attack of a hostile, persecuting enemy. But surely one of its cruelest aspects was to be Satan's penetration into the church in the form of false teachers who would oppose the gospel with one of their own making and draw away the unsuspecting and unprepared (Acts 20:29-30). The term *terrible* characterizes the events of *the last days* as dangerously wild and out of control (compare Mt 8:28). The surprising thing is that this is not a prediction of the very end, but of the whole age begun by Christ which will conclude with his return. *The last days,* the age of salvation and the final opposition against God, were "now" for Paul and Timothy, and they are "now" for us as well. The appearance and threat of heresy is as much a part of this concluding stage of history as salvation and the church. Therefore Timothy was to view his trials as "signs of the times," reminders of the presence of the Enemy and the promise of victory. The reminder would keep him on his guard and at work, awaiting the return of Christ. Since we belong to the same epoch of time, we too must keep on serving in the same hope.

Characteristics of the Ungodly (3:2-5) The ungodly are those who oppose God. Verses 2-5 comprise a list of eighteen traits that presents a caricature of people totally concentrated on themselves and in opposition to God. Paul's tool here, the vice catalog (1 Tim 1:9-10; 6:3-5), functions like a "wanted" poster, though its intention includes both identification and denunciation. While the caricature may be excessive, it makes absolutely clear the wickedness of the false teachers. But anyone whose life conforms to this list, in any part, bears marks of unbelief, whatever claims to faith might be made. With that thought in mind, we might do well to view this as a Christian's checklist of possible areas needing attention.

The theme of the first four items is selfishness. *Lovers of themselves* are those who place themselves first in all things. Perhaps the only rival for their attention is money, which they also love. This love is a source of evil (1 Tim 6:10) because it separates one from God (Lk 16:13-14). Selfish people are naturally *boastful* and *proud* (compare Rom 1:30). Completely lacking in humility, they speak to draw attention to themselves and in their thoughts see themselves at the center of the universe. The fallen world is the source of this boastful pride (1 Jn 2:16), and God stands in opposition to it (Jas 4:6). Perhaps the difference between the false teacher and the struggling Christian here is only a matter of degree or of sensitivity to the sin of selfishness. Either way we ought to do something about it.

Next come two terms that describe destructive behavior. *Abusive* talk tears down other people, usually to build oneself up (see notes on 1 Tim 6:4). Equally dangerous for the family relationship is these people's (flagrant) disobedience to parents. In Paul and Timothy's day this sin set one off as fundamentally rebellious at heart, for the attitude toward parents was understood as a reflection of a deeper attitude toward God (see Ex 20:12; Deut 21:18-21; 1 Tim 1:9). They set themselves above the feelings of others and the authority of their parents—not only is this extremely selfish, but it is also destructive behavior. Have you ever observed these attitudes in the church?

Four negative *un-* words follow. *Ungrateful, unholy,* "unloving" (NIV *without love*) and *unforgiving* each depict the opposite of a characteristic of true faith. Attitudes generated by a deep-seated selfishness that threatens relationships seem to be in mind. Holiness is a matter of inner purity (see on 1 Tim 2:8; Tit 1:8), so *unholy* is probably a broad description of vile thoughts and motives (1 Tim 1:9).

The next two terms focus on speech and behavior. *Slanderous* refers to the destructive use of the tongue to spread false rumors and lies about others. Other passages (1 Tim 3:11; Tit 2:3) imply two things: people prone to slander others destroy the church, and there are such people in the church. Conduct that is *without self-control* (or undisciplined) is equally destructive to oneself and to others. In contrast, self-control is a qualification of those who would serve the church (see the discussion at 1 Tim 3:2; Tit 1:8).

As the list continues, two more *un-* terms identify ungodliness as both ruthless and cold. *Brutal* (or "untamed," "savage") served equally well to describe fierce lions and people who act like them. *Not lovers of the good* is another opposite to a quality required in church leaders (Tit 1:8). It suggests a proclivity for evil and a complete lack of moral sensitivity.

Verse 4 closes the list with four items that help in applying the general list of "pagan" failings directly to the false teachers troubling the Christian churches. *Treacherous* (NIV) might be better translated "traitors," for it is the treachery of betrayal of the faith and the faithful that is in view. *Rash* (or reckless) describes these people as those who, out of selfishness, act without thought for others or for possible consequences. A corollary of this thoughtless evil is a badly mistaken view of one's own

3:2-5 *Without love (astorgos)* means void of all natural love, particularly that "love that binds people in some natural group—the love of the family" (Morris 1981:114, also 114-17). See also Barclay 1975:216. The pagan practice of exposing/abandoning unwanted babies was the supreme illustration of this destructive lack of love.

importance (being *conceited*). The self-absorbed, self-gratifying orbit of the ungodly is described well with the phrase *lovers of pleasure rather than lovers of God*. Those who exhibit the qualities listed belong to the world, not to God.

The vice list ends here, but the caricature of the false teachers does not. The Greek sentence continues in verse 5 to describe one of the most fatal flaws of the heresy. Paul explains that they have a *form of godliness* but deny *its power*. To understand this text, we begin with the term *form,* and there are two possibilities. *Form (morphōsis)* might mean "outward appearance," giving the sense "from outer appearances they seem to be godly." This would make Paul's statement a description of deceptive, superficial godliness or godliness that amounts to ascetic practices and endless religious discussions (compare Barrett 1963; Kelly 1963; Brox 1989; Fee 1988). The excoriating list of vices in 3:2-5 that leads up to this statement certainly makes it clear that Paul is not commending such behavior. However, another inference might be intended. His concern may be less with the deception of asceticism and more with the distorted shape of their concept of Christian spirituality (= *godliness):* it was a static concept, consisting mainly of knowledge, which pertained to the cognitive, spiritual or theoretical level. In this case the whole phrase may mean more generally "they make a claim to godliness (with their claim to know God) but deny this claim with their powerless lives."

Either way, Paul has deception in mind. Now with the phrase *denying its power* in the second half of verse 5 he unmasks this deception. In Romans 2:20 he fenced with opponents who were similar in some respects. In speaking there to the "spiritual" Jews, he apparently acknowledged that they "have in the law the embodiment [= *form* in 2 Tim 3:5] of knowledge and truth." The problem is that this knowledge of God had no effect on their behavior (Rom 2:21-29). They preached it but didn't practice it. Worse yet, they believed that simply having this knowledge and the few superficial outward signs of "Jewishness" (circumcision, observance of certain rituals and regulations) amounted to true spiritu-

---

For *brutal (anēmeros)* see Dibelius and Conzelmann 1972:116; they cite Epictetus *Diss.* 1. 3. 7: "and others [of us become like] lions, wild and savage and *untamed.*"

The word behind *slanderous (diabolos)* had become a title or name for the devil (2:26; Jn 8:44).

ality. Paul says a true relationship with God is not a matter of knowledge alone, but of knowledge and practice (obedience) of what is known. Head knowledge without practical results is useless (see also Tit 1:16). In each case Paul submits the evidence of ungodly behavior to show that each group, with its failure to relate the knowledge of God to practical living, had "denied" (or shut off) the *power* that transforms lives. The Spirit, the source of this power (1:7-8), seeks to enable believers to apprehend the knowledge and truth of God with the mind and heart *and* implement these things in their lives. This is genuine *godliness.*

Timothy's opponents held that what the Spirit does he does in the spirit, and *godliness* is measured only by one's knowledge, not behavior. What one knows in the Spirit need have no necessary relation to what one does in the flesh (see commentary at 1:6). People who insist on teaching such things must be avoided.

This inconsistency between knowledge and practice, saying and doing, is still with us. There are still those who in their teaching fall out of balance on one side or the other, making Christianity all a matter of invisible belief in Christ ("it is all grace, how you live makes no real difference"), or all a matter of living a good life no matter what one believes ("after all, no religion has the exclusive claim to morality"). Each excess falls far short of genuine Christianity and poses its own dangers to people.

More personally, we all wrestle with the challenge of getting knowledge in our heads down that tortuous path to the place where performance occurs. True godliness is seen in action. If our faith in God (through belief in Christ) is not producing a corresponding visible renovation of lifestyle, we are not experiencing genuine *godliness.* It was said above that the difference between the false teacher and the struggling believer might be one of degree. But instead of asking ourselves if we have enough of these ungodly tendencies to qualify, we should view any one of them as an indication of the need to seek God's forgiveness and

---

3:6 Some have taken this statement as an indication that the false teachers concentrated their proselytizing efforts on women, and they cite 1 Timothy 2:11-15; 5:15 and Titus 1:11 in support (see Dibelius and Conzelmann 1972:116; Hanson 1982:145-46; Barclay 1975:220-22). It is more likely that they had targeted and found a hearing in homes, where women would have been alone during daytime hours; see Stott 1973:88-89; Kelly 1963:195-96. Paul's

power for change. Above all, we must not turn a blind eye to this kind of behavior simply because "it's just human nature." Christ came to renew human nature, and genuine life in the Spirit is the demonstration that this renewal is under way.

The Ungodly False Teachers (3:6-9) Paul's thought now turns from the command to avoid the opponents to a final description of their methods and depravity. And although he has an eye to certain specific developments as he makes these final remarks about false teachers, he leaves for us a pattern that is instructive today.

First, false teachers prey on people who are vulnerable. They tend to pick off the spiritual stragglers. The image Paul raises is one of sneaky infiltration: *they are the kind who worm their way into homes* (v. 6). In this case they had found success in certain homes (literally, "the" homes) or certain kinds of homes where vulnerable people lived. And in this case they captivated certain women. It was probably a very strategic move on the part of the false teachers to target these women: their position within households (perhaps as matrons) likely made them women of some means, who could support the movement. But the problem was not that they were women; rather, it was the kind of people they were: *weak-willed . . . loaded down with sins . . . swayed by all kinds of evil desires.*

This description explains the susceptibility of these victims and crosses the centuries to speak freshly to us. The time element suggests that the sins that *loaded down* (or overwhelmed) these women were accumulations from the past that continued to determine behavior in the present. Unconfessed sin forms a barrier in our relationship with God, and it renders the decision-making faculty (the conscience) ineffective (1 Tim 4:2). Such "baggage" weakens the resolve not to sin and gives strength to the desires of our sinful nature. In fact, Paul's language describes equally well the unbeliever (Eph 2:3), which shows the seriousness of this situation. Those who have not broken free from the bondage

---

language (too harsh to be a generalization—*weak-willed* or *"silly" women, gynaikaria*) better fits a reference to specific instances of this kind of success; see Fee 1988:272; Kelly 1963:195.

Sexual sin on the part of the false teachers is not chiefly in mind, though *all kinds* is broad enough to include it.

to sin are most susceptible to false teaching.

Verse 7 tells us one final thing about these victims. Their failure to distinguish between the false teaching and the true gospel and respond to the latter was not for lack of trying to learn. *Always learning* may depict these women as religious aficionados, ever eager to take up the latest spiritual fad. Or it may emphasize the futility of their search for truth: no matter how hard they tried, their hearts were veiled to the gospel (2 Cor 4:4). Probably both elements are present. Sin and lack of discernment neutralized their ability to apprehend God's truth. The importance of the mind, of human decision, in the salvation process surfaces in Paul's term for that process here: literally "to come to the knowledge of the truth" (see on 2:25). These women may have been victimized by ruthless impostors, but their refusal to come to terms with their own sin made them easy targets and willing victims.

What an incredibly accurate assessment of our modern situation! Consider not just the movement to rediscover the mysteries of the East but the whole drive to get to the bottom of the spiritual side of life. Religions, cults and societies are tried on as if they were new clothes, then discarded when they seem not to fit. How can they fit when they cannot deal with the ultimate problem of sin? Some "seekers of truth" avoid the Christian message because its focus on sin is too negative, too guilt-inducing. But the fact of the matter is that Christianity holds the key to breaking free from sin's bondage, while the trendy alternatives only deny that the problem exists.

Second, false teachers stand in direct opposition to *the truth* (v. 8). To illustrate this, Paul compares them with Jannes and Jambres, who, according to tradition, were two of the sorcerers who opposed Moses in Egypt. They opposed God through their actions, and so do false teachers by teaching another gospel (compare Gal 1:6-8). Paul's concern here was for opposition to fundamental doctrines (2:18) and ungodly behavior.

Third, false teachers have *depraved minds* (v. 8). That is, they are incapable of apprehending the truth of the gospel. For Paul, "the mind" represented the consciousness of a person, the faculty of rational deci-

---

3:8 The names of the magicians, Jannes and Jambres, do not appear in the Old Testament, but the tradition about them is well attested in Jewish literature and was current in Paul's

sion-making. It plays an essential role in accepting and adhering to the gospel. He relates it to *the truth* (the objective content of the gospel) here and in 1 Timothy 6:5. And the condition of the false teacher's mind *(depraved,* 2 Tim 3:8; *corrupt,* 1 Tim 6:5; Tit 1:15) prevents acknowledgment of the truth and is connected with rejection of the gospel (see also Tit 1:15). Even so, this condition does not appear to be irreversible (2:25).

Fourth, when measured by the standard of the apostolic faith, false teachers fail the test. Just as Timothy would be approved by his faithfulness to the gospel in word and life (see on 2:15), so these by their word and life *are rejected.*

Finally, whatever progress false teachers seem to make, in the end their failure is certain: *their folly will be clear to everyone.* This was an important word to Timothy, who at the time saw only their spreading success, enough so that he was tempted to concede. Pharaoh's magicians could compete only so long, and finally in the face of God's power they went down in defeat (Ex 8:18-19; 9:11). This word, which echoes the assurance of God's promises to his people (2:19-21), may well be our source of hope when wolves come in among us.

The presence of false teachers in the church should not surprise the wary Christian. It is one front of the battle that the enemy continues to wage with God and his people. But while their qualities and folly are obvious enough for the balanced Christian to see, the threat they present is no less dangerous. Avoidance of their teaching must be matched with careful attention to our faith and lifestyle (our godliness). The accumulation of sins that made some susceptible in Timothy's day can make us susceptible as well.

The Charge to God's Worker (3:10-17) Much the same advice is given to Timothy in this paragraph. Paul's goal for Timothy surfaces in verse 14: *continue in what you have learned.* But to do so effectively in a turbulent situation requires looking in at least two directions. In verses 10-13 Paul reminds him to learn from the pattern of life and

---

time. See the Cairo *Damascus Document* (CD 5:17-19; used by the Qumran sect) and the Targum Pseudo-Jonathan (1:3; 7:2; commenting on the contest recorded in Exodus).

service that he saw up close in the apostle. Then Paul urges reflection on the source of that life, Scripture, and on the impact that this has already had on Timothy's spiritual history.

Timothy had the great privilege of receiving training directly from Paul. Verse 10 refers to this special relationship in terms of discipleship: *know all about* means "follow and practice what has been taught." This is a reminder of a life he had already adopted and that he knew worked. And his firsthand knowledge of that life implied responsibility.

With martyrdom imminent, Paul, in one sweeping statement (vv. 10-11) summarizes (1) his ministry, which he is passing on to Timothy, with three terms, (2) the life of faith, with four standard Christian virtues, and (3) the reality of suffering, through reflection on his experiences. For Paul, ministry involved a commitment to the apostolic doctrine *(my teaching;* see 1 Tim 1:10), to the gospel as the source of salvation and to teaching about the Christian life, all of which were being challenged by false teachers. Conduct *(my way of life)* was not to be separated from correct doctrine (as the false teachers had done), for it was meant to flow out of and "adorn" this message (Tit 2:10). With the importance of these two aspects settled, a final broad one is mentioned: commitment or *purpose.* Paul's resolute *purpose* was clear—to serve Christ faithfully; and in his case that meant preaching the gospel to the Gentiles. Timothy had joined in this work and now must carry it on without Paul.

Next, the terms *faith, patience, love* and *endurance* depict the balanced life of faith (see on 2:22; 1 Tim 4:12; 6:11). The last of these leads to the theme Paul most wants to emphasize.

Paul does not expand on the purpose of suffering in this letter. Instead, we, along with Timothy, learn simply that it is a normal part of the Christian experience. The false teachers' triumphalistic outlook made no room for suffering, but the fact that Paul needed to remind Timothy shows that facing this fact is no easy matter for the balanced Christian either. Timothy's faith had taken root and grown in the *persecutions* and *sufferings* experienced by the apostle in Antioch (Acts 13:50), Iconium (Acts 14:2-6) and especially Lystra (Acts 14:19-20), where Paul found

Notes: 3:13 The term *impostors (goētes;* "magicians," "sorcerers") places the false teachers into the category of the magicians who opposed Moses, but does not imply that they practiced sorcery (see Delling 1964:737-38).

him. In light of this history, the present struggle was nothing new. The apostle might just as well have said, "You have been there before [from the beginning], you are there now, and you will be there again." To suffer for Christ is normal, and not just for apostles and their disciples.

In fact, everyone who wants to live a godly life in Christ Jesus will be persecuted. Verse 12 draws all faithful Christians into the discussion. Yet it is a verse that we pass over too quickly. First, the *godly life in Christ Jesus* is Paul's term for the life of genuine salvation (see on 1 Tim 2:2 and throughout). But it does not come automatically. The Christian must decide to want to live this way for Christ. Because God's intervention in willing lives produces dramatic visible change (godliness) and a new set of values and priorities, God's enemies respond with persecution. Verse 13, which alludes to the false teachers *(evil men and impostors* who seem to attack the church and its teachings relentlessly, *deceiving and being deceived),* was an immediate application of this truth for Timothy.

But what about us? Christian life in the West or perhaps even in much of the world these days does not seem to carry much of a price tag. Certainly the truth of verse 12 will be more evident in Muslim countries. But has it no application to us? Should we go out looking for persecution? Or is it compromise in the so-called gray areas of life that makes this verse so distant? I firmly believe that genuine godliness evokes a combative response in unbelievers, even if the prevailing attitudes or laws make room for religious freedom. Do we shy away from taking a stand for Christ in the workplace, neighborhood, school or family because we value human acceptance more than God's? If Paul's concept of godliness is understood and embraced by us, we can expect in some measure to pay the price of following Christ.

We have passed over the last part of verse 11 until this point. Suffering for the faith is normal, but so is the Lord's "rescue." Paul, writing from prison, cannot have meant rescue from persecution, but rather rescue in the form of the power to endure, to carry on in spite of such pressures, and perhaps rescue from death. But, as 4:18 shows, death may be the result of suffering for the faith, and the promise of God's rescue (to his

---

Deceiving and being deceived is a stock phrase for charlatans, who through their deceptive practices deceive themselves; see Dibelius and Conzelmann 1972:119.

eternal kingdom) is still good.

So Timothy, by drawing on the rich heritage of his own past (training received as Paul's assistant, training in the faith that went back to his family; see on 1:5), was to *continue* in what he had learned and believed (v. 14), the life of faith and faithful service to Christ. And whatever he had been taught had its source in the Scriptures, which God's servant must feed on daily.

In one sense this turn of thought also begins with the past. Timothy had already learned the importance of the Scriptures for a healthy spiritual life. As a Jewish boy (even with a Gentile father), he had probably from an early age been instructed in the Old Testament. But the focus has changed to the present through the present-tense command *continue* (v. 14) and the description of the Scriptures' "present" relevance in verse 15, *which are able to make you wise for salvation.*

Let us consider Scripture's present relevance. First, *all Scripture is God-breathed.* This is a statement of its origin. Paul has in mind the Old Testament Scriptures, not because the apostles' teaching lacked authority but probably because the opponents had so misused them. At that time the Old Testament represented the revelation of God, his communication to human beings, that had been written down; but it is certainly correct to extend his meaning to include the New Testament. This Word contains the wisdom necessary to lead one to salvation. Jesus said that the Old Testament Scriptures "testify about me" (Jn 5:39), and this was the common understanding of the apostles (Acts 3:24). The Scriptures declare God's promises and the plight of humans trapped by sin. They also declare God's solution, the appearance of God's Servant whose suffering would pay the price of our release. Paul was not concerned to distinguish between the authority of the Old Testament canon and the proclamation of the gospel by Jesus and himself, for the latter message was the authoritative continuation of God's revelation of grace. It brought to clarity what the prophets of Israel taught—"anyone who trusts

---

3:16 The alternative translation—"all God-inspired Scripture is useful . . ." (see Barclay 1975:229; Barrett 1963:114-15; compare ASV)—which Barclay, for example, thinks brings out the distinction Paul wished to make between the Jewish/Christian Scriptures and the man-made writings of the Gnostics and the heretics, is possible. However, as Fee (1988:279) points out, the syntax of 1 Timothy 4:4 supports the NIV. The divine origin of Scripture ensures its usefulness in leading to salvation (v. 15) and for teaching and training (vv. 16-

in him will never be put to shame" (Rom 10:11, quoting Is 28:16) and "everyone who calls on the name of the Lord will be saved" (Rom 10:13, quoting Joel 2:32)—by announcing that the lordship and resurrection of Jesus Christ from the dead form the focal point of our faith and our cry to God for salvation (Rom 10:9). Ultimately, the Scriptures are relevant and supremely useful because they are in their entirety *God's* Word.

Second, the relevance of Scripture may be seen in its various uses. Paul lists four of these uses. *Teaching* includes instruction in doctrine and matters of Christian conduct, and in this context the emphasis is more on building up the community of believers than on proclaiming the gospel to unbelievers. This was Timothy's responsibility in the churches (see on 1 Tim 4:13 and notes), but generally it is the work of elders, pastors and others appropriately gifted (1 Tim 3:2; 5:17; Tit 1:9; compare Eph 4:11; 1 Tim 2:11-12).

Rebuking and *correcting* are also to be accomplished from the Scriptures. Together these terms describe the task of disciplining and adjusting the conduct and doctrine of erring believers. Scripture properly understood is the standard of both holy living and teaching. False teachers and erroneous doctrine are of course uppermost in Paul's mind, but it is to Scripture that we should turn in all cases of sin in the fellowship (see 1 Tim 5:19-20).

Training in righteousness expresses the positive goal of teaching and disciplining. Here *righteousness* describes the observable Christian life (1 Tim 6:11; 2 Tim 2:22). The application of Scripture's principles to our lives by gifted teachers in the congregation enables us to make progress in the life that is pleasing to God.

Finally, the relevance of Scripture may be seen in its complete sufficiency for living the Christian life. Verse 17 closes the passage with a statement of purpose *(so that)* that reaches not only to *the man of God* who must carry out the tasks enumerated in verse 16 but to all believers. Constant study of God's Word (see on 1 Tim 4:6-16) equips one to do

---

17). Hanson (1982:152) suggests that the issue is the extent of the Scriptures' inspiration: every passage (Paul) versus only some parts (the heretics).

3:17 The phrase, which the NIV translates *thoroughly equipped,* consists of the striking combination of an adjective (*artios;* "equipped," "perfect," "complete") and its cognate verb (*exartizō;* "to equip," "to fit"). The language envisions one who, through training, has been specially shaped to perform a task.

all that God requires, because it contains the knowledge of God's will. Paul says in Ephesians 2:10 that we have been saved "to do good works"—that is, saved in order to bear tangible fruit in our lives, particularly in service to others and in our relationships with others (compare Gal 5:6, 22-23; 6:9). This "other-oriented" description of Christian living *(thoroughly equipped for every good work)* is linked inseparably here with nourishment from the Scriptures.

□ Final Charge to Timothy: Fulfill Your Ministry (4:1-8)

For the third time in these two letters to him (1 Tim 5:21; 6:13-14), Paul issues a solemn charge to Timothy. The substance of the charge is a command to carry out to completion the gospel ministry. Paul's changed circumstances account for the more solemn tone of this charge, and the motivating factors underline Timothy's responsibility and hope of reward. What was meant to urge Timothy on to the heights of faithfulness can do the same for us.

The Witnesses (4:1) If Christians were able to grasp the fact fully that God is with them, really and continually present, and that they live their lives in his presence, their zeal to live holy lives would be far more evident. But the invisibility requires faith. And with so much that is visible clamoring for our attention, we think and act as if the invisible were unreal or blind.

This is not a modern problem. While the Israelites were in the wilderness, the emblems of God's presence with them were the pillar of cloud and the ark of the covenant. They still lived as if God were far away. But a clear look at God is a life-changing experience, as Moses (Ex 34:6-8) and Peter (Lk 5:1-9) discovered. Even as they needed to be reminded of God's promise—"I will be with you"—we need to take the truth of the presence of God and Christ down from the shelf, dust it off and meditate on it. Perhaps it will awaken in us "the fear of the Lord," a powerful inspiration to holy living and faithfulness.

Paul calls God and Christ Jesus to witness the turnover of the ministry from apostle to assistant, and his charge to Timothy is therefore a charge that binds. But just as important is the comforting thought of God's continual availability to his people as they live and serve (see on 1 Tim

5:21; 6:13).

A second incentive to faithfulness is the certainty of Christ's judgment of believers on "that day" (4:8). Some understand this event in the case of believers as an assessment by Christ of our Christian service, a time for receiving rewards and perhaps failing to receive them (1 Cor 3:12-15). Paul, however, seems to teach that it is the believer's entire life that comes under the Lord's final scrutiny (1 Cor 4:2-5), and it does not appear to be a "rubber-stamp" affair. The fact of this impending review is given as strong motivation for Timothy to complete his ministry—faithfulness now has a bearing on the outcome then.

Third, Paul's charge is given with a view to the hope of the consummation of all things. *His appearing* is a way of describing the Second Advent of Christ as a decisive entrance (see on 1 Tim 6:14; 2 Tim 1:10). When he comes, salvation will be completely perfected and the struggle with sinful flesh will be over.

From a broader perspective, this event will mark the arrival of *his kingdom*—we might add, in a full and final way. God's kingdom is God's power, and here Paul conceives of an existence characterized by this dynamic power. On the one hand, Jesus declared and demonstrated its arrival, and its presence in the world is seen wherever and whenever God's people become instruments of God's power. But on the other hand, as with our experience of salvation, the final and full manifestation of God's kingdom awaits the return of Christ. Then God's power will be our pure and never-ending environment. Now this remains a promise, a matter of hope, and most importantly a hope whose fulfillment is also contingent upon the completion of the church's evangelistic mission. God's people must work faithfully and diligently in view of the End.

The Charge (4:2) The charge itself is to take up where the apostle has left off. This is a call to ministry, and as such it has immediate application to those called to vocational Christian service today. Yet its application does not stop there, for God's plan is that all believers participate directly in the church's ministry.

Five commands combine to summarize "ministry." *Preach the Word* casts Timothy in the role of a herald, making proclamation on behalf of the King (1:11). Christian ministry centers on the Word of God, God's own expression of his will for people whom he desires to bless. If God had not spoken, we would not have known about him. Since it is through his Word that he continues to speak with his people, ministry first and foremost must be the communication of his Word.

Second, ministry means availability and preparedness. Paul's adverbial phrase *in season and out of season* is the call to be ready. It brings to mind the doctor on call in the emergency room, or an obstetrician whose schedule must be determined by need, where readiness and availability might be the difference between life and death. It is "available" Christians who will be able to seize the moment and win people for Christ or come to the aid of struggling brothers and sisters in the church.

Ministry must also include the less desirable tasks related to correction of erring members of the fellowship. Together, *correct* (1 Tim 5:20; Tit 1:9, 13) and *rebuke* (Mk 1:25) cover the territory from the patient kind of correction carried out through teaching (with the goal of improvement) to the sterner variety of authoritative warnings or prohibitions (designed to bring about an immediate halt). While the danger of false teachers is uppermost in Paul's mind here, the leader especially will have to deal with church members who persist in sinful behavior for other reasons (compare Mt 18:15; 1 Tim 5:20).

"Encouragement" (see 1 Tim 1:3; 2:1; 4:13; 5:1 [see notes]; 6:2) is a very practical kind of exhortation from biblical texts which urges practical, lifestyle responses. It is the proclamation of Scripture that says, "This is what it says; let's do it."

The phrase *with great patience and careful instruction* applies at least to the three aspects of ministry just considered, but may apply to all five. This views ministry from the perspective of attitude and content. *Great patience* is an attribute ascribed to God (1 Pet 3:20; 2 Pet 3:15) which pictures his commitment to human beings in terms of ceaselessly waiting and working to bring them around to salvation. Given the resistant hearts that Timothy was encountering, he would need God's patience in good measure. Equally, he had to pay careful attention to the content of what was taught (1 Tim 4:16). Slow response might tempt one to alter one's teaching, but only sound teaching can produce sound, healthy Christians (see on Tit 1:9).

The First Reason (4:3-4) Verses 3 and 4 introduce one of the reasons *(for)* behind the charge to Timothy. Because of the presence of false teachers and apostasy in the church, Timothy's undivided attention and sustained service are required. Again, this development, already in progress, is regarded prophetically *(the time will come)* as a typical characteristic of "the last days" (3:1; 1 Tim 4:1). But in this case the problem is viewed more from the angle of weak, sinful believers who are willing to be duped. Paul describes those who have surrendered to worldly values and sinful passions of various sorts (see on 2 Tim 2:22; Tit 2:12), so much so that these things determine the kind of teaching they will listen to. *Sound doctrine,* which produces whole Christians (see on 1 Tim 1:10), is opposed to a life based on worldly values and passions, for it calls for rejection of them. The picture Paul gives is of weak believers who, unwilling to break free from the old life and give themselves fully to the new, grew dissatisfied and curious (with *itching ears)* for a "spiritual" answer that is more convenient. The false teachers were only too ready to provide a satisfying alternative, which Paul calls *myths* (see on 1 Tim 1:4; Tit 1:14) in contrast to *the truth,* the apostolic doctrine (see on 2:18; 1 Tim 6:5; Tit 1:14). And these teachers will bear their portion of the guilt, but the culpability of the weak who *turn their ears away from the truth . . . to myths* (v. 4) is also clearly in view (see on 3:6).

The Charge Repeated (4:5) The combined thoughts of deceitful and dangerous false teachers and weak Christians eager to be led astray turn Paul's thoughts back to the charge to Timothy. He must be different. And the difference is measured first in terms of balance. *Keep your head in all situations* is precisely what many believers in those churches were failing to do. As a result, they acted rashly, with muddled thinking, uncritically accepting the false doctrine.

Second, in contrast to the false teachers (who had written suffering right out of their manual on discipleship—see on 1:3-8) and their followers, God's servant must be willing to *endure hardship* for the sake of the gospel. This is the major theme of this letter (1:8, 12; 2:3, 9, 12; 3:11, 12).

The charge closes with the reminder to *do the work of an evangelist* (Acts 21:8; Eph 4:11). Here, as also implied in verse 2, Paul expressly hands on to his successor (and through him to the church—2:2) the mission to proclaim the gospel to the Gentiles. The concluding summary command urges that the whole charge to ministry be faithfully executed.

The Second Reason (4:6-8) A second equally immediate reason (*for*, v. 6) behind this charge to Timothy is the apostle's imminent death. Although the passage is intensely personal, its main purpose, which is motivational, emerges in verse 8: Paul's testimony and promise of reward provide a model for all.

A Death Worth Dying (4:6) In one respect, the death of an innocent person may seem a senseless waste. But as Paul sets before us a model, he reveals the true value and meaning of a life spent in faithful service to the Lord. To do so he employs the metaphor of a *drink offering* that he used earlier in Philippians 2:17. The Old Testament sacrificial system provides the background to Paul's imagery (Num 15:5, 7, 10; 28:7). Of course, the imagery of wine being poured out suggests a figurative description of death as the pouring out of blood. But Paul describes his whole life of service and devotion, culminating in his death, as a sacrificial "pouring out" to the Lord (Num 28:7), an expression of worship (compare Rom 12:1) that is acceptable to the Lord.

Is such an offering sensible? Consider the more recent words written by Jim Elliot, the missionary to the Auca Indians who gave his life for the Lord: "He is no fool who gives what he cannot keep to gain what he cannot lose" (Elliot 1957:247).

The apostle's death was imminent, unavoidable this time, as the second metaphor of *departure* suggests (compare Phil 1:23). Yet his death as his final token of worship was no senseless defeat. Timothy was to draw from this model the motivation to carry on the struggle, to bring his own worship to God.

A Life Well Lived (4:7) Paul's testimony continues with a description (built from three phrases) of a life of faithful service that should be the goal of every believer.

A dominant image in Paul is the Christian life and ministry as athletic

---

Notes: 4:7 *Finished the race (ton dromon teteleka)* corresponds almost exactly to the language Luke used to report Paul's speech to the Ephesian elders in Acts 20:24: "if only I may finish the race" *(teleiōsō ton dromon mou).*

competition. His readers were very familiar with the Olympic-type games and the high degree of training, endurance and discipline, let alone skill, that were required of the victor. So it is not surprising that Paul reflects on the course of his life in this way. He has *fought the good fight* (or "competed in the games"—1 Cor 9:25) that Timothy is still to fight (2:5; 1 Tim 6:12; 1:18). He has *finished the race* (Acts 20:24; 1 Cor 9:24).

The last statement says plainly what the two metaphors imply: he has *kept the faith.* If *the faith* here refers to the approved Christian faith, then, against the background of heresy, fidelity to Christ and the gospel is meant. It may be, however, that Paul's whole ministry is viewed as a sacred trust that he has faithfully discharged (1:12; 1 Tim 1:11). In the present context the former is more likely, but the two explanations overlap, and fidelity is central in either case. Paul has said elsewhere that "those who have been given a trust must prove faithful" (1 Cor 4:2). His final proof of faithfulness to God's Word and to his calling was given to the executioner in prison in Rome.

The Reward for Faithfulness (4:8) As close as Paul was to glory, his reward remained a future promise. What was the reward he expected to receive? He returns to athletic imagery to explain. The *crown* he envisions is the wreath awarded to the victor (see 1 Cor 9:25). He further describes it as *the crown of righteousness.* This has been taken by some to mean a reward for an upright life. Probably, however, Paul means the righteousness that God bestows (on the basis of faith), envisaged here as the reward for faithfulness to Christ.

It may be objected that Paul teaches that righteousness (or justification) is already the possession of the Christian on the basis of faith in Christ (Rom 3:21-31). And this is true. But just as with the gift of salvation, which we now experience only in part, Paul can also say that "we eagerly await . . . the righteousness for which we hope" (Gal 5:5). It is this complete righteousness that Paul expects the Lord to confer on him. Does Paul now envision righteousness as something to be earned? No. But the athletic imagery implies the need for a life of faithful response

For the view that *kept the faith* means preservation of the gospel message, see Hanson 1982:155-56; Stott 1973:114; Guthrie 1957:169-70. For the view that "loyalty to a trust" is in mind, see Fee 1988:289; Kelly 1963:209.

on the part of Christians; God has given salvation and righteousness and along with them the responsibility to work out, implement and perform the new life in the power of the Holy Spirit.

The award ceremony will take place *on that day,* the day of Christ's return (1:12, 18). Thus the reward remains an object of hope. But Paul in his confident hope in God and in his faithful life and ministry provides a model for all believers. For the promise of God's righteousness is a promise to all, with one qualification—*who have longed for his appearing.* In this qualification several things become apparent. Paul describes a life lived in anticipation of Christ's return. Christians are to be those who from the moment they learn of it live for the return of Christ. The false teaching had basically eliminated the need for Christ's return, for it taught that the resurrection had already occurred and salvation was complete. As a result, those affected by such doctrines lived either in the past or only for the moment.

Many modern Christians living in comfort and economic security are equally confused. In reality salvation is yet to be completed; sin and evil are yet to be destroyed. Christians are to carry on a struggle against sin in the flesh in full awareness that the present experience is not complete but can indeed be one of growth and victory. This understanding of the need and significance of Christ's return for God's people will transform a believer's life. Endurance, perseverance and faithfulness make perfect sense in the light of Christ's future appearance. Paul's life bore these marks, and his reward is sure. All who follow him may be assured of the same reward.

□ Closing Instructions, Personal Notes (4:9-18)

The more intimate nature of 2 Timothy probably accounts for the greater length given to discussing Paul's personal situation and needs and the movements of individuals known to Paul and Timothy. This section is primarily designed to explain Paul's need for Timothy to visit. At this stage, although he knows there is no release from this imprisonment, Paul does foresee a length of time in custody before his end, and he urges Timothy to come to his aid.

Notes: **4:10** Paul claimed to have reached as far as Illyricum in his gospel ministry (Rom

Paul and His Coworkers (4:9-13) Verses 9-13 mention seven of Paul's coworkers, whose movements have left Paul in a lonely position. Crescens, whom we know nothing about, had gone to Galatia (v. 10), presumably for the purpose of ministering there. Titus, a better-known associate of Paul (see introduction), had similarly departed for Dalmatia, across the Adriatic Sea from Italy and north of Macedonia (on the west coast of modern Bosnia-Herzegovina). Both of these seem to have been sent from Rome back to areas in which Pauline churches had made inroads. Tychicus, an inhabitant of Asia Minor, joined Paul's work around the time of his Ephesian ministry (Acts 20:4). He delivered the letters to the Ephesians and Colossians (Eph 6:21; Col 4:7) and may have been the one who relieved Titus in Crete at an earlier time (Tit 3:12; see introduction). Paul sent him to Ephesus, almost certainly to minister there.

Allusions to two other persons connected to Paul's work tell a more poignant tale. The first is Demas, whom Paul mentions first in urging Timothy to hurry to Rome because he had *deserted* and *gone to Thessalonica* (v. 10). I have heard whole sermons based on the three references to Demas in the New Testament. They do tell a story, but we never learn the final outcome. In Philemon 24 and Colossians 4:14 Demas is listed along with other faithful assistants of Paul. Here, however, we read of his desertion, which disappointed Paul greatly. No details are given. Perhaps Thessalonica was his home. But that his faithfulness flagged is attributed to love for *this world,* literally "the present age." Paul describes the object of Demas's affections as this fallen world influenced by sin, with values opposed to God's, rather than "the age to come" (compare 4:8), where the Christian's faithfulness will be rewarded and hopes will be fulfilled. Demas may have left out of fear of being too closely associated with one who was to be put to death. In any case, the attraction of this world is its false promises of comfort and ease. It may offer these things on one level, but to accept the offer and live by its values is to reject the way of the cross. Demas's desertion illustrates how even service alongside a spiritual giant does not remove one from the dangers of the world. Faithfulness does not simply rub off. It is not appropriate for

---

15:19); Dalmatia bordered this district on the west side.

us to shake a finger at Demas but to learn from him, for his weakness is latent in all of us.

Then there is Mark (v. 11). Timothy was to bring him along, because, Paul said, *he is helpful to me in my ministry.* We might pass over this easily except for the fact that this is the very John Mark who once left the work of Paul and Barnabas (Acts 13:13) and whom for this reason Paul was unwilling to take along later (Acts 15:38). I first thought of Mark as an encouraging example when a professor of mine, introducing his course on the Gospel of Mark, told us, "Take heart! If Christ could bring victory out of the failings of Peter and Mark (both New Testament authors), he can make something out of us." Apparently, at least in the eyes of Paul, Mark had failed. But by the time he had written Colossians, Paul had received him back into the work as a trusted coworker, and that is how he is described here: *helpful* (or "useful," 2:21) *to me in my ministry.* Mark's life had its "hiccups." But by God's grace and with the help of Christian leaders willing to allow for growth and willing to forgive, his story became one of success.

That left only Luke with Paul in Rome (v. 11). He may have been Paul's secretary in the writing of this letter (and 1 Timothy and Titus; see introduction), and Paul does not minimize his usefulness to him here. But the rest of his coworkers have departed, and there is still work to be done in Rome.

Timothy, therefore, is to go to Paul quickly. Coming from Asia Minor in the vicinity of Ephesus, Timothy could take the route to the port town of Troas and from there take the road around to Macedonia and make his way to Rome. At some point Paul had left his *cloak* (a woolen outer garment for winter) and *scrolls* with someone named Carpus (probably a Christian in that city). Timothy is to retrieve the clothing and the scrolls. The latter may refer to Paul's copy of the Old Testament. With the added phrase *especially the parchments,* Paul probably specifies which books he means ("that is, those made of parchment"; see notes on 1 Tim 4:10).

4:13 *Scrolls (biblia)* could be a reference to any books, including the writings of the Old Testament.

4:14-15 It is possible that the Alexander of this passage and 1 Timothy 1:20 (probably the same) is the same one mentioned in Acts 19:33. That he was involved in Paul's arrest (or rearrest, since this explanation assumes a first and second Roman imprisonment) might

An Enemy of the Gospel (4:14-15) The warning about *Alexander the metalworker* in verses 14 and 15 is probably connected with Timothy's travel plans. Alexander was vehemently opposed to the gospel and had done Paul *a great deal of harm.* Fee (1988:296) makes the plausible suggestion that this Alexander may have been the one named in 1 Timothy 1:20, apparently a believer turned heretic and one of the ringleaders of the movement in Ephesus (and therefore explicitly mentioned). Having been excommunicated, he left Ephesus with much resentment and perhaps had a hand in Paul's arrest. This is speculation, of course; but whoever he was, he had proved himself an enemy of the gospel and was apparently in the region, and Timothy was to be on guard. *The Lord will repay him for what he has done* echoes the Old Testament consolation of the righteous who suffer in the midst of the prospering wicked (Ps 28:4; 62:12; Prov 24:12; Rom 12:17-21). Whatever God's opponents might do to impede the gospel or harm us, God has the final say. Fear need not immobilize us.

The Lord's Help (4:16-18) In fact, Paul concludes this section with a strong reminder of the Lord's sufficiency in his servants' times of need. One has the feeling that Paul sees himself in his experience of imprisonment as following in Jesus' footsteps. Jesus (and the early church) made use of Psalm 22 in interpreting his own suffering (Mt 27:29, 39, 43, 46), and Paul seems to reflect on that psalm and ideas associated with it in this final section. Desertion (Ps 22:1 [21:2 LXX]), deliverance (22:4, 8, 21 [21:5, 9, 21 LXX]), salvation (22:5 [21:6 LXX]), the Lord's nearness (22:11, 19 [21:12, 20 LXX]), and references to the mouths of lions (22:13, 21 [21:14, 22 LXX]) and the supreme power of God all suggest that Paul was greatly influenced and encouraged by this psalm.

At my first defense (v. 16) probably refers to an initial hearing (similar to a modern arraignment to determine the existence of sufficient grounds for a trial) before the final trial (rather than a first imprison-

---

be indicated by the verb translated *did [me a great deal of harm] (endeiknymi),* which sometimes bore the legal meaning of "inform against" (so Fee 1988:296; Knight 1992:467).

4:16 For the view adopted here, see Fee 1988:296; Kelly 1963:218; Dibelius and Conzelmann 1972:124; Guthrie 1957:175-77. For the view that Paul refers to his first imprisonment see Eusebius *Historia Ecclesiastica* 2. 22; Lock 1924:119; Hendriksen 1965:326.

ment). At that time no one stood by Paul; everyone *deserted* him. On the one hand, according to Kelly (1963:218), no one came forward to represent him or give testimony in his behalf, and on the other, those who were with him *deserted.* Apparently either this statement excludes Luke or he had not yet arrived. But that is really unimportant, for Paul is emphasizing how the Lord was near (see Acts 23:11; 27:23), that he gave the necessary strength (Phil 4:13), and that therefore, though all had departed, in the Lord's strength alone he has been able to continue the work given to him: making the gospel known to *all the Gentiles.*

The Lord's intervention also took the form of rescue, and Paul views this from two perspectives. His allusion to *the lion's mouth,* against the background of Psalm 22, refers to physical death, from which Paul had been spared (on more than one occasion, 2 Cor 11:23). And while Paul's portion of the work is still to be finished, this protection will be assured. But ultimately the Lord's faithfulness extends to his rescue to eternal life *(his heavenly kingdom).* No evil worked against God's people can keep them from this goal (compare Rom 8:31-39). Paul's own experience of Jesus' travail was his opportunity to learn of the Lord's strength for endurance and promise of protection.

It seems that it is when circumstances least warrant hope in God that the conviction and experience of God's promises to stand near and deliver grow most clear to the righteous. Paul's hope of salvation was never more certain than when he wrote these final words. The doxology, which proclaims the Lord's *glory,* is the fitting conclusion to this reminder of the presence, power and rescue of God (see on 1 Tim 1:17; 6:16).

□ Closing Greetings (4:19-22)

As was typical in letters of that day, Paul's letters frequently ended by asking that greetings be given to certain individuals with whom the recipient would be sure to have contact. He also took the opportunity to pass on greetings from mutual friends on his end. These personal touches reflect concern and genuine feeling; Paul wanted those greeted to be sure of their significance to him. Instead of closing with a wish for "all the best," Paul wishes them God's best with a benediction.

Greetings (4:19, 21) Priscilla and Aquila show up here not for the first time in Paul's letters (Rom 16:3; 1 Cor 16:19). Luke tells us that this couple had come to Asia Minor from Rome at the time when Claudius had expelled all Jews from the imperial city (Acts 18:2). Paul made their acquaintance in Corinth, where he lived with them for some time (18:18). Then when Paul was en route back to Syria/Antioch, they all stopped off at Ephesus, where Aquila and Priscilla were left and Paul began to preach (18:26). By the time Paul wrote Romans, they had moved back to Rome (Rom 16:3). Yet when Paul wrote 2 Timothy they had apparently returned to Asia Minor, probably in the vicinity of Ephesus. Their open home and skillful assistance (their instruction of Apollos and their house-church ministry) came at the tricky Corinth-Ephesus stage of the work. They were probably a couple of some means, owners of a successful business, but Paul remembers best their courage and sacrifice for the gospel (Rom 16:4: "they risked their lives for me") and their hospitality (1 Cor 16:19). Their willingness to put everything on the line for God makes them fine examples for Christian couples in all walks of life today.

Paul mentions *the household of Onesiphorus* here for the second time in this letter (see 1:16). Onesiphorus's loyalty moved Paul deeply, and if it also cost him his life, as this greeting to his household may imply, then there is all the more reason for Paul to remember his family in this way.

Greetings are also sent back to Timothy from the Roman fellowship in verse 21. Timothy may have met previously the four individuals who are singled out from the whole church (three men and a woman—the last three names are Latin). Or perhaps they were key figures in the church. Early tradition names Linus as bishop of Rome. But nothing more is known of Eubulus, Pudens and Claudia.

Personal Details (4:20-21) Two more of the team are mentioned in closing. The name Erastus appears elsewhere (Rom 16:23) in reference to a Christian in Corinth "who is the city's director of public works." Acts 19:22 mentions another Erastus (a helper of Paul), whom Paul sent along with Timothy to Macedonia. Unless the one in 2 Timothy is another person altogether, he is probably the one mentioned by Luke. Trophimus is probably "the Ephesian" mentioned in Acts 21:29. The significance of these two to Timothy would probably go back to the role they played in the Ephesian period of Paul's ministry. But beyond that (whether Timothy had sent queries about them) we cannot be sure. It is also not clear from the Greek whether Paul meant that he had to "give up" Trophimus to sickness *in Miletus* or, as the NIV interprets it, that Paul personally *left* him *sick* there (see discussion of Tit 1:5 in introduction).

Consequently, the bearing of this note on a reconstruction of Paul's travel plans is difficult to ascertain. Timothy learned, however, that Trophimus was no longer in active service. The repetition of the earlier request, now with a time limit added (v. 21; compare 4:9), makes it unlikely that Paul intended Timothy to visit Trophimus on his way to Rome. Instead, Timothy was to ensure that he left soon enough to cross the Adriatic Sea before winter weather (November to March) closed it to travel. There was also the matter of getting Paul's winter cloak to him in time to be of use. Fee (1988:301) posits from this note a late spring/ early summer time of writing, and this seems reasonable.

The Benediction (4:22) Paul's personal blessing to Timothy is a prayer that the Lord be continually with his spirit (Gal 6:18; Phil 4:23; Philem 25). *Spirit* here refers to the spiritual dimension of human life, that dimension in which the Lord communicates and has fellowship through the Holy Spirit (Rom 8:16). This is probably just as much a prayer that Timothy be able to perceive the Lord's presence.

To others, including those whom Timothy was to greet but perhaps also members of the Ephesian and other congregations in which Timothy had been at work, Paul extends the blessing *grace be with you [all]*. This term encompasses the whole of God's love and concern for his people (see on 1 Tim 1:2; 6:21). Thus it is a wish that they will continue to draw meaning and purpose from a life lived responsively in this orbit.

Outline of Titus

COMMENTARY

Titus

☐ Greeting (1:1-4)

How many of us really know who we are and why we are here? Of course, we all have names and our own personal histories. We have goals, dreams and characteristics which we feel give us a special identity, and these things are certainly to be valued. But when we think about reason for being, personal identity and meaning in life, do we do so with God and his will in mind?

The letter to Titus lays that challenge, among others, before us today. Much of the letter encourages rather ordinary believers, who occupy all walks of life, to consider their lives in every facet as an expression of the will of God. In fact, once life is considered in this way, the thought of "ordinariness" departs from Christian thinking about life. No matter what path God has given us to walk, we are intended to be a vital piece in God's missionary plan to reach the rest of the world. Each "piece" has meaning, each human life has inestimable value and usefulness to God, and this realization is a tremendous source of joy, satisfaction and peace. But to comprehend this, we may need to make some adjustments in the way we view life. Let's begin, then, with a look at how Paul defined his own life. Although he was an apostle, the pattern of his thinking ought also to be ours.

As he does in the opening greeting of 1 Timothy, Paul again identifies formally his status and his office and then identifies and blesses the intended recipient. In comparison with 1 Timothy, however, the apostle, using very compact language, describes in more detail his Christian *raison d'être*. This sets the tone and introduces the main theme of the letter.

The Sender (1:1-3) Paul uses two terms to introduce himself in verse 1. *Servant of God* occurs only here in the Pastorals (see "servant of Christ Jesus," Rom 1:1; Phil 1:1). It describes Paul as one who is under compulsion, committed to faithful service as a slave to a master. It also indicates his submission to the will of God. *Apostle of Jesus Christ,* as we have seen at 1 Timothy 1:1 (though there it is "Christ Jesus"; compare 2 Tim 1:1), signifies Paul's selection for service and his sending by Christ himself. This is a technical designation of one to whom Christ's authority has been delegated.

From the accounts in Acts and his own letters, it is very apparent that Paul lived to serve God. It is also apparent that he wanted to see this motivation duplicated in the lives of others. The greeting in Titus reflects both of these interests as Paul describes what makes life meaningful for him. Both the compact form of the description (in fact, the entire greeting, vv. 1-4, consists of a single sentence) and its central place in the message of the letter recommend a closer look.

1. The purpose of Paul's ministry (1:1). Three main phrases combine to describe what made Paul tick. The first two focus on purpose, and that purpose was the salvation and spiritual growth of others. He lived to bring *God's elect* to faith and maturity in Christ (compare 2 Tim 2:10). This language reflects the belief in God's election, his sovereign choice and preservation of a people for himself (compare 2:14). At the same time Paul clearly understood his ministry to consist of calling in, by proclaiming the gospel, those who would belong to God.

The second phrase continues without a break in the Greek sentence to define the first phrase in terms of *knowledge of the truth*. This is a description of salvation based on a rational decision about the gospel (the truth; compare 1 Tim 2:4; 4:3; 2 Tim 2:25; 3:7). But in Crete, as in

Notes: 1:1 For the Pauline understanding of God's people as *God's elect* see Romans 8:33; Colossians 3:12; 2 Timothy 2:10 (see the notes at 1 Tim 6:12). It is one of several related concepts, including "predestination," "calling" and "foreknowledge" (growing out of an Old Testament understanding of God—Ps 105:43; Is 65:9) by which the formation and sustaining of a people for God is described as resting ultimately in God's sovereign choice.

1:2 Affirmation of the utter truthfulness of God appears alongside references to his promises (Num 23:19; Heb 6:18). The term Paul uses *(apseudēs)* has the ring of an attribute.

Ephesus, the traditional meanings of "truth" and "gospel" were disputed by false teachers. For this reason Paul adds the important qualification *that leads to godliness.* The "truth" that his ministry was concerned with produces genuine Christians. *Godliness* throughout the Pastorals defines the Christian experience as a balanced and holistic life in which correct knowledge of God affects every part of life (see notes on 1 Tim 2:2).

Consequently, Paul conceived of his life's task not simply as planting seeds of faith but also as producing strong, mature and fruitful Christians. His purpose was accomplished only when people were well on their way to maturity in Christ.

2. The basis of Paul's ministry (1:2-3). The third phrase, set off somewhat from the first two by a change of preposition (the first two phrases share the same one), also describes Paul's apostleship. The NIV interpretation repeats the substance of the first two phrases, *faith and knowledge,* suggesting that Paul's meaning is that these "rest on" hope. But in the long sentence the three main phrases are parallel, each describing *apostle.* Thus it is Paul's ministry that is based on *the hope of eternal life.* Or to put it another way, the reason for Paul's apostolic calling *is* the hope of eternal life.

This word *hope* means different things to different people. Often the way we use it ("I hope tomorrow will be a nice day," "I hope I get the job") implies uncertainty. But Christian hope has an entirely different quality about it, for it is grounded on the promises of God. The remainder of verses 2-3 provide one of the finest illustrations of the certainty of Christian hope in eternal life.

Paul divides time into two parts to emphasize the certainty of our hope. First, before time God made the promise of eternal life (v. 2). That is, it was part of his eternal will that his people would enjoy eternal life. Furthermore, God's promises are not like human promises, because God cannot lie.

The NIV translation *before the beginning of time (pro chronōn aiōniōn)* accurately captures the "pretemporal" meaning of Paul's phrase (Rom 16:25-26; 1 Cor 2:7-10; Eph 1:4; Col 1:25-26).

Paul employs the formula "before time began—now" (compare "formerly—now"; see below on 3:3-4) to emphasize that the present is the age of salvation, the age of fulfillment (see Towner 1989:63-64).

Paul's argument reaches full force, however, with the shift in time that occurs in verse 3. Here Paul says that God manifested his word at the proper time (NIV *his appointed season*), and he links this manifestation in some way to preaching. In what sense did/does God bring his word to light through preaching? Paul's thought here is important for an understanding of the role of proclamation in God's plan of redemption. God first demonstrated the certainty of his promise (that is, *his word*) in sending his Son who died and was resurrected. Paul does not mention this explicitly here (though compare 2 Tim 1:10), but the thought is implicit. This is virtually certain because the verb "manifest" (NIV *brought . . . to light*) and the "before time—now" (or, as here, "at the proper time") scheme in the New Testament usually depict together the divulgence of God's plan of salvation in Christ to the world or to the apostles (Rom 16:25-26; 1 Cor 2:6-7; Eph 3:4-7, 8-11; Col 1:26-27; 1 Tim 1:9-10; compare Gal 4:4; 1 Tim 3:16). Also, in the Pastorals the phrase "the proper time" refers to Christ's Incarnation or his Second Coming. Therefore, in saying, as the NIV interprets it, *at his appointed season he brought his word [his promise] to light,* Paul alludes to the historical appearance (ministry, death and resurrection) of Christ which forms the bedrock of Christian hope in eternal life.

But Paul's focus in this passage is on his (and our) place in God's plan to deliver eternal life. Now we see that God not only verified the truthfulness of his promise—the certainty of hope—in sending Christ but continues to do so *through the preaching entrusted to* Paul and the church. The thought here parallels 2 Timothy 1:9-10: there time is also divided into the "before" and the "now," and God fulfills his promise first in Christ's death and resurrection, second through the church's preaching of that event. Thus in God's plan the church has become not only the proof and recipient of hope's promise but also the channel through which *the hope of eternal life* is offered to the rest of the world.

Christian hope is built on the promise of God. That promise is good (1) because God does not lie and (2) because he sent his Son to keep

---

1:3 *His word* has been interpreted by commentators variously as a reference to (1) the preaching of the gospel (Fee 1988:169; Dibelius and Conzelmann 1972:131; Hanson 1982:170); (2) Christ as the *logos* (Walder 1923:110-15); or (3) God's aforementioned "promise" or "purpose as declared through the proclamation" (Kelly 1963:228). The reason

his promise. The gospel ministry, which exists to communicate this hope, extends the redemptive work of Christ's cross and resurrection into the "present" of the church. For by this means and this means alone God has chosen to execute salvation (1 Cor 1:18-31). The rest of Paul's instructions to Titus draw their meaning from this point, because only a healthy church will be able to carry out this plan of *God the Savior.*

It is important to get hold of the significance of ministry in Paul's thinking. Every believer's life has been uniquely designed with ministry in mind (Rom 12:6; 1 Cor 12:7). Paul's calling—to make known the truth of God and *the hope of eternal life*—is one in which we are all meant to have a part.

The Recipient (1:4) Paul wrote this letter to Titus. Although our knowledge of him is limited, it seems that he became a coworker of Paul's at an earlier time than Timothy (Gal 2:1, 3). He was a Gentile and may have come to faith through the apostle's ministry (as Tit 1:4 suggests). Paul found him well qualified to handle difficult situations, such as representing him in the Corinthian church (2 Cor 2:3-4, 13; 7:6-16; 8:16-24). When he received this letter, his situation was similar, for he had been deployed by Paul to establish and strengthen the church in Crete.

Crete is an island in the Mediterranean located south of the Aegean Sea. What we know of the church on Crete comes from this letter. Paul set foot on the island as a prisoner, en route to Rome (Acts 27:7-17), but the initial planting cannot be attributed to that brief visit. If Paul was personally involved in the initial Cretan mission, he probably did so within the period of release from his first Roman imprisonment. On the other hand, if his coworker(s) carried out the work by Paul's direction, the church may have been established on the island prior to his imprisonment (see introduction). In either case, the task assigned to Titus— to complete and put in order what was unfinished (1:5)—suggests a church (probably house churches in most of the districts) considerably younger and less organized than the church in Ephesus.

---

for choosing the latter interpretation is Paul's syntax, which requires that *his word* be the object of the verb "manifested"; by virtue of the continuity provided by the time sequence, *his word* is also parallel to the relative pronoun *which* and its antecedent, the promise of eternal life.

For all the Cretan believers to see (compare 3:15), Paul at once associates himself closely with Titus and validates his ministry. As with Timothy, *true son* establishes Titus's legitimate connection with the apostle's ministry. Paul's language may indicate that he himself played a part in bringing Titus to faith (see 1 Tim 1:2 notes). The further reference to *our common faith* reveals that their faith in Christ formed the basis of their personal and working relationship. The readers were to understand that Titus worked among them as Paul's delegate; they were to regard him (and his authority) as they regarded Paul.

The Blessing (1:4) This blessing, *grace and peace,* occurs regularly in the openings of Paul's letters (excepting 1 and 2 Tim). It is his wish that Titus enjoy God's unmeritable favor and unshakable peace. As Paul indicates, these blessings are the benefits of membership in God the Father's family and of participation in the salvation accomplished by Christ the Savior. For Titus and those who serve God, they are promises of divine provision and inner stability regardless of external circumstances. Paul's blessing also reminds the readers that the ministry initiated by God and Christ can be accomplished only by reliance upon them. Human means and strength are insufficient for the task.

□ Titus's Instructions (1:5-16)

Parenting is challenging work. When our first daughter was born, I was struck by our lack of anticipation of her basic needs: food, sleep, clean diapers—often at inconvenient times. But most parents discover that this stage is nothing compared with what is to come. The needs associated with the child's growth and maturity require greater attention and unconditional love from the parent. Encouragement builds self-esteem and propels the child forward to meet life's challenges. Correction instills and increases an understanding of right and wrong, as it teaches that human behavior has moral consequences. Parents must provide the child's life with structure and organization. In this way the young person learns about expected roles and responsibilities within the home and society, as well as lines of authority and the importance of interdepend-

Notes: 1:5 Paul seems to envisage the Cretan believers as making up a single church (consisting of house churches throughout the island), in which case the number of elders chosen in each locale would have depended on the size of the local congregation

ence among fellow human beings. Meeting these needs prepares the child for life as an adult. If all of this is taken seriously, parenting is not easy.

Parenting a church requires most of these same skills and responsibilities. As the church grows in numbers and maturity, its needs change much as those of the growing child do. When Titus received Paul's letter, the churches of Crete were still quite young, but quickly growing out of infancy. They had reached the stage where more structure was required, where church members needed to ascend to roles of leadership and where they could begin to carry on ministry independent of their spiritual parents. Preparing them for this was a task that fell to Titus. At the same time an element within the churches was introducing false doctrine that threatened the development of these Christians. Thus Titus's instructions include correction.

The tone and content of this passage are very similar to those of 1 Timothy. After a reminder to Titus about his purpose in Crete (1:5), Paul includes the same basic set of qualifications for the overseer/elder that he issued to Timothy (1:6-9) to guide him in his task. Then he calls Titus to correct the errorists (1:10-16).

Appointing Elders (1:5-9) Paul's strategy for church planting included the eventual selection of leaders from among the converts to oversee the ministry and spiritual growth of the community (compare Acts 14:23). In this way the missionaries could move on freely to expand the work in new and unreached areas. As Paul's team of trained coworkers grew, he entrusted a good deal of the work to them. In the case of the Cretan churches, Titus functioned in this capacity.

Paul spells out his purpose in appointing Titus to the work in Crete in verse 5. It has two parts. The first phrase Paul uses to describe this purpose might address the need for correction (of things gone wrong) or completion (of things as yet undone). The former possibility makes sense in view of the false teaching that Titus is to combat (vv. 10-16). But the second part of the purpose, to appoint elders, and the phrase

---

and the number of qualified candidates available. Considered as a whole, however, the rule would have been for a church to be ruled by a plurality of elders. On the offices in the church, see further at 1 Timothy 3:1.

"what is lacking" in the first part suggest that Paul means completion of the tasks that remain to be completed. Actually, since correcting the false teachers is linked to careful choice of leadership (v. 9), it may be best to combine the two possibilities as the NIV has done: *straighten out what was left unfinished.*

In any case, the second part of the purpose is clearly first on Paul's list of specific things that Titus is to finish. Precisely what went into the process of appointing elders is not clear. Certainly from the qualifications that follow we can guess that some form of evaluation played a part. But the situation in Crete, where the churches were younger, was not the same as that which we find in Ephesus, where a body of elders already existed (see 1 Tim 4:14). And any evaluation may have been carried out by Titus himself (compare Acts 14:23). The appointment of the elders would have been signaled by the laying on of hands (compare Acts 14:23; 1 Tim 4:14; 5:22) in the presence of the congregation. It is also impossible to determine how many elders would have been selected *in every town* (meaning "in the house church of each town"); but the general rule would probably have been a plurality of leaders.

Qualifications of the Elder/Overseer (1:6-9) To guide Titus in choosing leaders, Paul included the same basic office code (with certain modifications) that appears in 1 Timothy 3. Before we consider differences we should consider similarities. Most important, the purpose of this code is identical to that of 1 Timothy 3 in that it is meant to test the candidate's "blamelessness." The broad standard appears twice at the head of the list (vv. 6, 7; compare 1 Tim 3:2). Then the remainder of the verses place "blamelessness" into a concrete framework, treating the domestic, personal and ecclesiastical aspects of the candidate's life. It is equally obvious that the codes share most of the specific requirements; where terms are not duplicated, concepts generally are. In the end it is clear that whatever the circumstances of a church, its leadership must be of the highest moral standard in all aspects of life; to expect less is to place the church's reputation and ministry in jeopardy.

The code begins abruptly (for there is no break in the Greek sentence at the end of v. 5) in verse 6 by laying down the general standard of "blamelessness" (compare 1 Tim 3:10). Again, the examination begins in the domestic sphere, with fidelity in marriage. The reappearance of this qualification at the head of this list (compare 1 Tim 3:2, 12) excludes the possibility of compromise here. It should perhaps be pointed out that while "one-woman man" has sexual fidelity primarily in view, Paul undoubtedly expected the marriages of church leaders to exhibit mutual love and respect (Eph 5:22-33). The leader of the church must be a model of faithfulness in marriage.

Keeping the domestic concerns together, the remainder of verse 6 refers to the children of the elder and their behavior. But there is an interpretive problem here that we must pause to consider. The problem lies in the meaning of the Greek word *pista* in the phrase "having believing [or faithful] children." One view understands Paul to be limiting membership in the office to those whose family members all believe; *pista* can certainly bear this meaning. Another view is that the term means, more generally, "faithful" or "trustworthy" (1:9; 3:8; 1 Tim 3:11; compare 1 Tim 1:15; 3:1), which quality is then delineated in the phrase that follows. While the first view is possible, it seems to place more stringent requirements on the elder than does 1 Timothy 3:4. Moreover, in view of this parallel, Paul probably means that the elder's children are to be faithful in obeying the head of the house. In fact, the rest of the verse contrasts "faithful" with *the charge of being wild and disobedient,* which suggests a more general kind of faithfulness. The code asks that candidates for the office of elder not be those whose children will attract accusations of dissipation and rebellion (compare v. 10). This is very much in accord with 1 Timothy 3:4.

As we consider application of this quality today, a practical question arises regarding the length of time elders are to be held accountable for the behavior of their children. As used here, the term *children* views sons and daughters in relation to their parents. Within the household their status would be that of dependents. The instruction, therefore, restricts the elder's accountability to children who are not yet adults. And of course, then and now and from one culture to the next, entrance into adulthood is measured by different combinations of age and events (marriage, leaving home, beginning a career), which prevent us from drawing rigid lines (such as up until age eighteen or twenty-one). Nevertheless, it is reasonable to think that the attitudes and behavior of children still within the household provide an indication of the faithfulness of an elder in parenting. But while this formative influence is meant to prepare children for godly adult lives, it does not constitute a guarantee such that elders ought to be made responsible for the directions that their grown children might choose to take.

Verse 7 inserts the formal introduction of the code (compare 1 Tim 3:2), which uses the term *overseer.* Apparently, the terms *elder* and *overseer* were interchangeable (at least at this stage of the church's development and in this locale). Alongside the official title Paul introduces a significant theme that the NIV interpretation *(entrusted with God's work)* of the literal "as God's steward" fails to convey. By describing the overseer as God's steward, Paul calls to mind the image of the church as God's house (compare 1 Tim 3:5, 15; 2 Tim 2:20-21). In the secular household the steward was charged with the responsibility of managing the master's affairs. The church leader is equally obligated to God to discharge the duties of oversight in the church. Also, to be a "steward" was to acknowledge the requirement of utter faithfulness (Lk 12:42; 1 Cor 4:2).

In God's house faithfulness is required in every part of life. Therefore the examination of the potential steward's "blamelessness" extends to the personal life. First, Paul prohibits four kinds of behavior. Tendencies toward overbearing behavior and anger are indications of unfitness for working as part of a team. Such people do not listen to the views of others but rather force their wills on them, causing disunity. Arguments and quarrels were in fact characteristic of the false teachers (3:9). The implied opposite qualities of gentleness and amicability (1 Tim 3:3) are required of the leader who must lead as Christ does (2 Cor 10:1).

Equally to be avoided are those who are controlled by strong drink or who react with violence to people and situations. Such people are not able to control their own behavior and certainly should not be entrusted with the oversight of others.

Finally, the overseer must not be allured by *dishonest gain.* Complete honesty in financial matters and an attitude of detachment toward wealth (compare 1 Tim 6:7-8, 17-19) that leads to generosity are the signs of

---

1:7 *Elder* was taken over from Judaism, while *overseer* was borrowed from the Greco-

a leader who will be able to model faithfulness in these things before the congregation.

Verse 8 continues, without a break in the sentence, to enumerate some positive and observable characteristics of *blameless* conduct. The leader must be hospitable. This widely praised virtue in that day was practically a social obligation for the householder. It also became a mark of Christian behavior (Rom 12:13; 1 Pet 4:9). What sometimes passes for hospitality today (the entertainment of friends and church members, often with the expectation of a return invitation) is a rather dim reflection of the New Testament concept. The practice of hospitality among Christians was often urgent, sacrificial and risky: urgent because Christians might be forced from homes or jobs with no one to turn to but fellow Christians; sacrificial because material goods were often in short supply; risky because to associate oneself with those who had been forced out meant to identify with their cause. Thus hospitality required sacrificial sharing and stretching. It was a very practical expression of love, not a source of entertainment. While the practice of hospitality had primarily the needs of believers in mind, there is no reason that it could not be a way of showing concern for unbelievers. The importance of this practice for the church, in either case, required that a leader must model it for all (1 Tim 3:2; 5:10).

The leader must "love" *what is good*. Paul's term for this occurs only here in the New Testament (compare Wisdom 7:22). It is the inclination or devotion to things that are or that promote good. This trait was prized in the secular world, and it is easy to see that it would serve the church leader well in the task of oversight.

Self-control is a fundamental mark of genuine faith, and Paul refers to it frequently in these letters (see above on 1 Tim 3:2). Like most of these observable qualities, self-control was prominent in the secular understanding of respectability. Paul, however, emphasizes that the possibility of such conduct depends on the work of Christ (2:12) and conversion.

The remaining three qualities, *upright, holy and disciplined,* complete this profile of the blameless life. Uprightness was one of the cardinal

Roman (or Hellenistic) sphere, where it was applied to supervisors of various sorts. See discussion at 1 Timothy 3:1-13.

virtues in Greek thought. Here "uprightness" refers to behavior in relation to people that is *holy* in the presence of God (Lk 1:75; Eph 4:24; 1 Thess 2:10). *Disciplined* (or self-controlled) here means to be in full control of oneself (one's temper, moods, behavior and so on). This observable quality is truly a mark of the Spirit's work in an individual (Gal 5:23).

Paul's description of the *blameless* personal life is extensive. A person's life is capable of measurement because the characteristics of this life are observable. While Paul clearly teaches that genuine Christian conduct results from conversion (2:12), he does not shy away from presenting the church's leaders for the approval of outsiders, as his vocabulary and concepts for behavior show. Those who would lead the church and promote its cause must be respectable in the eyes of all people.

Verse 9 takes the qualifications for leadership into the area of ministry (compare 1 Tim 3:2). With the false teaching in mind, Paul instructs Titus to ensure that the leaders he chooses are committed to the approved doctrine of the church (compare 1 Tim 3:9). He calls it the *trustworthy* (or faithful) word. This *message* has been handed down by the apostles (literally, "it accords with 'the teaching' "). In other words, leaders must affirm as *the* Christian doctrine that which has the traditional apostolic stamp of approval. Elders must not be chosen from among those who have been toying with new doctrines.

There are two purposes *(so that)* for this commitment. First, only adherence to the "sound doctrine" (see on 1 Tim 1:10) will enable the leader to fulfill the ministry of encouraging and exhorting (that is, producing "healthy") believers. Second, it is only by means of correct doctrine that the leader can successfully refute the opponents (1:13; 1 Tim 4:6; 6:2-3; 2 Tim 3:16).

What qualifies a person to be an elder? Not management skill alone, but also a lifestyle that is proved to be pure and respectable within the church and on the outside. In public and in private the overseer must meet the high standard of "blamelessness." But as with the similar code

---

1:8 *Upright* and *holy* in classical usage described, respectively, "humanward" and "God-ward" behavior (see Fee 1988:175). But in the Hellenistic era the distinction had perhaps faded somewhat (Wisdom of Solomon 9:3); in 1 Thessalonians 2:10 (as here) the pair of terms describes the behavior of people in relation to other people.

in 1 Timothy 3, the emphasis in this teaching is often missed. "Blame-lessness" is more a measure of wholeness and balance than of perfec-tion. The code examines all dimensions of life for evidence of the Spirit's influence in each part. This kind of balanced "reading" means develop-ment toward maturity is under way. And Paul felt that "whole" believers were best suited for church leadership. The code serves equally as a yardstick of maturity for all believers. Both those in leadership and those in support positions will profit from a periodic look at the reference marks it provides; it will point out areas of neglect and areas of success, but it will always point us to maturity in the whole of life.

Titus's task of appointing elders from among recent converts (notice that in this case Paul cannot rule out recent converts; compare 1 Tim 3:6) must not have been easy. Nevertheless, the importance of the church's unity and evangelistic mission required that care be taken to select only leaders whose genuine faith could be measured by commitment not simply to the true gospel but to the Spirit's influence in every part of life.

Opposing False Teachers (1:10-16) Having concluded the list of qualifications for the elder with a reference to refuting error, Paul goes on to unmask the false teachers in the Cretan church. These opponents of Paul must have arisen soon after the churches were planted, but we cannot be certain exactly how this came about.

Heresy involves more than simply teaching an unorthodox doctrine. Just as the Christian message affects the whole life, heresy left unchecked penetrates deep into the community's and the individual's life and thought, leaving nothing undisturbed. But its subtle beginnings and se-cretive motives often make it undetectable until it has surfaced as a movement with increasing momentum. For this reason Paul identifies and unequivocally denounces the false teachers and their doctrine.

The False Teachers What kind of people would, in the name of Christianity, oppose the true faith? Paul's indictment of them, which is designed to expose and discredit them completely, begins by revealing

---

"Discipline" (or self-control; *enkratēs*) was a highly praised virtue, which one Cynic writer described, along with perseverance, as "the most honored of goods" (*The Epistles of Crates* 34. 3).

some telltale clues of heresy.

Far from being innocent seekers of truth, verse 10 portrays false teachers as willful and culpable. *Rebellious* (see v. 6; 1 Tim 1:9) describes them as consciously defiant and in opposition to Paul's authority and work. Paul characterizes their activity as "idle" or "mere talk," a reference both to their meaningless speculation and discussions and to the pagan quality of their "knowledge" (1 Tim 1:6). But it is as *deceivers* (v. 10) that false teachers do their most dangerous work; they willfully lead others astray. Paul's language places them into the same category as the heretics in Ephesus, who, by misrepresenting God's law and causing others to break it, come under its condemnation (1 Tim 1:8-10).

The description *those of the circumcision* (v. 10) provides a clue to the identity of those troubling the Cretan churches. As the term's use elsewhere suggests, the troublemakers were Jewish converts (Acts 10:45; 11:2; Gal 2:7-9, 12). Earlier Paul opposed Jewish believers in Galatia who were teaching the need to return to the ceremonies of the law to achieve righteousness. While this is not the same group, nor precisely the same teaching (see below), we can at least see that the influences of Judaism on the church had not yet ceased.

Paul's description is too brief to make absolutely plain the meaning of *ruining whole households by teaching things they ought not to teach* (v. 11). This may be a reference to the turning of whole house churches to the heresy, or possibly some part of their doctrine challenged traditional concepts concerning the household. To judge from 2:1-10, their teaching may have spawned a disregard for the accepted patterns of behavior in the various social relationships. Either way, the word *whole* here suggests that the influence of this doctrine was thorough. In Ephesus disruptions resulted from a misunderstanding of salvation and the times, and something similar may have been at work in Crete. These false teachers disrupted the unity of the church and endangered the church's reputation with those outside, who valued highly the traditional social structure.

False teachers can also be detected by their false motives. These

---

1:12 Crete was known for its lack of wild beasts (Pliny *Natural History* 8. 83), which made the proverbial description of Cretans as *evil brutes* (literally, "wild beasts") ironic

"Christian" teachers in Crete were seeking to make a profit from their ministry. Such financial motives expose the false teacher's selfish desire to benefit more than the hearers from the "ministry" (compare 1 Tim 6:5-10).

The description Paul has thus far given has drawn out the obvious faults of the false teachers. When their attitudes, methods and motives are exposed, there can be no doubt that these people are evil. Paul puts the cap on this exposé with his surprising quotation of Epimenides (v. 12). He calls this ancient religious teacher, from the sixth century B.C., *one of their own [that is, the false teachers'] prophets.* This first connection probably lies in their common profession, teaching religious fables, and in their common homeland, Crete. But how does Paul mean the citation to be understood? Cretans had acquired the name *liars* because of their claim that the tomb of Zeus was on Crete. Thus a reference to religious deceit is at the heart of the saying. These false teachers have fulfilled Epimenides' prophecy in their own generation by propagating a religious lie. The rest of the quotation, *evil brutes, lazy gluttons,* associates the false religious claim with uncontrolled, wanton behavior. Notice how closely Paul's description of the errorists corresponds to the three-part saying: they are *deceivers* (v. 10), rebels and disrupters (vv. 10-11), with minds set on money (v. 11). Clearly, in the case of these Cretan heretics, the ancient forecast held true. Today the religious lies propagated by cult leaders (those that draw attention away from the gospel) belong to the same category. Their purpose is to attract attention to the leader or the cult's ruling elite. Their result is self-gratifying behavior on the part of the leaders and ignorance on the part of naive followers.

Paul describes the false teaching in verse 14 with two terms. The first, *Jewish myths,* is similar to the "myths and genealogies" mentioned in 1 Timothy 1:4. Together with the reference to *genealogies* in 3:9, the term probably indicates a peculiar use of the Old Testament (see 1 Tim 1:4 and notes). Verse 15 implies that they were preoccupied with ritual purity, which suggests that the false doctrine had some affinity with the

and striking. For references to the ancient sources, see Dibelius and Conzelmann 1972:136-37; Quinn 1990:107-8.

teaching about foods and defilement in Colosse (Col 2:16-23) and Ephesus (1 Tim 4:3). Verse 16 may reflect a claim on their part to special knowledge: *they claim to know God.* However, Paul's language is too general to allow us to be sure of this, and it is better to understand the statement in Jewish terms as a claim to be zealous and exacting in their approach to "the faith."

The second term in verse 14 describes the false teaching as "commands of men." This is a technical term, which goes back to Isaiah 29:13, for teaching of human origin that is added to God's revelation (the NIV somewhat obscures this nuance). Jesus picked it up in his denunciation of Jewish regulations about clean and unclean things (Mt 15:9; Mk 7:7). And Paul describes the ascetic practices in Colosse with this term (Col 2:22). Ironically, adherence to such regulations, which to the false teachers indicated holiness, was actually an indication of how far they had strayed from *the truth* (of the Christian message; v. 14).

Paul operated on the basis of Jesus' principle "Nothing outside a man can make him 'unclean' by going into him. . . . What comes out of a man makes him 'unclean' " (Mk 7:15, 20). This Paul translates in verse 15: *To the pure, all things are pure, but to those who . . . do not believe, nothing is pure* (compare Rom 14:14). Purity that counts comes only through faith in Christ. The heretics' obsession with external purity grew out of unbelief and rejection of the gospel. In their false teaching they cut themselves off from the One who could cleanse them. Their rejection of *the truth* (v. 14) signaled the corruption of their *minds* (v. 15). The mind, the organ of rational discernment, plays an important role in accepting the truth (1 Tim 6:5; 2 Tim 3:8). These teachers' obsessive behavior and evil motives signaled equally the corruption of their consciences, for it is by the conscience that faith and knowledge issue in behavior (see on 1 Tim 1:5; 4:2).

Ultimately, as Paul explains in verse 16, the condition of these opponents was paradoxical. Their profession to know God was contradicted by their outward behavior. The excoriating description that closes the passage heightens this paradox: (1) *they are detestable,* though they strive to avoid "detestable" things; (2) they are *disobedient,* though they strive to be exactingly obedient; and (3) they are unable to bear any spiritual fruit (good deed), though they claim to know God. One thing is clear from Paul's denunciation of the false teachers: they present a danger to the church and to themselves, a danger that cannot be ignored but must be confronted.

Opposing False Teachers As we have seen, confronting false teaching is a task that falls to the leadership of the church. Titus and the leaders he selected were to handle this matter in Crete.

The gravity of the situation is reflected in the two commands that Paul gives. First, Titus is to "silence" (literally, "stop the mouths") of the heretics (v. 11). This must mean to "take the wind out of their sails," or to take away the momentum they had established, by publicly correcting their false doctrines with the approved teaching of the apostle. Second, he is to *rebuke [correct, reprove] them sharply* (v. 13). The graphic adverb used only here and in 2 Corinthians 13:10 implies the use of force that is backed up by authority. Confronting false teaching calls for decisive, firm correction, for the church's ministry and the spiritual health of believers are at stake.

But the goal of correction is not simply to protect the gospel. Correction also seeks *(so that*—v. 13) to restore the erring one to spiritual health (1 Tim 1:20; 2 Tim 2:22). Paul employs the verbal form of the term used elsewhere to describe the gospel as "health-producing" (v. 9; 1 Tim 1:10; 6:3) to convey this thought. This health comes only from acceptance of *the faith.* Turned around, as they were, these lying and perverse heretics could still be brought to repentance through confrontation with the true faith.

☐ Instructions for Godly Living (2:1-15)

In the months before his execution by the Nazis, Dietrich Bonhoeffer wrote: "I fear that Christians who stand with only one leg upon earth, also stand with only one leg in heaven." His concern was for Christians who had disengaged themselves from the world, who could stand by and watch atrocities committed as if the Christian message or individual Christian responsibility had no bearing whatsoever upon earthly affairs.

The fact of the matter is that the Christian faith intends full engagement in the world. Certainly the origin of this new life is otherworldly. Certainly Christian values are not those of the world. Certainly Christian hope takes us beyond this world. But it is in this world that God has called Christians to live, and it is this world's inhabitants that Christians must reach with the gospel. Engagement of this kind requires Christian credibility and participation in the life of the world.

Credibility especially depends on living, as far as possible, in a manner that the world considers to be respectable. "Respectability" was an important concept in Paul's day. But the values connected with it have always been subject to change. Therefore, the Christian life is first and always to be a clear expression of the will of God.

The church's respectability in the world was very much in Paul's mind as he addressed the various groups in the Cretan churches. This is evident from the patterns of behavior he encourages in 2:1-10, patterns that would have pleased any upright person in that day. It is equally evident in his affirmation of the social categories by which orderly community or civil life was defined. In verses 2-10 he divides the church according to customary social categories (generations, sexes, slaves), and he employs the household-code form of teaching to emphasize that Christians must practice a renewed or reformed quality of behavior within those categories (see commentary at 1 Tim 2:1).

This type of teaching encouraged participation in the social structure rather than withdrawal from it. Exemplary (Christian) behavior within the traditional relationships would help maintain or increase the church's credibility in the eyes of the world and promote the evangelistic mission. But Paul does not simply adopt secular rules of behavior. Whatever affinities this lifestyle might have with secular moral ideals, only faith in Christ can produce the Christian, reformed version (vv. 11-15). This is what Paul means by godly living; and godly living is what this passage is about.

Godly Living and Social Groups (2:1-10) It had been Paul's practice to urge Christians to remain in the place in life that they occupied at the time of conversion (1 Cor 7:8, 17, 20, 24). This meant, among other things, that becoming a Christian did not release one from social assignments. And the organization of roles and behavior in the church was not to diverge *unnecessarily* from the greater social structure.

But the emphasis on *unnecessarily* should not be missed. It implies limitations. As important as the mission mandate was to Paul, he would not do just anything to make the gospel appealing to the unbeliever. The church must live within the world, which is fallen, and within cultures, which in various ways express this fallenness, but it must do so critically, measuring everything against the Word of God. It will undoubtedly find that much of any given culture can be accepted, worked with and (in Christ) improved upon; but wherever the culture encourages or advocates behavior that violates the will of God, the church must make its stand for God, whatever the consequences (compare Acts 5:29). The point to be observed in this context is that responsible Christian living within society, which promotes mission *while not compromising God's values*, is a part of God's will.

Apparently, revolutionary teaching was penetrating the Cretan communities through the opponents' doctrine. The visible effects produced in the churches would not go unnoticed by the outsider; doctrinal subtleties, however, tended to be an "in-house" affair, invisible or irrelevant to the outsider. Consequently, Paul's instructions aim to restore social stability and protect the church's witness.

The Sound Doctrine and Social Ethics (2:1) Christian ethics and the Christian message are meant to be inseparably and harmoniously related. Paul's command in verse 1 binds Titus to this principle. He does so because the opponents had rejected the message and perverted the concept of a Christian way of life.

Sound doctrine, the approved teaching of the Christian faith which produces spiritual health, is the immovable foundation of the Christian life. What is taught about Christian living must be *in accord with* (or correspond to) it. Paul measures this in two ways.

First, the Christian message is the source of the real Christian life. It is salvation through Christ that has introduced this new manner of life (2:12). Without the message there can be no Christian ethics. Consequently, many of the terms that describe aspects of godly living in verses 2-10 represent the possibilities of belief and in principle do not have their beginning in human effort. Here Christian and secular "respectability" part ways.

Second, the Christian manner of life accords with the Christian message by serving its missionary purpose. It adorns the gospel and makes it attractive to those who look on (2:5, 8, 10).

This opening command is therefore not simply a transition to bring the readers from 1:16 to the practical teaching of 2:2. Rather, it reminds Titus and Christian teachers that Christian ethics to be *Christian* must emerge from, correspond to and serve the message of the Scriptures. Furthermore, every believer's lifestyle must be subjected to the test of biblical principles; the alternative is to allow our lives to be shaped and approved by a value system that is opposed to God's.

Older Men (2:2) Older men must live lives of observable respectability or dignity. To emphasize this, Paul uses language that, as we have seen elsewhere (1:8; 1 Tim 3:2-3), belongs to the constellation of terms borrowed from secular ethicists. *Temperate, worthy of respect* (or "respectable," "serious") and *self-controlled* (or "sensible") tend to overlap in meaning. But the implication of a dignified lifestyle that is free from overindulgence, dissipation and foolish behavior in general is clear. As Paul's use of common terms suggests, this lifestyle would be readily recognizable. Christianity does have a mystical, incomprehensible element to it, but its manifestation in life communicates in a language understood by all.

The rest of verse 2 suggests, however, that Christian respectability has a deeper source. What the NIV has interpreted as three additional aspects of acceptable behavior *(and sound in faith, in love and in endurance)* could, by virtue of the participle "being sound," express instead the cause or means of the behavior described above. For Paul the most basic constituents of Christianity are *faith* and *love* (see notes on 1 Tim 2:15): the vertical, personal relationship with God through Christ and the horizontal dimension of "good deeds" characterized by love (compare Gal 5:6). *Endurance* here speaks of commitment to this life. The more traditional triad was "faith, hope, love" (1 Cor 13:13; Col 1:4-5); but if the situation called for it, *endurance* might occur as a fourth virtue (1 Thess 1:3) or replace "hope." Given the presence of heresy in these churches, *endurance* gave this instruction the emphasis on perseverance that Paul wanted to express.

Within the social structure, older men are to be the models of dignity, respectability and wisdom. Paul knew that if this does not hold within the church as well, Christianity cannot hope to compete in the world. At the same time, the language of this instruction suggests that the absence of respectability means divergence from the faith.

Older Women (2:3-4) Paul's instructions to the older women have the same goal *(likewise)* of Christian respectability. In their case, respectable behavior amounts to "reverence," which above all means avoiding "slanderous talk" and "drunkenness," and *teaching what is good.* The term Paul chose to refer to "reverence" was used to characterize the conduct of priestesses, which suggests that he is advocating that Christian women fit an exceptional type. "Slanderous talk" and "drunkenness," on the other hand, were among the vices commonly associated with the negative type of older women in Greco-Roman society.

The positive quality of "teaching good things" reminds older women that they are responsible to model the acceptable and respectable life for younger women. The adjective *teaching what is good* denotes informal teaching by lifestyle, as verses 4-5 show. It leads directly to the stated purpose of their instruction *(then they can train the younger women,* v. 4). "Good things" in this context are acceptable patterns of behavior. But the term contains a hidden implication: one teaches with one's life either good things or bad things; pursuit of the acceptable lifestyle will ensure teaching that is good.

This is a resource the church today could draw on much more than it does. We have bought into the notion that older people have had their day of usefulness and ought to make way for the young. But the principle here is quite the opposite. With age and experience come wisdom, and many older women have discovered secrets of godly living in relation to their husbands, children and neighbors and in the workplace that could save younger women a lot of unnecessary grief. And when the unavoidable trials come to the young woman, who better to guide her through than an older sister who has been through it before? Somehow the church must see that younger women have contact with older women. The leadership must encourage (and equip further) specially gifted older women to seek younger women who desire to be trained.

Younger Women (2:4-5) Contained in the instruction to the older women is instruction to younger women as well. In Paul's teaching format, which is limited to the most typical categories of society, *younger women* means younger married women, for in that day most would have been married. Such a woman was to excel in the socially acceptable role of the homemaker, and therefore domestic concerns dominate. Paul's choice of verb, *train*, is related to a word that means "self-control," "prudence," "moderation" and "discretion" (2:2, 5; 1 Tim 2:9; 3:2). Though it can mean "to bring back to one's senses" (which might imply that some young women had been influenced by the false teaching; 1:11), perhaps Paul chose it to underline the theme of discretion and self-control in outward Christian behavior.

Although there were exceptions (and Paul envisaged one; see below), for the young woman of that day respectability generally meant marriage. Within marriage she was to *love* her husband and children. To the honorable Jew or Gentile in that day, the presence of this kind of love indicated an exceptional wife. The Christian wife who sets an example of love sends a powerful message that is understandable even to those outside the church.

The next two terms, *self-controlled* (or "sensible"—2:2; 1 Tim 2:9; 3:2) *and pure* (1 Tim 2:15; 4:12; 5:2, 22), seem to digress from the theme of domesticity. However, in that they probably refer to sexual conduct, they are quite appropriate to discussion of a wife's Christian conduct. If the matter of love just mentioned is settled, self-control and purity are bound to follow.

Next, another pair of words either instruct the young woman *to be busy at home* and *kind* or together mean "to be an efficient homemaker." In either case, the emphasis on skill in managing the home is typical of Paul's (and secular) thinking about the young woman's acceptable role (1 Tim 2:15; 5:14). A reference to "kindness" undoubtedly would remind the young woman to pay attention to those around her as she goes about her daily business.

Finally, submission to the husband is mentioned. This is a typical feature of New Testament teaching about the role relationship of the wife to the husband (Eph 5:22; Col 3:18; 1 Pet 3:10) and again is obviously in touch with the secular idea of marriage. However, Paul's concept of "submission" contained notions of mutuality of respect and love and thus clearly transcended the secular notion.

Compared with the discussions in Ephesians 5 and Colossians 3, Paul's

Notes: 2:5 To put the modern discussion of the implications of "submission" into

"subordination" teaching in Titus 2:5 is abbreviated; he has left off instructions to the husband that would emphasize mutuality of responsibility, and he has added the purpose of protecting God's Word (see below). There are two possible explanations for the "harsher" appearance of 2:5 (see on 1 Tim 2:11-15): (1) All that is set forth in Ephesians is implied; he writes briefly and addresses the more serious problems surrounding the home and women in the home. (2) The instruction is indeed intended to be stricter; disruption in the church that affected the women led Paul to clamp down on women to protect the church's reputation in the world. Given the fact that there is really nothing here that Paul does not say in related passages (he simply passes over the husband's role), the first alternative seems best. Perhaps we should (1) acknowledge the special problems in the Cretan Christian households, (2) consider Ephesians 5 as a more thorough treatment of marriage and (3) focus on the purpose (see below) of the wife's full engagement in the institution of marriage.

There is no question that the behavior of the Christian wife taught here would have pleased the pagan critic. In fact, this lifestyle has the outsider in mind, as the purpose (*so that*) of verse 5 reveals. One of Paul's concerns was to protect the Christian message (*the word of God;* compare Col 1:5; 1 Thess 2:13) from charges that it encouraged disrespectful or revolutionary behavior. The Old Testament prophets feared that God's name would be slandered by the nations because of the ungodly behavior of God's own people (Is 52:5; Ezek 36:20-36; see 1 Tim 6:1 and notes). This same theme receives a more distinct missionary interpretation in the New Testament: respectable behavior, which bears witness to the power and truth of God, enhances the church's witness (1 Thess 4:12; 1 Tim 6:1; 1 Pet 2:11-12).

There was, however, an important exception to the rule of marriage, and in view of the modern situation we should pause to consider it. In Paul's thinking, for a Christian woman (or man) to remain single had many advantages for ministry (1 Cor 7:1, 7, 8, 32-34), but it required a special gift (Mt 19:11-12; 1 Cor 7:7). The advantages led Paul to encourage those with this gift to remain single. But alongside the advantages

focus, compare Knight 1992:307-10, 316-18 and Padgett 1987:39-52.

of singleness were dangers in the form of temptation. So the qualities of self-control and sexual purity (v. 5) were to be clearly evident (compare 1 Cor 7:2, 5, 9) among the unmarried. A single Christian woman would be expected to exhibit a lifestyle that avoided any suspicion of immorality.

If anything, the challenges that face the single Christian woman (and man) today are even greater. With greater freedom, mobility and responsibility, combined with society's indifference to sexual behavior, the temptations have multiplied. Yet God's will has not changed. Purity and self-control must characterize the lifestyle of the single Christian woman. And the "countercultural" message she sends will be received all the more clearly.

Younger Men (2:6-8) Verses 6-8 address instructions (in the third person, through Titus) to younger men and blend them with instructions to Titus himself (v. 7). The effect is similar to that achieved in 1 Timothy 5:1-2, where Timothy receives instructions as a member of an age group which generally apply to all members of that age group. What constitutes godly respectability for this group?

Paul draws from the same class of terms to describe observable Christian behavior. First, young men are to maintain a sensible and respectable bearing in all aspects of life (vv. 6-7; the NIV interpretation, *self-controlled,* captures just a part of this term's intention, and without a break in the Greek sentence between *self-controlled* and *in everything,* the latter belongs with the former).

Then Paul instructs Titus (as he did Timothy in 1 Tim 4:12) to be an example of "good works," which means in his visible expression of genuine faith. In his conduct Titus is thus to be the antithesis of the false teachers (1:16).

This contrast continues as the thought turns to ministry. First, Titus must teach, as the NIV interprets it, with *integrity.* The term envisions avoidance of the corruption introduced by the heretics. Moreover, since verse 8 takes up the thought of the content of Titus's teaching, "with *integrity*" probably focuses on motive of teaching; of course, the false

---

2:9 Depending on training and ability, a slave might serve as a tutor, a doctor or a

teachers' motives were manifestly corrupt (1:11).

Second, in his teaching he must exhibit seriousness, the dignified bearing that bespeaks the importance of the Christian task. In contrast, the opponents were unruly, arrogant and rebellious (1:10).

Finally, Titus's message (not *speech* as in the NIV) is to be "sound"—that is, "healthy" (and health-producing; see 1 Tim 1:10)—in its doctrine, and untainted by the false beliefs (v. 8). This true gospel cannot be condemned by those outside the church as giving rise to disorder and unseemly behavior.

What is the motivating force behind this instruction? The purpose clause *(so that)* shows that the opinion of the outsider to the faith is in view (though some argue that the opponent in mind is the false teacher; see notes). The early church had to deal with criticism of its "new religion" constantly (1 Pet 2:12; 3:9-16). In Titus's case, the distortion of the gospel and related upset in behavior caused by the false teachers did not make the matter of relating to the world any easier. However, exemplary conduct, pure motives, dignified bearing and sound teaching leave no basis for the outsider's allegations. The outsider will be silenced and even put to shame for slandering those who are innocent. But Paul does not seek solely to legitimate the new religion in this way; his concern is to protect the gospel, continue the evangelistic mission (2:5, 10; 1:1-3) and at the same time encourage a lifestyle that exemplifies God's will for humankind.

Titus's lifestyle and ministry must be exemplary. They must bear the marks of dedicated commitment to the genuine Christian faith. In this way all basis for slander is removed and the way forward for the gospel is opened.

Slaves (2:9-10) Since slaves were part of the Hellenistic household, it is quite possible that the false teachers' disruption of Cretan households (1:11) accounts for the kind of disrespectful behavior among slaves implied by this set of instructions. Something similar had occurred in Ephesus (see 1 Tim 6:1-2).

What is godly behavior in the case of Christian slaves? Propriety in the

---

manager of the household or business (see further Bartchy 1973:72-82). See further the discussion at 1 Timothy 6:1 commentary.

master-slave relationship was clearly defined in the ancient world. While despotism and cruelty among masters were generally disdained, in practice the bulk of the load in maintaining a peaceful relationship was borne by the slave. The slave was to be obedient and respectful toward the master at all times.

Paul did not dispute this arrangement. Rather, with the customary exhortation, he commanded slaves to be models of decency in their respective roles. "Subordination" (or "subjection") was the traditional abbreviation for willing acceptance of the realities of this social institution and compliant, respectful behavior within it (1 Pet 2:18; "obey" is equivalent, Eph 6:5; Col 3:22). This meant complete recognition of the master's authority.

The remainder of the instructions break this general command into specific applications. First, slaves must seek *to please* their masters. Only by doing their best could this level of satisfaction be reached. Slaves were generally motivated to this level of excellence by the hope of freedom; Paul does not rule out such a hope, but his motivation is different (compare 1 Cor 7:22-23; Col 3:23-24).

Next, Paul urges that Christian slaves be fully compliant. *Not to talk back* suggests that Paul is thinking of the stereotype of the ill-mannered, unruly and rebellious slave. One of the first ways that people under authority use to express rebellion is verbal challenges: sarcastic comments given under the breath, defiant contradictions. Generally speaking, orders must not be questioned (especially) by Christian slaves.

The last two items pertain to the slave's performance of household responsibilities. Many slaves managed their masters' business interests and were responsible for any money involved. A Christian slave must not be caught with a hand in the till or embezzling or juggling the books. Rather, the genuine faith of a Christian slave will be reflected in complete honesty and trustworthiness.

This description of the subordinate slave makes use of the secular vernacular. But Paul shows where the difference between respectability and *Christian* respectability lies in the purpose he describes. For the third time, a purpose clause *(so that)* connects appropriate conduct within a particular social institution to Christian witness. Slaves were known to be attracted to new religions, often with disruptive results.

Christian slaves were to behave in such a way that they would actually validate the "new religion" in front of their skeptical masters. Obviously, excellent behavior and full respect for authority which the slave attributed to the Christian message would make it attractive to the master. Slaves in their humble circumstances either helped or hindered the gospel's penetration.

What appears at first glance to be a time- and culture-bound instruction to slaves applies to all who find themselves under the authority of someone else. But times have changed. For a number of reasons, the modern employer, supervisor or teacher does not necessarily expect to be treated with respect by those under his or her charge. As a social value, respect for those in authority is a thing of the past, even though disrespect is regarded as a disruptive force (affecting the quality of education and workmanship). But it is just at this point that a Christian can step into the confusion and make a powerful impression. Where all around there is disrespect or indifference to those in authority, a Christian's respectful attitude and speech, backed up by good performance, will demonstrate that God's message of salvation produces positive, visible results. This is an opportunity for witness that we must not miss.

The Basis of Godly Conduct (2:11-15) It might be asked, Why should Christians pursue this respectable and dignified life? Surely God's people should turn from sin; but what warrant is there for endorsing such a mundane form of respectability? Actually, it is not mundane at all, if it is properly understood. It is a part of God's plan. This is what Paul meant to prove in this passage.

The language of this text, especially verses 11-14, is majestic and somewhat allusive. Content, tone and form suggest the passage was probably originally constructed for a baptismal service. Its use of terms that were widely popular made it applicable in this context in which Paul seeks contact with the outsider. But despite these points of contact, the theological basis for the new life that Paul establishes places this life into an entirely different category.

The Appearance of the Grace of God (2:11) It may seem strange to us to speak of God's grace "appearing." Pagans used the term *grace* to signify divine or regal beneficence—something good done by a god or king for those who could not do for themselves. For the Hebrew and the Christian, however, *the grace of God* is the essence of God's covenant with humankind. It signifies God's unmerited love. The language of verse 11 shows that this grace culminated or found full expression in a particular event. But what event does Paul mean?

The verb *appeared* is a technical term for the manifestation or "epiphany" of a god (or hero) to bring help. Paul (or his material) has borrowed this concept to denote the "appearance" of Christ (2 Tim 1:10), and elsewhere in these letters the term refers to the second, future "appearance" of Christ (2:13; 1 Tim 6:14; 2 Tim 4:1; compare 2 Thess 2:8). It is this historical event that gives full expression to God's grace.

This event, too, brought help. But the help associated with God's grace, *salvation,* transcends any pagan notions of help or deliverance from physical calamity. It is salvation from sin and sin's extensive, destructive results. *Salvation* is an adjective in the Greek sentence which describes something intrinsic to *grace:* God's grace is not simply beneficent in purpose, it means to save.

This event is unique in another respect. In scope it is universal, reaching in some way *to all men.* This does not mean that all people respond to the appearance of Christ—to his birth, ministry, death and resurrection—with equal acceptance. In fact, the change to *us* below (vv. 12, 14) implies the need for belief. But as a means of salvation God's grace in Christ is offered to all. Compared with pagan beliefs in patron gods who might deliver a city from crisis, the claims of Christianity are startling.

Thus Paul's logic begins with the event of Christ's incarnation and earthly ministry. But his main point is yet to come.

The Purpose of the Appearance (2:12-13) Without a break in the Greek sentence, verse 12 gets right to the point. Christ appeared to "teach" *us* to live a new life. Thus we might say that "living" or "how to live" is God's curriculum. In this respect, Christ (or God through the medium of his grace) followed a long line of teachers. Moreover, Paul's material employs the Greek teaching model in this description. In Greek thought, education *(paideia;* here the verbal form of this term occurs) produces virtue. Paul makes good use of this model here, but while maintaining contact with secular ideas, he describes the Christian counterpart to virtue in a way that it is placed on an entirely different level.

1. The new life and conversion (2:12). Part of the earliest gospel message was the call to repent (Mk 1:15). It meant "to change the mind," to leave behind an old way, a godless way, and turn to follow God. Paul's material here uses a different word, "deny." But the thrust is the same. The original language of this verse makes it clear that pursuit of the new life below is actually contingent upon this denial. As the NIV interprets it, *say "No,"* this denial is to be final and almost vocal. Of course, if the event of baptism lay behind this creed, it would indeed have been a vocal pledge.

What is to be denied if we are to pursue life? It is the way of this world. *Ungodliness* is a general reference to all that is anti-God (3:3). *Worldly passions* are the sinful impulses that express themselves through the body (1 Jn 2:15-16). Together these two expressions summarize the old life, the life natural to the inhabitants of this world before they have the knowledge of God.

But the appearance of Christ demands that the old way be abandoned. A conscious choice of denial must be made. It is the first step in a new life.

2. The new life (2:12). The goal of God's curriculum is the living of a new life. After the old way has been abandoned, what then? If Christianity ended there, it would consist of a life of avoidance. We could sum it up with a divine "Thou shalt not." But the focus in this passage (and above in vv. 1-10) is actually on "being" or "living," and a far more appropriate and positive summary is "Thou shalt."

As we saw, the Greeks thought that education would lead to virtue. Now Paul translates that into Christian thinking. His translation is really more of a transliteration, for he describes the Christian's new life with three terms that designated cardinal virtues in Greek ethics. In doing this he emphasizes again that Christian conduct should be observable.

The new life is described as *self-controlled* and *upright.* We have come across these two terms already in the description of the lifestyle of the church leader (1:8). "Self-control" was to be exercised over the impulses and sensual desires common to human life (see discussion on 1 Tim 3:2). "Uprightness" is a more general description of observable "rightness" in all aspects of life.

If only these two terms were used to describe the qualities of the new life, one might get the idea that Christianity is acting a certain way, putting on an acceptable performance. The third term, however, at least as Paul uses it, takes us beyond that to show that true spirituality is meant. *Godly,* as a description of life, brings together faith in or knowledge of God and its visible outworking in life ("godliness," 1:1; see notes on 1 Tim 2:2). It is Paul's term for genuine Christianity. Consequently, the life to be lived as a result of Christ's entrance into human history (v. 11) is not only characterized by visible respectability but is also born of the knowledge of God.

Further, it is the antithesis of the old life. Formerly the values of the world shaped life (v. 12), but now a new set of values and goals define life in Christ (compare 3:3-4; Rom 6:20-22; 11:30-32; Gal 1:23; 4:8-9; Eph 2:1-22; 5:8; Col 1:21-22; 3:7-8; Philem 11; 1 Pet 2:10).

Finally, the new life introduced by the appearance of Christ pertains to the present time. Christianity or spirituality is not something that is unattainable or something that is proper to life outside of this world. The time reference *in this present age* focuses readers' attention on the now. Salvation may not be complete (or completely realizable) until the return of Christ; but it has made possible a new quality of life *in this present age.* With the Christian possibility goes Christian responsibility to live fully engaged in this world.

3. The new life and the forward look (2:13). While it is true that genuine spirituality is not foreign to existence in this present age, it is also not wholly at home in it. Salvation has begun, but the struggle with sin (and therefore imperfection) hinders the believer from experiencing it in full. Consequently, an important aspect of the new life is the forward look to the culmination of redemption in Christ's return. This is not to be confused with "living in the future" or "living for tomorrow." It is rather an acknowledgment that the Christian's hope is ultimately beyond this world.

Paul's material uses language that was used of kings and emperors to describe the Christian's hope in Christ's future appearance. *The blessed hope* means "the hope that brings blessing." As the rest of the verse

Notes: 2:13 For the first interpretation see Fee 1988:195-96; Hanson 1982:185; Houlden 1976:150-51; Barrett 1963:137-38; Guthrie 1957:200; and see especially Harris 1992:173-85.

indicates, this hope consists of another "appearance." The NIV's *glorious appearing* smooths out the cumbersome Greek sentence (literally, "the appearance of the glory of the great God"). However, "glory" is probably not to be taken as an adjective but rather as that which will appear. It picks up the theme of an ultimate manifestation of God's glory at the close of history (Is 24:23; 35:2; 40:5; 58:8; 60:1), which in the New Testament is understood to be the return of Christ (Mt 16:27; 24:30; 2 Thess 1:10).

But there is a question whether the following appellation, *our great God and Savior, Jesus Christ,* is of one person, Jesus Christ, or of two, God the Father (great God) and our Savior, Jesus Christ. Depending on the interpretation, we have either a unique, direct affirmation of the deity of Christ or an unprecedented reference to God's accompaniment of Christ at his Second Coming.

In favor of the first interpretation: (1) In the Greek sentence, one definite article *(the)* governs the two nouns, God and Savior, which ordinarily would imply a reference to one person. (2) *God and Savior* was a title current in religious writings during the first century, usually denoting a single deity. (3) The use of epiphany language in the New Testament is primarily limited to Christ, and in the Pastorals there is a strong tendency to describe each "appearance" of Christ in this way (1 Tim 6:14; 2 Tim 4:1; 2 Tim 1:10; 4:8).

In favor of the second interpretation: (1) It is unusual, perhaps unprecedented (compare Rom 9:5), for Paul to refer to Christ as "God." (2) It is argued that in the epiphany passages of the Pastorals there is a tendency to distinguish between God and Christ (1 Tim 6:13-14; 2 Tim 1:9-10). (3) Paul tends to emphasize Christ's dependence upon God in the Pastorals, so that a reference to Christ as God would be out of character.

On the whole, grammatical and background considerations recommend the first interpretation. It is best to conclude, therefore, that *the blessed hope* is the hope in God's ultimate manifestation of glory in the return of Christ. Paul affirms that Christ is God. The use of epiphany

For the second view see Kelly 1963:246-47; Dibelius and Conzelmann 1972:143; Brox 1989:300.

language ("appearance") in this passage for both events of Christ not only implies the "helping" character of these events but also characterizes the present age between them. What began with Christ, salvation and a new manner of life (vv. 11-12), will be brought to completion only with his return (v. 13). The present age, and life in it, thus takes its meaning from these two reference points. The past reference point is certain, historical; it is the substance of the gospel message. The future reference point is based on the past event, but its time is uncertain, requiring hope and the expectant forward look.

The Significance of Christ's Sacrifice (2:14) The identification of the God and Savior as Jesus Christ at the end of verse 13 leads to a discussion in verse 14 of the actual outworking of God's *grace* (v. 11). The language of this description was well known and would have immediately struck a chord with the readers; Paul's material combines a saying of Jesus (that the early church made good use of) with well-known citations from the Old Testament, which together explain the significance of Christ's death for the formation of God's people.

Verse 14 describes the death of Jesus Christ as an offering/sacrifice that was made for those who could not make it themselves.

First, the verb *gave* (and indeed the entire saying—*who gave himself for us*) portrays Christ's death as a ritual offering made specifically to atone for sins (Rom 4:25; 8:32; compare Gal 1:4). Although here the traditional saying of Jesus is attenuated (compare Mk 10:45; 1 Tim 2:6), the same thoughts are in mind.

Second, the note of willingness is emphasized, for it is said that he *gave himself.* Consequently, it cannot be said that Christ's death was an accident that took him by surprise. This death had'to occur; it was an intrinsic part of God's plan of salvation (Acts 2:23).

Third, the phrase *for us* reveals that this offering was both representative and substitutionary. In giving himself as a sacrifice, the God-Man represented sinful humans, almost as a modern-day attorney would take a case. Furthermore, his death *for us* was a death rightly required of people; he stepped in as our substitute and suffered what is rightfully our punishment for sins.

Christ's redemptive death, understood in this way, is without question the ultimate illustration of God's grace. The act originated in God's plan, was executed in behalf of undeserving people and accomplished their salvation. But the theme of Christian living that runs throughout Titus 2 suggests that Paul's focal point in verse 14 is on the purpose or result of this event, which the following clause introduces.

Two metaphors and two Old Testament passages combine to describe the purpose of Christ's sacrifice (of course, from the church's standpoint this purpose is now result!). The first metaphor is that of redemption: the offering was designed *to redeem us.* For the first readers this statement would have conjured up a picture of being bought out of slavery or servitude through a ransom. It was the practice in ancient warfare for conquerors to make slaves of captives. *Redeem* described the process of paying for such a prisoner's release. In a different context, slaves might secure redemption by having the right to ownership of them transferred to a god. Either picture naturally suited a description of Christ's redeeming work in the life of a believer: though a person was formerly enslaved to sin (Jn 8:34), Christ himself paid the price of manumission, setting the believer free to serve God. As the imagery of Psalm 130:8 reveals, the servitude or bondage from which we are released is *all wickedness* (literally, on the Old Testament model, "lawlessness")—a state of complete opposition to God's law.

This description of purpose continues with the metaphor of washing or purification: the offering was designed *to purify . . . a people* for himself. Here the imagery is not of baptism (compare 3:5; Eph 5:25-26). Rather, as the Old Testament context of the citation suggests (Ezek 37:23), "washing" denotes God's act of purifying or sanctifying his wayward people from the defilement of idolatry—claiming a people out of the sinful world. The early church understood this action to be executed ultimately in the shedding of Christ's blood.

Consequently, God's action in Christ purified a peculiar people of God. This idea goes back to Exodus 19:5, where God's purpose in establishing a covenant with Israel is revealed (Deut 7:6; 14:2; 28:18; compare Eph 1:14; 1 Pet 2:9). In response to God's grace, the new people were to observe God's law (Deut 26:18). In New Testament and Pauline terms this is translated into being "zealous for good works." Salvation results in works of the Spirit (see notes on 1 Tim 2:10).

God's grace (v. 11) in Christ's self-offering (v. 14) has established a special people for God's own possession (v. 14). Set free from sin's bondage and purified, they are able to pursue a manifestly new manner of life, characterized by good works. From the interweaving of Old Testament citations it is clear that the early church viewed itself as being continuous with Israel, the true Israel, enjoying the fulfillment of God's Old Testament promises to his people. Jesus' death is the decisive event in the fulfilling of God's promise to create a special people for himself.

More Instructions to Titus (2:15) Paul's thought turns briefly to remind Titus of his duty in relation to the doctrine just laid down *(these . . . things* refers at least to vv. 1-14, perhaps also to 1:5-16). In the original Greek sentence three verbs combine to describe Titus's responsibility toward the Cretan churches. First, he must *teach* (literally, "speak") this doctrine. Thus at the outset Paul emphasizes the need to communicate not only the practical teaching of verses 1-10 but also the content of the creedal material in verses 11-14, particularly as the latter provides the reason and basis for the former.

The following two verbs, *encourage and rebuke,* reveal the two main thrusts of communication. *Encourage* can also mean "urge" and "exhort." In any case, it is a positive use of Christian doctrine for edification. *Rebuke,* however, is corrective in its thrust and implies that Paul's teaching is also designed to get wayward believers back on track (1:13; 2:1). Of course, uppermost in Paul's mind here are the effects of the false teaching on the conduct of individual Christians in Crete.

As one chosen by God to serve the churches, the Christian teacher or leader has authority to carry out such a command. Titus, as the apostle's delegate, shared Paul's authority. The gravity and need of the situation required that the people recognize that this doctrine was to be accepted and responded to as God's instruction. These were not merely helpful suggestions, but divine commands.

It is in view of this delegated authority that the personal command is given: *Do not let anyone despise you.* Obviously, neither Titus nor any Christian leader can control the feelings and actions of others. And in

---

Notes: 3:1 "Doing good" is expressed in slightly different, though clearly related, ways in the relevant New Testament passages: the Greek of Romans 13:3 is *to agathon poiei,* while 1 Peter 2:15 has *agathopoiountas;* the present passage recasts these phrases as "ready to do every good deed" *(pros pan ergon agathon hetoimous einai).* The change to "every

this situation Paul anticipated opposition to his delegate's authority (1:9-10, 13; 3:10). But for his part Titus was to insist on his authority (and not allow others to ignore him or "go over his head") and behave in a commendable manner (so that no one would question his suitability to lead). Christian leaders should keep in mind that authority and exemplary behavior are to be inseparable.

□ The Church in the World (3:1-8)

Biblical Christians are by definition in a predicament. Christians must live *in* this world, but they are not *of* this world. As the Father sent Christ into this world to minister, so he sends believers to be ministers in the world (Jn 17:14-18).

Titus 2:1—3:8 is concerned with living in this world. The previous passage stresses engagement in the world, by enforcing Christian respectability in a way that shows sensitivity to accepted social rules and relationships. At this point the question of the Christian's general attitude toward all people and political institutions is raised. What is the Christian's obligation in relation to the world—that is, to its unbelieving inhabitants and its political structure? The early church had to deal with this question (1) because it was compelled by Christ's missionary mandate to reach the world with the gospel, a task that requires interaction, and (2) because the political system was generally opposed to the exclusive claims of Christianity.

What Paul has to say in Titus 3 is not new, but reflects agreement with both his own earlier thinking and that of 1 Peter 2:13-17. The instruction in 3:1-8 divides into three parts: verses 1-2 give the instructions; verses 3-7 give the theological foundation for the behavior that is prescribed; and verse 8 adds a missionary motive.

Christian Living in the World (3:1-2) Christian conduct outside of the church is to be sensitive in two directions, to government authorities (v. 1) and to all people (v. 2).

---

good deed" corresponds to the style and language of the Pastorals (1 Tim 5:10; 2 Tim 2:21; 3:17; Tit 1:16; compare 2 Cor 9:8; Col 1:10; 2 Thess 2:17); the use of "all" with the singular "good deed" places the emphasis on activity that is habitual.

Paul's injunction to recognize the state is firmly embedded in the New Testament church's ethical code. Here we find a command common to other New Testament "household codes" at the head of a list of virtues (see 1 Tim 4:12; 6:11; 2 Tim 2:22; 3:10). It is likely that Paul and other New Testament writers drew on and adapted teaching from a common source to which the "household code" belonged (see on 1 Tim 2). This aspect of the teaching encouraged the church to respect the government; a form of the verb "to be subject to" is typical of this kind of teaching (Rom 13:1, 5; 1 Pet 2:13). Essentially, the instruction calls for Christians to participate in this level of the social structure (as far as possible) according to society's rules.

Participation as such takes two courses. "Obedience" is left unexplained, but presumably it corresponds to Romans 13:6 where a specific example of doing what is obligatory (paying taxes; in 1 Tim 2:2, obedience takes the form of praying for—and thereby expressing loyalty to—government leaders) underlines the need to do what the "system" requires. Subjection to the state—that is, adherence to and recognition of this institution—means obeying the rules.

Yet subjection also necessitates the more active expression of the Christian life which is (according to the early church's code) traditionally termed "doing good" (Rom 13:3; 1 Pet 2:15). This was the attitude of the respectable, loyal citizen. As with the other two passages cited and throughout the Pastorals, "doing good" is Christian existence portrayed in tangible ways in the life of the believer or the community (collectively) as the observable manifestation of the Holy Spirit. Paul has stressed in other contexts that this "expression of the Spirit" will include socially responsible behavior (Tit 2; 1 Tim 2:8-15; 5:1-2, 9-14; 6:1-2).

At verse 2 the church's responsibility toward all people comes into view. The tradition seems to have influenced Paul here to connect this responsibility and the responsibility to the state (compare 1 Pet 2:13, 17). Essentially, the instructions advise the Cretan Christians to make as few waves as possible by living in a way that fosters good relations. In the area of speech, Christians are not to be known as those who slander others. Rather, in speech and conduct (that is, in the totality of life; see discussion at 1 Tim 4:12) they are to be known for peaceableness, gentleness (NIV *considerate*) and meekness *(humility)* toward all people.

Misunderstanding these qualities leads to what has been called "door-mat Christianity." But in reality they have nothing to do with passivity. Peaceableness is a conscious mode of response that allows one to resist taking a violent course in difficult situations, often sacrificially, in order to save relationships. Gentleness (or consideration) is an attitude that quiets personal concerns to make room for the concerns of others. And meekness *(humility)* is that balanced perception of oneself that makes it possible to regard others as more important (compare Phil 2:3-4). In fact, the last two qualities describe Christlikeness, the basic disposition of Christ toward others (2 Cor 10:1; compare 1 Tim 3:3; 2 Tim 2:25). Paul's language portrays Christian living in relation to all people as reasoned forbearance in every aspect of life, the putting of the concerns of others ahead of one's own.

The Basis for Christian Living in the World (3:3-7) In this passage Paul lays down a foundation for leading a life in the world that is demonstrably different from that of unbelievers. In the first place he is explaining a reason; the connecting word "for" is omitted by the NIV. But he does not specifically tell his readers whether he is addressing the question of why we *ought* to live this life or why we *can* live it. Perhaps his material answers both of these questions.

The Appearance of God's Kindness and Love and the Possibility of Change (3:3-4) The crux of the matter is a fundamental change or transition that has occurred. To emphasize this change Paul uses a device that he has put to good use elsewhere; verse 3's *at one time* is to be taken with verse 4's *but when* (compare 1:2-3; 2 Tim 1:9-10). The force of this formula is to focus attention on this change, for with it (and only with it) does human life enter into a new age of rescue.

Before discussing the nature of this rescue, Paul describes the characteristics of life without Christ. Although there is an element of identification here, since Paul includes himself in the description *(we too;* compare 1 Cor 15:9; Gal 1:13-14; Phil 3:1-10; 1 Tim 1:13, 16), the point of describing the old way of life is to emphasize that the change that makes new life possible has indeed occurred. And we must not miss the fact that in selecting the items he does, Paul is presenting the false teachers, who have been troubling these communities, as living illustrations of life outside of Christ. *Foolish, disobedient* and *deceived,* the first three terms, are the sorts of words he has used to describe the heretics. Foolishness is a stubborn refusal to acknowledge the truth. Disobedience is a culpable condition involving the choice to live in opposition to God (1:16). Underlying these traits is deception. This particular term was often descriptive of the purpose or result of false prophets (2 Tim 3:13; compare Mt 24:10-12; 1 Thess 2:3; Rev 2:20). The source of deception is false teaching, be it worldly philosophies or distorted Christian doctrine. The message to believers is clear: stay away from the doctrines of the false teachers.

As the list continues, the image becomes one of enslavement to *passions and pleasures.* This is life lived as if its purpose were to satisfy one sensual desire after another (NIV *all kinds of).* Paul has already described the old life of sensuality in this way (2:12; 1 Tim 6:9; 2 Tim 3:6; 4:3). But here the added note of bondage shows this lifestyle to be an addiction; once one is on this merry-go-round, it is difficult to get off.

The remainder of the list views this life in relation to other people. *We lived in malice and envy* characterizes this life (the exact opposite of the life of faith; see the comments on 3:2 and 1 Tim 2:2: "living in all godliness and holiness") as totally absorbed with the destruction of others to preserve oneself. This manner of life both attracts hatred to the one so living and promotes hate. It is a vicious mode of existence from which rescue is desperately needed.

And so the rescue came. Verses 4-7 consist of a single, densely packed sentence of theology, originally probably part of a liturgical creed. Paul modifies and inserts the material at this point to describe the experience of becoming a Christian.

Verse 4 delivers the second half of the transition formula introduced in verse 3: *At one time . . . but when.* What made the Christian life a possibility was an event in history, an event in which the grace of God was manifested. Here the phrase *the kindness and love of God our Savior* describes the appearance of Christ as the fullest expression of God's grace and love toward humankind. This description delves more deeply into the nature of the event than does the very similar statement in 2:11. *Kindness (chrēstotēs)* is a Pauline word in the New Testament. Its use in Romans 2:4 and 11:22 shows God's kindness to be an instrumental factor in bringing people to repentance. The link in our passage between God's kindness which "appears" and Christ, the embodiment of this kindness, is then clear in the salvation his appearance brought. Though it may be accidental, the Greek *chrēstotēs* sounds very similar to the Greek *Christos* (Christ), suggesting an intentional interpretation of God's *kindness* at the outset. The second term, *love* (NIV), is literally "love for humanity" *(philanthrōpia)*. God's fatherly love for humankind is thus declared to have been expressed in Jesus' incarnation.

As we noted above (2:11, 13; 1 Tim 6:14; 2 Tim 1:10), in describing this event as an epiphany or "appearance," Paul draws on the current religious theme of the advent of a god to bring help and deliverance. The appearance of Christ is this type of event par excellence. Its purpose—as the title *God our Savior* and the main verb of this sentence, *saved* (v. 5), show—was to save or rescue *us* from the life of slavery to sin described in verse 3. The event is a matter of historical record, so the life it introduced (vv. 1-2) is a real possibility. A rescue plan of epic proportions was carried out when Christ came in the flesh.

Salvation and Change (3:5-7) Verses 5-7 explain in rich detail and from several perspectives the nature of the salvation that this event brought.

Salvation and God's mercy (3:5). First, the cause of our salvation is solely God's mercy. While from the standpoint of human need Jesus' crucifixion could be explained as "for our sins" (1 Cor 15:3), from the standpoint of God's love it was *because of his mercy.* This mercy of God is the equivalent of the loving-kindness of God that in the Old Testament (Hebrew *ḥeseḏ*) formed the basis of the covenant relationship with Israel. Salvation in Christ has its origin in the very same place. It is God reaching toward humankind to put us into relation with himself, not (as the phrase *not because of righteous things we had done* shows) the reverse. Human effort is excluded: salvation is not something that a person can merit (Rom 3:21-28; Gal 3:3-9; Eph 2:8-9; 2 Tim 1:9).

Salvation and the Holy Spirit (3:5-6). Second, it is the Holy Spirit who applies salvation to us. But the three metaphors that occur in this connection—washing, rebirth and renewal—require a closer look. If you have been in the church for a while, you probably feel comfortable with such terms; they have become Christian jargon, and we hardly question their meaning. In fact, though, such words put off outsiders to the faith, and our frequent easy use of such jargon leaves them rightly wondering whether we really do understand what we believe.

A check of the commentaries confirms that the meanings of these words and their relationships are not settled matters. The main possibilities can be arranged as follows (see Dunn 1970:165-70 and Fee 1988:204-5).

1. through the washing of rebirth
and
(through) renewal by the Holy Spirit

2. through the washing that produces rebirth and renewal,
(the washing being) by the operation of the Holy Spirit

Arrangement 1 above has two separate events in mind: Roman Catholic commentators divide them into baptism and confirmation (others take them as conversion and confirmation), but some groups have seen in this arrangement a reference to conversion and a subsequent baptism in the Holy Spirit.

Arrangement 2 can be taken as a reference to baptism, during which or through which rebirth and renewal occur, the Holy Spirit being the agent of washing. Or 2 can be taken as a reference to the conversion/initiation event in which the individual receives the Spirit and is thus cleansed, reborn, renewed and incorporated into the community of faith. Either way, one (more complex) event—washing by the Spirit—is envisaged.

While it is well to keep in mind that these verses represent a liturgical formulation and are therefore not necessarily meant to be precise statements of theology, the following points speak against interpretation 1 (two separate activities) and favor 2 (one complex activity). First, the two metaphors, rebirth *(palingenesia)* and renewal *(anakainōsis)* are practically synonyms and thus express a unity. This is even more likely since there is just the single preposition *through* governing the phrase; ordinarily, where two conceptually related ideas are involved yet two separate activities are meant, the preposition would be repeated to ensure that the distinction is made by the reader. Then the reference to the outpouring of the Spirit in verse 6, an allusion to Pentecost (see below), suggests that the role of the Spirit is central in the thinking of verse 5—thus it is probably best to understand verse 5 as referring to one event of washing by the Spirit which produces two closely related effects, rebirth and renewal.

In other words, the tradition Paul draws on at this point seeks to emphasize the gift of the Spirit in the salvation process. And based on verse 6, which takes up the traditional imagery of washing and water in *poured out* to describe the Spirit's life-giving and renewing work, the reference to *washing (loutron)* in verse 5 is most likely a reference to spiritual washing rather than to the rite of water baptism (compare Eph 5:25-27).

Rebirth and *renewal* describe the work of the Spirit. *Rebirth* is a coming back to life from death, an apt description of the new life in contrast to the old one of sin and death (v. 3; on the Spirit and [re]birth see Gal 4:29; 1 Cor 4:15 with 2:4). As explained in Romans 6:4-11 and Philippians 3, by faith in Christ one is enabled to participate in Christ's resurrection life even now. *Renewal* expresses almost synonymously the idea of "re-creation" (compare 2 Cor 5:17). These two terms bring together the whole change associated with conversion and life in the new age of salvation—restored fellowship with God and new, eternal life.

Salvation and history (3:6). Verse 6 spells out in greater detail the historical reference point of salvation alluded to in verse 4 *(when . . . appeared).* It consists of two things. First, the verb *poured out* takes the readers back to the description of the outpouring of the Spirit on the day of Pentecost (Acts 2:17-18, 33). Second, verse 6 brings the thought back to the work of Christ, through which God's plan became concrete reality. The phrase *through Jesus Christ our Savior* is an abbreviation for Christ's historical ministry of teaching, healing, sacrificial death and resurrection, and its results (v. 5). As the preposition *through* indicates, it was this Person and his work that made possible the gift of the Holy Spirit (Jn 16:7; Acts 2:33).

The whole passage has been establishing the basis for a new way of life (vv. 1-2), and it is a historical basis. The perspective from which the new possibility is viewed is that of salvation history, God's kingdom intersecting time and space: verses 3 and 4 announce the great turning point for human ethics—Christ's appearance. God the Father (vv. 4-5), the Holy Spirit (vv. 5-6) and Jesus Christ (vv. 4, 6) are joined together in the work of salvation (compare 1 Cor 12:4-6; Eph 1:3-14; 4:4-6).

Salvation and justification (3:7). Paul's material views salvation from one more familiar perspective, justification by grace. Justification, as it is often pointed out, is salvation seen from a forensic or legal perspective. It is the judge's declaration of righteousness. But the grounds are not that the defendant has been found to be free of guilt. Rather, the defendant's guilt has been paid for by another—Christ—and so it is a matter of grace, an unmerited participation in Christ's righteousness. Paul often coordinates salvation and justification or uses the terms almost synonymously (Rom 10:10). Sometimes he maintains a distinction between them, making the "righteousness of God" the understood condition for receiving the gift of salvation. This is probably the intention here.

Salvation and hope (3:7). What is the goal of God's redemptive work? It is eternal life (Rom 2:7; 5:21; 6:22-23; Gal 6:8). Through justification, the believer takes up the privileged position of an heir, as Paul often points out (Rom 3:24; 4:13-14; Gal 3:6-29; 4:6-7). The unique thing about God's family is that every Christian shares this position equally. None is entitled to a greater share than another, for the object of inheritance is eternal life (compare Mt 19:29; Lk 18:18). But the inheritance is yet to be received, so it remains an object of hope. Nevertheless, the certainty of God's past acts in Christ guarantees the certainty of what is still to be fully obtained (see above on 1:2).

Consequently, Christians can boldly live the kind of life prescribed in verses 1 and 2, because God has intervened in human history to bring about a change. The whole salvation complex—rebirth and renewal, justification and hope—is reality, grounded in the historical events of Christ's ministry and death/resurrection and in the outpouring of the Holy Spirit. But to experience the new reality, the believer must actively decide to step forward; the reality of the Christian possibility is not

---

Notes: 3:8 Barclay (1975:302) translates the verb *devote (phrontizō)* with "think and plan how," which brings out well Paul's emphasis on the concentration of the mind (compare the similar tone of Rom 8:5-6).

The verb *doing (proïstasthai)* is used elsewhere in the New Testament in relation to leadership in the church (Rom 12:8; 1 Thess 5:12; 1 Tim 3:5, 12; 5:17) and home (1 Tim

experienced through reciting a creed but by performing it in faith.

The Motive of Christian Living in the World (3:8) While many versions of the Bible view verse 8, with its "faithful saying" formula, as beginning a new paragraph, it is important to see its relation to the preceding teaching. Here Paul attaches a strong motive for living the life described in verses 1-2, the possibility of which verses 3-7 subsequently demonstrate.

Rather than creating a division, the assertion *this is a trustworthy statement,* which refers back to at least verses 4-7 (so Knight 1979:95), bonds verse 8 to the preceding discussion. As in its other occurrences (1 Tim 1:15; 3:1; 4:9; 2 Tim 2:11), this formula calls the readers to a fresh acknowledgment of what has been their common confession. The reason for doing so in this case, as in the others, is to encourage the readers to live the life that the theological statement declares to be a possibility. Verse 8 is a succinct conclusion to the whole of the teaching on the Christian life given in Titus. In it Paul drives home three points that we must not miss.

First, the Christian life is a life of active performance. We must not mistake this emphasis as evidence that Christian morality or ethics boils down simply to doing the best that is humanly possible. This instruction is for *those who have trusted in God,* and therefore the role of the Spirit and faith is assumed (Rom 8:4-17; Gal 5:16). Yet at the same time we must not misconstrue Christianity as a gift from God that operates independently of the one who has received it. The truth is, the reality of the new life in the Spirit is discovered only by those who dare to be actors instead of audience. This comes through clearly in the purpose given for Titus's emphasis on *these things* (Christian living, vv. 1-2, and especially its theological basis, vv. 3-7): *so that* believers *may be careful to devote themselves to doing what is good.* Here concentration of the mind is combined with effort. A decision to perform is integral to the Christian life.

3:4). Here (and in 3:14) the meaning is "to engage in"; however, as Quinn (1990:234) points out, this term has a history of use to describe the performance of duties in the household, which may mean that 3:8 alludes to the model of the church as household as it urges Christians to perform "good deeds."

Second, as it is performed this life will have visible results. Paul describes this performance with the term "good deeds." This is Christian life viewed from its visible outworking (2:7; 2:14; 3:1; see notes on 1 Tim 2:10). The nearest practical application of the term is to be found in the Christlike lifestyle outlined back in 3:1 and ahead in 3:14. Performed in this way, the genuine Christian life contradicts the claims of the false teachers, who ultimately denied God with their lifestyle completely devoid of good deeds (1:16).

Third, the living out of this life will benefit *everyone*. Herein lies the motive. In this new sentence Paul brings this qualitatively new life (the second *these things* = good deeds) to bear on the lives of others. It is because this life of faith is inherently and manifestly good (NIV *excellent*) that it is able to be of benefit to everyone. But of what benefit? For several reasons it is likely that Paul is speaking from a missionary concern for those outside the faith. First, the unambiguous reference to believers in the first half of verse 8 suggests that the reference to *everyone* at the end is primarily to unbelievers (the same contrast appears in 3:1-2). Then, as in 2:5, 7-8, 10-11 and 3:2, so also in this case: the importance of the visible attractiveness of the Christian life is that it might point others to belief in God. Paul's thought is that since God's love in Christ has transformed the lives of those who have believed (3:3-7), the manifestation of that love in their lives (3:1-2, 8) should have similar results in the lives of others. Mission is one of the primary reasons for the performance of the Christian life in the world.

□ Final Instructions and Greetings to Titus (3:9-15)

This letter draws to a conclusion in much the same way as it began. First, in 3:9-11 Paul instructs Titus regarding the false teachers that were trou-

---

Notes: 3:10-11 Does this type of warning imply that Paul envisioned the possibility of a true believer forfeiting salvation? This may be to simplify a complex issue. When Paul addressed troubled churches, he assumed that they contained genuine and nominal believers (compare 2 Tim 2:19-20), but he treated all the same, calling them to test the genuineness of their faith (2 Cor 13:5) and warning them of the dangers of falling away (1 Cor 10:1-13; 2 Tim 2:12).

3:10 Behind the word *warn* (NIV) is the Greek noun *nouthesia* (a literal translation is "after a first and second warning"). It means to shape the thinking with instruction or warning; in relation to God's dealings with Israel (Job 40:4; Wisdom of Solomon 11:10; 12:2,

bling the Cretan churches (compare 1:10-16; Rom 16:17-20). Then, as he often did, Paul adds in 3:12-15 some personal instructions (compare 1:5-16), greetings and a closing blessing (compare 1:1-4).

Confronting the False Teachers (3:9-11) The somber tone of these verses reflects the gravity of the situation that Titus faced in the Cretan churches. Paul focuses on the utter uselessness of the false teaching and the depravity of the heretics. Yet a note of hope, however muted, is sounded.

Paul's instruction in verse 9 is to refuse to enter into the false teachers' dialogue (see 1 Tim 4:7; 6:20). Apparently, the arcane nature of their doctrine, which, as *genealogies* and *quarrels about the law* suggest, built upon a novel use of the Old Testament (see on 1:14; 1 Tim 1:4 notes; 1 Tim 6:20), led to a great deal of bitter controversy. In fact, throughout the Pastoral Epistles it is controversy (see notes at 1 Tim 1:4) and strife (NIV *arguments*) that most typify the opponents and their false doctrine (1:10-12; 1 Tim 1:4-7; 6:3-5; 2 Tim 2:23). The final evaluation of the false message and its results as *unprofitable and useless* stands as the exact antithesis of genuine Christianity *(profitable for everyone, v. 8)*.

Paul's way of dialoguing with the false teachers and those they have attracted is on an individual basis. But rather than talk theology with the *divisive person,* Titus is to *warn* (or "admonish") that person "once and twice." As in 1 Timothy 5:19-20 and 2 Timothy 2:25, the purpose of this confrontation is to induce the erring brother or sister to repent, and the admonition is understood to be positive instruction given within the context of a caring relationship. Verse 10 may be the apostle's abbreviated reference to the disciplinary procedure that Christ taught the apostles (Mt 18:15-17; Lk 17:3). If so, then Paul means that an individual confron-

26) and in the New Testament usage (mostly by Paul—Rom 15:14; 1 Cor 4:14; 10:11; Eph 6:4; Col 1:28; 3:16; 1 Thess 5:12, 14; 2 Thess 3:15), the goal of "admonition" is correction, not condemnation.

The Greek term behind *divisive* is *hairetikos,* from which the technical terms *heretic* and *heresy* developed. Paul's use of the term (1 Cor 11:19; Gal 5:20) is clearly negative but descriptive only of dissension that disrupts fellowship, not of parties that can be distinguished by a false system of doctrine. The term begins to reach the latter stage of meaning in 2 Peter 2:1 (see also Ignatius *Letters to the Ephesians* 6. 2; *Letter to the Trallians* 6. 1).

tation, if fruitless, is to be followed up with a visit to the erring party by
two or more believers (see Deut 19:15). If the second attempt also fails,
then the recalcitrant one is to be avoided—that is, treated as an outsider
to the faith. Although the idea of excommunication is expressed more
clearly in Matthew 18:17, *have nothing to do with him* must mean the
same thing in view of the tone of finality of the description in verse 11.
Something (presumably acceptance of the false doctrine) has turned the
unresponsive one away from God (compare 1 Tim 6:4-5; 4:2). In this
"turned" condition, the continuation of sin (the NIV *sinful* is better
translated "he keeps on sinning") shows the rejection of the warning.
Finally to refuse to heed the apostolic warning is tantamount to pro-
nouncing sentence on oneself (compare Lk 19:22; Gal 2:11).

There is a warning in this instruction (especially in combination with
1 Tim 4:2; 6:4-5; Deut 32:20) for all who will hear. False doctrine, like
the practice of idolatry, will turn one's heart away from God; it may not
be possible to detect precisely the point at which the turn becomes
permanent, but that this point can in fact be reached is indicated by the
descriptions in the verses cited above.

There is also a question to be asked. On the basis of this and other
related passages (Mt 18:15-17; 1 Cor 5:9-13; 1 Tim 1:20; 5:19-21), is not
church discipline a matter to be taken seriously? The unfortunate reality
of sin in the church (see 2 Tim 2:19-21) would seem to call for an
affirmative answer. Experiences of excessive and unfair judgments have
left their mark on the church. So has the spirit of toleration, which,
though positive in many respects, often leads to indifference when practiced uncritically. The fact of the matter is that both the Christian community and the individual must be protected from sin. And the procedure taught in the New Testament is designed for this purpose. Properly
executed, it allows the leadership to encourage purity of doctrine and
behavior as erring individuals and groups are given every reasonable
opportunity to acknowledge their error and turn from it. The process is
meant to be a positive one of reclamation, and the church must keep
this in mind. Yet it also provides for the judgment of separation to be

Notes: 3:12-15 See Romans 16:1-2, 1 Corinthians 16:5-12 and Colossians 4:7-9 for other
examples of closing personal instructions. Concluding greetings occur in most (see Rom

administered (though still with hopes of reclamation) in cases of stubborn refusal to turn from sin. Paul's letters to the Corinthians show something of the difficulty and stress connected with church discipline; they also reveal how desperately it is needed. Things are no different today.

Closing Personal Notes (3:12-15) In the closing verses of the letter, Paul instructs his assistant concerning transfer of personnel and related logistics, and sends greetings and a blessing.

Paul mentions four individuals and one place name. At the time of writing, either Artemas or Tychicus was to replace Titus in the work on Crete. Nothing more is known about Artemas. Tychicus, however, was a well-known traveling companion of Paul (Acts 20:4; Eph 6:21; Col 4:7; 2 Tim 4:12). Assuming the plan held good, apparently it was Artemas who replaced Titus—not Tychicus, who is placed in Ephesus in 2 Timothy 4:12. With the arrival of his replacement, Titus was to make his way to Nicopolis, where Paul planned to spend the winter. Nicopolis was a busy port town on the western coast of Greece. It was actually known for its harsh winters; many travelers from all parts would have been forced to spend the winter there, so that Paul could continue his ministry despite the impossibility of travel. Titus later turns up in Dalmatia, up the coast from Nicopolis (2 Tim 4:10). Zenas the lawyer and Apollos (Acts 18:24-19:1; 1 Cor 1:12) were probably the bearers of this letter to Titus.

It was not at all unusual for Paul to have asked Titus to assist these two with their continued journey (Rom 15:24; 1 Cor 16:6, 11; 2 Cor 1:16). In fact, he uses this occasion to again instruct the whole congregation to live out the genuine Christian life. Verse 14 repeats exactly the phrase *to devote themselves to doing what is good* that occurs in verse 8. But in this case an additional phrase defines the "good deeds" as those that meet (literally "for" or "unto") *daily necessities,* referring to the needs of these travelers. The living out of genuine Christianity (performing good deeds) has both practical and evident results.

16:21-24; 1 Cor 16:19-20; Phil 4:21-22; Col 4:10-15), and blessings occur in all of Paul's letters.

As Paul usually did in closing his letters, he communicates his genuine feeling of friendship and partnership (and that of the other team members with him) to his coworker. This would have been a reminder to Titus and the church not only of the prayer support for the work in Crete but also of the true love and fellowship that exists among believers and sustains one who is engaged in God's service.

The closing wish, *grace be with you all,* is equally an expression of affection. The grace of God is the source of salvation (3:5) and all blessings; so to have God's grace *with* us is to have access to all that he can provide (see on 1:4; 1 Tim 1:1; 6:21).

Bibliography

Aune, David E.
1983   *Prophecy in Early Christianity and the Ancient Mediterranean World.* Grand Rapids, Mich.: Eerdmans.

Barclay, William
1975   *The Letters to Timothy, Titus and Philemon.* The Daily Study Bible. Rev. ed. Philadelphia: Westminster Press.

Barrett, C. K.
1963   *The Pastoral Epistles.* New Clarendon Bible. Oxford: Clarendon.

Bartchy, S. S.
1973   *First-Century Slavery and 1 Corinthians 7:21.* Society of Biblical Literature Dissertation Series 11. Atlanta: Scholars Press.

Brown,
Harold O. J.
1984   *Heresies: The Image of Christ in the Mirror of Heresy and Orthodoxy from the Apostles to the Present.* Grand Rapids, Mich.: Baker Book House.

Brox, Norbert
1989   *Die Pastoralbriefe.* Regensburger Neues Testament 7. 5th ed. Regensburg, Germany: Pustet.

Bruce, F. F.
1954   *Commentary on the Book of the Acts: The English Text with Introduction, Exposition and Notes.* New International Commentary on the New Testament. Grand Rapids, Mich.: Eerdmans.

1982   *The Epistle to the Galatians: A Commentary on the Greek Text.* New International Greek Testament Commentary. Grand Rapids, Mich.: Eerdmans.

Bruggen,
Jakob van
1981   *Die geschichtliche Einordnung der Pastoralbriefe.*
               Wuppertal, Germany: R. Brockhaus.
Clark, Stephen B.
1980   *Man and Woman in Christ.* Ann Arbor, Mich.: Servant.

Delling, G.
1964   "γόης κτλ." In *Theological Dictionary of the New
               Testament.* 1:737-38. Edited by G. Kittel and G. Friedrich. 10
               vols. Grand Rapids, Mich.: Eerdmans.
.Dibelius, Martin,
and Hans
Conzelmann
1972   *The Pastoral Epistles.* Hermeneia. Philadelphia: Fortress.

Donelson, Lewis R.
1986   *Pseudepigraphy and Ethical Argument in the Pastoral
               Epistles.* Tübingen, Germany: Mohr (Siebeck).
Dunn, James D. G.
1970   *Baptism in the Holy Spirit.* London: SCM.

Easton, B. S.
1948   *The Pastoral Epistles.* New York: Scribner's.

Elliot, Elisabeth
1957   *Shadow of the Almighty: The Life and Testament of Jim
               Elliot.* New York: Harper & Brothers.
Ellis, E. Earle
1957   *Paul's Use of the Old Testament.* London: Oliver & Boyd.
1989   *Pauline Theology: Ministry and Society.* Grand Rapids,
               Mich.: Eerdmans.
Evans, Mary
1983   *Woman in the Bible.* Downers Grove, Ill.: InterVarsity Press;
               Exeter, U.K.: Paternoster.
Fee, Gordon D.
1988   *1 and 2 Timothy, Titus.* New International Biblical
               Commentary. Peabody, Mass.: Hendrickson.
Forthcoming.   "The Pastoral Epistles." Chap. 11 of *God's Empowering
               Presence: The Spirit in the Letters of Paul.* Peabody, Mass.:
               Hendrickson.
France, Richard T.
1977   "Exegesis in Practice: Two Samples." In *New Testament
               Interpretation.* Edited by I. H. Marshall. Exeter, U.K.:
               Paternoster; Grand Rapids, Mich.: Eerdmans.

Furnish, Victor P.
1984   *II Corinthians.* Anchor Bible 32A. New York: Doubleday.

Goppelt, Leonhard
1982   *Theology of the New Testament.* Vol. 2. Grand Rapids, Mich.:
               Eerdmans.
Gundry, Robert H.
1970   "The Form, Meaning, and Background of the Hymn Quoted
               in 1 Timothy 3:16." In *Apostolic History and the Gospel.*
               Edited by W. W. Gasque and R. P. Martin. Grand Rapids,
               Mich.: Eerdmans.
Gunther, John J.
1972   *Paul—Messenger and Exile: A Study in the Chronology of
               His Life and Letters.* Valley Forge, Penn.: Judson Press.
Guthrie, Donald
1957   *The Pastoral Epistles: An Introduction and Commentary.*
               Tyndale New Testament Commentary. Grand Rapids, Mich.:
               Eerdmans; Leicester, England: Inter-Varsity Press.
1962   "The Development of the Idea of Canonical Pseudepigrapha
               in New Testament Criticism." *Vox Evangelica* 1:43-59.
1979   *New Testament Introduction.* 3rd ed. Downers Grove, Ill.:
               InterVarsity Press.
1981   *New Testament Theology.* Downers Grove, Ill., and Leicester,
               England: InterVarsity Press.
Hanson, A. T.
1968   *Studies in the Pastoral Epistles.* London: SPCK.
1982   *The Pastoral Epistles.* New Century Bible Commentary.
               London: Marshall, Morgan & Scott.
Harris, Murray J.
1976   "2 Corinthians." *The Expositor's Bible Commentary.* Grand
               Rapids, Mich.: Zondervan.
1992   *Jesus as God: The New Testament Use of "Theos" in
               Reference to Jesus.* Grand Rapids, Mich.: Baker Book House.
Hawthorne,
Gerald F.
1983   *Philippians.* Word Biblical Commentary 43. Waco, Tex.:
               Word.
Hendriksen,
William
1965   *Exposition of the Pastoral Epistles.* New Testament
               Commentary Series. Grand Rapids, Mich.: Baker Book
               House.

Hengel, Martin

1977   *Crucifixion in the Ancient World and the Folly of the Message of the Cross.* Philadelphia: Fortress.

1983   "Hymns and Christology." In *Between Jesus and Paul.* London: SCM Press.

Houlden, J. L.

1976   *The Pastoral Epistles: I and II Timothy, Titus.* Pelican New Testament Commentaries. London: Penguin.

Hultgren, Arland J.

1984   *I and II Timothy, Titus.* Augsburg Commentary. Minneapolis: Augsburg.

Hurley, James B.

1981   *Man and Woman in Biblical Perspective.* Grand Rapids, Mich.: Zondervan.

Jeremias, Joachim, and A. Strobel

1975   *Die Briefe an Timotheus und Titus; Der Brief an die Hebräer.* NTD. Göttingen, Germany: Vandenhoeck & Ruprecht.

Johnson, Luke T.

1987   *1 Timothy, 2 Timothy, Titus.* Knox Preaching Guides. Atlanta: John Knox.

Karris, Robert J.

1979   *The Pastoral Epistles.* New Testament Message. Wilmington, Del.: Michael Glazier.

Kelly, J. N. D.

1963   *A Commentary on the Pastoral Epistles.* Harper's New Testament Commentaries. New York: Harper.

Knight, George W.

1979   *The Faithful Sayings in the Pastoral Letters.* Grand Rapids, Mich.: Baker Book House.

1992   *The Pastoral Epistles: A Commentary on the Greek Text.* New International Greek Testament Commentary. Grand Rapids, Mich.: Eerdmans.

Kroeger, Catherine C.

1986   "1 Timothy 2:12—A Classicist's View." In *Women, Authority and the Bible.* Edited by A. Mickelsen. Downers Grove, Ill.: InterVarsity Press.

Ladd, George E.

1975   *I Believe in the Resurrection of Jesus.* Grand Rapids, Mich.: Eerdmans; London: Hodder & Stoughton.

Lewis, C. S.
1961   *A Grief Observed.* New York: Bantam Books.

Lock, W.
1924   *A Critical and Exegetical Commentary on the Pastoral
                Epistles (I and II Timothy and Titus).* International Critical
                Commentary. Edinburgh: T & T Clark.
McDonald, J. I. H.
1980   *Kerygma and Didache.* Society for New Testament Studies
                Monograph Series 37. Cambridge, U.K.: Cambridge Univer-
                sity Press.
Malina, Bruce J.
1981   *The New Testament World: Insights from Cultural
                Anthropology.* Atlanta: John Knox.
Martin, Ralph P.
1977   "Approaches to New Testament Exegesis." In *New
                Testament Interpretation.* Edited by I. H. Marshall. Exeter,
                U.K.: Paternoster; Grand Rapids, Mich.: Eerdmans.
Metzger, Bruce M.
1971   *A Textual Commentary on the Greek New Testament.*
                London: United Bible Societies.
Moo, Douglas J.
1980   "1 Timothy 2:11-15: Meaning and Significance." *Trinity
                Journal* 1:62-83.
Morris, Leon
1955   *The Apostolic Preaching of the Cross.* Grand Rapids, Mich.:
                Eerdmans; London: Tyndale.
1981   *Testaments of Love.* Grand Rapids, Mich.: Eerdmans.

Moule, C. F. D.
1982   "The Problem of the Pastoral Epistles: A Reappraisal." In
                Essays in New Testament Interpretation. Cambridge, U.K.:
                Cambridge University Press. (Reprint of *Bulletin of the John
                Rylands University Library* 47 [1965]: 430-52.)
O'Brien, Peter T.
1982   *Colossians, Philemon.* Word Biblical Commentary 44. Waco,
                Tex.: Word.
Osborne, Grant R.
1992   *The Hermeneutical Spiral.* Downers Grove, Ill.: InterVarsity
                Press.
Osburn, C. D.
1982   "*Authenteo* (1 Timothy 2:12)." *Restoration Quarterly* 25:1-
                12.

Padgett, Allan
1987   "The Pauline Rationale for Submission: Biblical Feminism
               and the *Hina* Clauses of Titus 2:1-10." *Evangelical Quarterly*
               59:39-52.
Payne, Philip B.
1981   "Libertarian Women in Ephesus: A Response to Douglas J.
               Moo's Article '1 Timothy 2:11-15: Meaning and
               Significance.' " *Trinity Journal* 2:169-97.
Pfitzner, V. C.
1967   *Paul and the "Agon" Motif.* Novum Testamentum
               Supplement 16. Leiden, Netherlands: Brill.
Prior, Michael
1989   *Paul the Letter-Writer and the Second Letter to Timothy.*
               Journal for the Study of the New Testament Supplement Se-
               ries 23. Sheffield, U.K.: JSOT.
Quinn, Jerome D.
1978   "The Last Volume of Luke: The Relation of Luke-Acts and
               the PE." In *Perspectives on Luke-Acts.* Edited by C. Talbert.
               Macon, Ga.: Mercer.
1990   *The Letter to Titus: A New Translation with Notes and
               Commentary and an Introduction to Titus, I and II Timo-
               thy, the Pastoral Epistles.* Anchor Bible 35. New York:
               Doubleday.
Sandmel, Samuel
1972   "Myths, Genealogies and Jewish Myths and the Writing of
               the Gospels." In *Two Living Traditions: Essays on Religion
               and the Bible.* Detroit: Wayne State University Press.
Scholer, David M.
1986   "1 Timothy 2:9-15 and the Place of Women in the Church's
               Ministry." In *Women, Authority and the Bible.* Edited by A.
               Mickelsen. Downers Grove, Ill.: InterVarsity Press.
Sider, Ronald J.
1977   *Rich Christians in an Age of Hunger.* Downers Grove, Ill.:
               InterVarsity Press.
Skeat, T. C.
1979   " 'Especially the Parchments': A Note on 2 Tim 4.13."
               Journal of Theological Studies 30:173-77.
Spicq, C.
1969   *Saint Paul: Les Epîtres Pastorales.* 4th rev. ed. 2 vols. Études
               Bibliques. Paris: Gabalda.
Stauffer, E.
1964   "ἑδραῖος κτλ." In *Theological Dictionary of the New
               Testament.* 2:362-64. Edited by G. Kittel and G. Friedrich. 10

vols. Grand Rapids, Mich.: Eerdmans.

Stott, John R. W.

1973   *Guard the Gospel: The Message of 2 Timothy.* The Bible
            Speaks Today. Downers Grove, Ill., and Leicester, England:
            InterVarsity Press.

Towner, Philip H.

1989   *The Goal of Our Instruction: The Structure of Theology and
            Ethics in the Pastoral Epistles.* Journal for the Study of the
            New Testament Supplement Series 34. Sheffield, U.K.: JSOT
            Press.

Turner, Nigel

1976   *A Grammar of New Testament Greek (by James Hope
            Moulton).* Vol. 4, *Style.* Edinburgh: T & T Clark.

Verner, David C.

1983   *The Household of God: The Social World of the Pastoral
            Epistles.* Society of Biblical Literature Dissertation Series 71.
            Chico, Calif.: Scholars Press.

Walder, E.

1923   "The Logos of the Pastoral Epistles." *Journal of Theological
            Studies* 24:310-15.

White, John

1993   *Money Isn't God: So Why Is the Church Worshiping It?*
            Downers Grove, Ill.: InterVarsity Press.

Wilson, Stephen G.

1979   *Luke and the Pastoral Epistles.* London: SPCK.

Winter, Bruce W.   "Providentia for the Widows of 1 Timothy 5,3-16." *Tyndale
1988   Bulletin* 39:83-99.

Witherington,
  Ben, III

1988   *Women in the Earliest Churches.* Society for New Testament
            Studies Monograph Series 59. Cambridge, U.K.: Cambridge
            University Press.